BORDER DIPLOMACY

BORDER DIPLOMACY

The *Caroline* and McLeod Affairs in Anglo-American-Canadian Relations, 1837–1842

Kenneth R. Stevens

THE UNIVERSITY OF ALABAMA PRESS
TUSCALOOSA AND LONDON

Library of Congress Cataloging-in-Publication Data

Stevens, Kenneth R., 1946–
    Border diplomacy : the Caroline and McLeod affairs in
Anglo-American-Canadian relations, 1837–1842 / Kenneth
R. Stevens.
        p.   cm.
    Bibliography: p.
    Includes index.
    ISBN 0-8173-0434-7
    1. Northeast boundary of the United States. 2. United
States—Foreign relations—Great Britain. 3. Great Britain—
Foreign relations—United States. 4. United States—
Boundaries—Canada. 5. Canada—Boundaries—United
States. I. Title.
E398.S9   1989
327.73041—dc 19   88-31658
                                                            CIP

British Library Cataloguing-in-Publication Data available

FOR NANCY

the best Friend I've ever known

Contents

PREFACE

Long after Americans and Britons signed treaties ending the Revolutionary War and the War of 1812, ill will between the two nations simmered under the surface of their relations and periodically boiled over. In the mid-nineteenth century, Americans were still squabbling with the British and their subjects in Canada over borders, sovereign rights and responsibilities, and the American republican experiment.

Some of the antagonism arose from a fundamental difference in attitude toward democracy. Britons believed that democratic government was inadequate to control the baser elements of a population. Further, they disliked the aggressiveness and arrogance of their former colonists. Americans sensed and resented this contempt; in turn, they regarded British aristocratic pretensions with scorn and believed that country sought world domination. In view of such attitudes, even relatively minor incidents threatened to erupt into violence between the two nations. Such was the case in 1837, when British troops set fire to the American steamer *Caroline* in American waters, killing a United States citizen, and in 1840, when the state of New York arrested a Canadian, Alexander McLeod, for the murder.

These incidents have been mentioned in American history textbooks and have been examined in relation to problems in Anglo-American relations in such scholarly works as Howard

Jones's *To the Webster–Ashburton Treaty*, which analyzes the myriad conflicts leading to that accord, and as an example of the "diplomacy of menace" that Wilbur Devereux Jones describes in *The American Problem in British Diplomacy*. They have also been discussed as episodes in the history of American and British administrations in such works as James C. Curtis's *The Fox at Bay* and Oliver P. Chitwood's *John Tyler*.

Yet these events, taken together, are not simply examples of diplomatic relations or political problems for particular administrations. The clash of attitudes and loyalties along the American-Canadian frontier also demonstrates the instability of the border region, socially as well as politically, and conflicting motives of patriotism and political opportunism in both the American and British governments.

The young democracy was still trying to establish the limits of federal and state authority, and the results were not always predictable: John Tyler, a states'-rights Whig, championed the federal government's exclusive right to conduct foreign policy; and Governor William Seward, who would later become secretary of state, advocated New York's right to try a foreign national for crimes committed in the name of his government. The "McLeod law" of 1842 helped clarify the national government's dominance over foreign affairs.

Further, the United States was still trying to establish itself as a member of the community of nations, guided by commonly accepted principles of international law. In his official response to the *Caroline* raid, Secretary of State Daniel Webster articulated a stance that not only showed the United States' acceptance of the law of nations but also established a principle—the *Caroline* doctrine—that is still applied today.

Thus, the *Caroline* and McLeod affairs, occurring as they did at a pivotal moment in American history, reveal how the republic began to mature in its relations with its long-established forebear, refined its own definitions of state and federal powers, and established itself as a nation contributing to as well as influenced by international law. Perhaps most hopefully for the future, the affairs also demonstrate that, despite provocative actions from unruly forces on both sides, nations can pull back from the brink of war and resolve their difficulties through negotiation.

Research for this book was done in public and private papers in the United States, Britain, and Canada (including many available only in manuscript form) and from contemporary newspaper accounts of events along the border and in Congress.

I would like to express my gratitude to those who have aided in the completion of this book.

At Indiana University, it was my good fortune to work under the direction of Maurice G. Baxter, Robert H. Ferrell, and David M. Pletcher. Each has read this manuscript more than once and over the years has offered many helpful suggestions for both research and writing. Any of my skills as a historian and teacher are attributable to them.

Friends and colleagues have generously provided advice and encouragement. Included in this group are my former coworkers at the Papers of Daniel Webster project at Dartmouth College, particularly Assistant Editor Alan R. Berolzheimer, Correspondence Series Editor Michael J. Birkner, and Editor-in-Chief Charles M. Wiltse. I owe a special debt to the late Mary Virginia Anstruther, who extended to me a thousand kindnesses and whose contributions to the body of knowledge about Daniel Webster have never been recognized beyond those who worked with her on the project.

Thanks also go to my colleagues in the history department of Texas Christian University, all of whom have supported me in this effort, and especially to Grady McWhiney, who has given me the benefit of his expertise and untold hours of his time. Jamie Gleason, the best departmental secretary in the world, typed much of this manuscript.

A number of people have kindly read all or part of this work and have made helpful suggestions: Terry H. Anderson, Joyce S. Goldberg, Wilbur Devereux Jones, Stephen E. Maizlish, and Donald E. Worcester. Howard Jones, in particular, offered invaluable advice and was a patient as well as insightful critic.

I am indebted to the staffs of the National Archives, the Library of Congress, the Public Archives of Canada, the British Historical Manuscripts Commission, and the British Public Records Office, as well as other depositories. Mary Giunta and Sara D. Jackson, of the National Historical Publications and Records Commission, and John McDonough, of the Manuscripts Division of the Library of Congress, have assisted me time and again over the years. My appreciation is also extended to Karl Kabelac, manuscripts librarian at the University of Rochester library, and the library staffs at Dartmouth College and Texas Christian University.

This book was completed with the assistance of a travel-to-collections grant from the National Endowment for the Humanities (NEH) and supplemental funds from Texas Christian University and Dartmouth College. Deeply appreciated, too, are the encouragement and assistance provided Larry D. Adams, Jan Fox, and Michael D. McCracken, of Texas Christian University, and William B. Durant, of Dartmouth.

Finally and most important, I would like to thank my wife, Nancy, and my children, Sally, James, and especially John, who has been my boon companion during the final stages of this work.

BORDER
DIPLOMACY

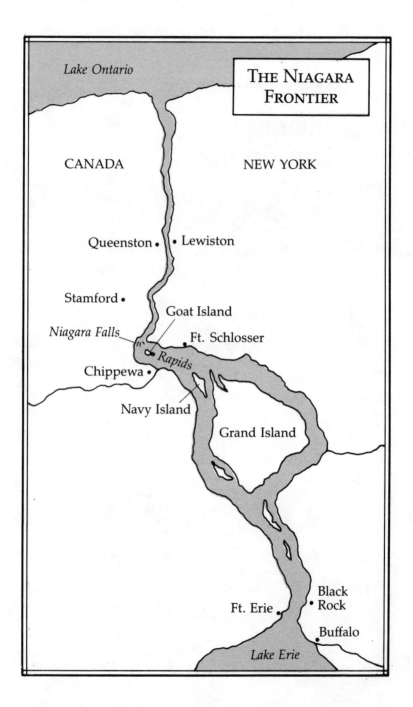

1

"Blood Has Been Shed"

For as long as any person can remember, the border between Canada and the United States has been peaceful. Americans travel to Canada without passports and usually comment on how alike are the two countries and their inhabitants. People who live along the border are often surprised to learn that amity between the two countries has not always existed. Automobile drivers who pass the juncture of Vermont, New York, and Quebec seldom realize that the dilapidated stone fortifications at Rouses Point are reminders of a less peaceful time, and tourists who cross the Niagara River between Buffalo and Fort Erie, Ontario, over the aptly named Peace Bridge little suspect that the river was once the scene of hostilities between the nations. But the fact is that, as recently as one hundred fifty years ago, Americans, Britons, and Canadians were skirmishing across the border and threatening war between the United States and Britain over Canada.

The troubles that came to the brink of war in 1837–38 had their beginnings at the end of colonial times, when Parliament, in 1774, passed the Quebec Act. This legislation restored the center of the old French western fur empire by defining the western boundary of Canada to include territory north of the Ohio River between the Alleghenies and the Mississippi. The measure also recognized the importance of the Catholic church in French Canada; it abolished test oaths, which had

1

barred Catholics from civil office, and restored the church's right to collect tithes and other fees. The act imposed English criminal law in the colony but restored French law in civil matters.[1] ✔

Inhabitants of the thirteen Atlantic colonies saw the Quebec Act as a plot. Several of the colonies had made claims to the area between the mountains and the Mississippi, and settlers had moved into the Ohio Valley. Most of the Atlantic colonists were Protestants who hated Catholicism. They saw the restoration of Catholic privileges and French law as the establishment of despotism on their flank. In October 1774 the First Continental Congress addressed a petition to Parliament, including among their complaints that the Quebec Act had established a "religion fraught with sanguinary and impious tenets."[2]

Britons and loyal Canadians suspected with justification that the English colonists to the south had designs on Canada. Late in May 1775 the Second Continental Congress invited the "oppressed Inhabitants of Canada" to join in "defence of our common liberty." Outraged by Congress's earlier address to Parliament, Canadians denounced the "perfidious, double-faced" Americans and proclaimed loyalty to the king. In the face of Canadian refusal to join the cause, the United States launched military expeditions against Quebec. The invaders tried to present themselves as a liberating army, but their actions alienated Canadians. American General David Wooster antagonized Quebec's Roman Catholics by forbidding Mass on Christmas eve. ✔ After an assault against the walls of Quebec City failed, his troops retreated in disarray, terrorizing the countryside.[3]

Although there was no conquest of Canada during the Revolution, American leaders remained convinced that its acquisition was inevitable. John Adams bluntly declared that "as long as Great Britain shall have Canada, Nova Scotia, and the Floridas, or any of them, so long will Great Britain be the enemy of the United States." Writing to his British friend David Hartley, Benjamin Franklin argued that England should cede all its North American holdings to the United States because they would eventually be taken anyway.[4]

In the years after the Revolution, mutual suspicion and hostility continued. Following the Peace of 1783, the British government encouraged colonial loyalists to migrate to Canada. Most brought anti-American prejudices that the British government valued, but many were more American than they realized and did not adapt. On the whole, they brought as much dissension as they did stability.

After the Revolution, about thirty thousand displaced loyalists went to Nova Scotia and what is now called New Brunswick. In the American revolutionary setting, they had been "pillars of conservatism," but in Canadian society many of them were soon marked as "dangerous radicals." The refugees to Nova Scotia were promised land and expected the means to create a society that would prove the "envy of all the American states." In the meantime, they were placed in refugee camps where, British officials complained, they were "indolent and mutinous." When allotment of land grants began, many complained because they could not make their own choices. One frustrated British official observed that their "cursed republican, town-meeting spirit has been the ruin of us." Equally distressing, in the provincial assembly the loyalists raised issues often heard in America, but never in Canada, about compensation for royal officials, collection and disbursement of public revenues, and the system for administration. It became apparent, too, that not all the immigrants were true British loyalists. Many who came to Nova Scotia were "late loyalists" who came not out of loyalty but merely for economic gain.[5]

The same problems prevailed with loyalists farther west in Canada. Revolutionary refugees from northern New York and New England expected that they would be allowed to settle along the St. Lawrence in the region south of Montreal. Quebec Governor Frederick Haldimand was concerned about the effect of the English and Protestant loyalists on French Catholic Quebec and just as worried about their nearness to the undefended American border. He decided that they should be located in the frontier area northwest of the junction of the St. Lawrence and Ottawa rivers and extending along the north shore of Lake Ontario, a region known as Catariqui. Many loyalists, however, resisted Haldimand's plan and held "indignation meetings" protesting government policy. Some ignored his orders and moved into closed territory at Missisiquoi Bay, on the northern shore of Lake Champlain. He resisted the movement by threatening to burn squatters' houses, but he could not halt their contentiousness. Settlers in the Catariqui region complained about terms on which land was granted and about the wildness as well as the remoteness of their allotments. Again, some of them proved to be "late loyalists." Settlers at Kingston learned to their distress that one of their number had been the executioner of the British spy Major John André.[6] ——

Americans saw the War of 1812 as an opportunity for easy acquisition of Canada. Former President Thomas Jefferson declared that its capture would be "a mere matter of marching." Kentucky Congressman Richard M. Johnson—later elevated to the vice-presidency as "Rumpsey Dumpsey Johnson," the killer of "Tecumsey"—said that the "Great Disposer of Human Events" intended that the St. Lawrence and the Mississippi should belong to the same people.[7]

Americans had reason to be confident. Along the thousand-mile frontier, British forces in Canada numbered only 5,000 regulars and 4,000 militia. In Upper Canada, the area most vulnerable to attack from the United States, the British commander, Major General Sir Isaac Brock, had only 1,600 regulars. Against them stood an American army of 7,000 men and 690,000 militia. The population of the United States was seven million, but Canada had only 500,000 inhabitants and was underdeveloped. It lacked roads necessary to move troops, and its main settled areas—York and Montreal—were almost islands in the wilderness that failed to serve as rallying points. British leaders were as concerned about the situation as Americans were confident. Major General Brock declared that Canadians were convinced that "this Province must inevitably succumb."[8]

But, from the beginning, Americans were disappointed in their expectations. According to their plan, Major General Henry Dearborn would lead his forces against Montreal by way of Lake Champlain, but the effort stalled when his militia refused to cross the border into Canada. Farther west, Major General William Hull crossed into Canada from Detroit in July 1812 with the intention of capturing the area between Lakes Huron and Erie.

He anticipated Canadian collaboration, or at least acquiescence. Among his first acts, he called on inhabitants to greet American troops with a "cordial welcome" and informed them he had come to free them from British tyranny. After making dire threats against Canadians who opposed the American invasion, he retreated back to Detroit, where the next month he surrendered to Brock without a fight.[9]

Victory in 1812 belonged to the British. At Fort Dearborn—now Chicago—Americans surrendered to British forces, then were massacred by Indians as they evacuated the post. At the Battle of Queenston Heights—across from Lewistown, New York—Brock was triumphant, though he lost his life.[10]

The next year, 1813, the United States again invaded Canada, though retaliation was prompt. In April, troops led by General Dearborn captured York, the capital of Upper Canada, and burned and looted government buildings as well as private houses. In December, soldiers burned the town of Newark, leaving the inhabitants without shelter. The American government disavowed these acts, but they engendered bitterness. British troops retaliated by burning Buffalo the same month. The next year, they burned and looted Washington, D.C.[11]

The War of 1812 strengthened Canadian nationalism. Just as Americans made Andrew Jackson a national hero because of New Orleans, Canadians remembered the heroic deeds of the always outnumbered but never outgeneraled Brock. Equally important, though war brought some devastation to the colony, it created a sense of permanence. Roads were improved, a sounder currency was established, and wartime provisioning brought prosperity.[12]

The War of 1812 hence brought to an end what one historian has termed the "peaceful American invasion" of Canada. During the war, the British government made strenuous efforts to reduce the American presence in Canada, which had been growing steadily over the years. Shortly after war was declared, the governor of Lower Canada, Sir George Prevost, ordered Americans living there to take an oath of allegiance to Britain. Those who refused were ordered to leave the province. In Upper Canada, settlers who claimed exemption from military service because of their American background received passports to return to the United States. At the end of the war, Colonial Secretary Lord Bathurst declared that Americans should be denied land grants and discouraged from settling in Canada. In 1815 the British government offered to transport settlers—especially British military veterans—from Scotland to Canada. The British government two years later dispossessed settlers, many of them American, who held lands without proper title in Canada. The new policy was to discourage any settlers whose loyalty might prove uncertain.[13]

As a consequence of the war, Canada's leadership became ultra-Tory and militantly anti-American. It included such figures as the Reverend John Strachan, Anglican rector of York, elected to the legislative council in 1820; Upper Canadian Attorney General John Beverly Robinson, a member of the provincial assembly from York; and William Allan, president of the Bank of Upper Canada. Together with other Tories, these individuals hoped to create a model aristocratic and class-conscious British society in Canada. They looked down on what they regarded as the "incorrigible republicanism and common democracy of America." Americans had not conquered Canada by force during the war, but these men believed that only eternal vigilance could protect it from the contagion of republicanism.[14]

Certainly the Americans bore watching, for they were ambitious and expansive. From their original coastal bases, they had acquired the vast Louisiana Territory and the Floridas. Although the phrase "manifest destiny" would not appear until the 1840s, the impulses guiding that urge were already evident. Americans believed their country was destined for greatness. Geographer Jedidiah Morse had proclaimed in 1789 that the "Mississippi was never designed as the western boundary of the American empire," and President Jefferson had informed James Monroe that he looked forward to a time when the United States would encompass the whole of North America, and perhaps South America as well.[15]

Britons and Canadians needed to look no farther than Texas for evidence of American perfidy. Colonists from the United States had moved there throughout the 1820s, swearing loyalty to the Mexican government. But in 1836 the settlers declared independence and sought annexation to the United States. These events provided an ominous portent of what could happen in Canada. Given opportunity, Sir George Arthur declared, Americans would "pour in upon us" as they had in Texas. The British minister to the United States, Henry S. Fox, feared that annexation of Texas as a slave state would result in an invasion of Canada by northern states to repair the sectional imbalance.[16]

A rebellion against royal authority in British North America during the winter of 1837–38 reawakened fears that Canada would eventually fall to the United States. Although Canadians had resisted American advances over the years, they felt some discontent with British colonial practices. In 1791 Parliament had divided Canada into lower and upper provinces along the Ottawa River and granted the colony representative government by creating elective assemblies. But the governors of the provinces retained power that limited the legislatures, including authority to convene and prorogue the assembly as well as to veto any measure. If the governor chose, he could avoid the assembly by relying on the legislative council (comparable to an upper house) and on his executive council of advisers, all of whom he appointed. The assemblies sought a larger share in government, and clashes occurred similar to those between royal governors and lower houses years before in the thirteen American colonies.[17]

Many Canadians had social as well as political grievances. In Lower Canada, the *habitants*, or French small-scale farmers, resented the feudal land system that prevailed there. The Catholic church and absentee landholders, many of them London speculators, owned nearly eight million acres. Tenants on these lands paid not only rent but also for improvements they made. They were obliged to work for the landlord but were denied hunting, fishing, and other privileges. In Upper Canada, the source of social discontent was the hold of the "Family Compact" on society. An oligarchy of loyalist families from the American Revolution, the Family Compact controlled the provincial government, economic institutions, and the Anglican church. Particularly galling, as in Lower Canada, was the status of land.

In an era of agricultural expansion in the neighboring United States, the government of Canada kept large tracts of land idle: the Church of England's reserve alone amounted to two million acres, and members of the Family Compact each held ten thousand to fifty thousand acres. Meanwhile, ordinary farmers clamored for more land. People who hoped to build an industrial order in the country also resented colonial government. Between 1815 and 1837, native industries increased, but the merchant-landowners and British officials opposed the free-trade principles championed by industrialists and rigidly maintained a mercantile system. Resentment grew among business-minded Canadians when they observed economic progress in the United States.[18]

For such reasons, resentment moved to rebellion. In 1834 the Lower Canadian assembly passed the Ninety-Two Resolutions demanding government reform and more independence. Patriots who opposed British rule began wearing clothes made from homespun fabric. Committees of correspondence provided direction for resistance and helped organize rebel government and military units.[19] In Upper Canada, the leader was William Lyon Mackenzie, a skilled but unfocused demagogue, who had arrived in the colony from Scotland in 1820 and established a reform newspaper, the *Colonial Advocate*. Elected to the provincial assembly in 1828, he was expelled in 1831 for libeling political opponents but was reelected several times. In 1834 he became mayor of Toronto. Serving in the assembly that year, he headed a committee on grievances and issued a report that became the platform of the reform group. The report condemned the Family Compact because its privileges harmed the populace. It objected to the preferential status accorded the Anglican church, called for an elected rather than an appointed legislative council, and demanded replacement of the executive council by a ministry responsible to the people.[20]

Political crises occurred in both Canadas in 1836. In September the Lower Canadian assembly turned down appropriations for government supplies. In London, Colonial Secretary Lord John Russell met intransigence with toughness. On March 6, 1837, he rejected Lower Canadian demands for the Ninety-Two Resolutions. When this became known in Montreal and Quebec, Patriots took to the streets, marched with the French tricolor, and sang the *Marseillaise*. In Upper Canada, provincial Lieutenant Governor Sir Francis Bond Head had similar problems. In March 1837, after a series of clashes, the assembly denounced the government and refused appropriations. Head responded by dissolving the legislature and calling an election. In the campaign, he managed to win a loyalist majority in the assembly, but the event had convinced many that only independence would end Canadian discontent.[21]

An unsuccessful rebellion broke out in Lower Canada in November 1837. The Patriots won their first encounter with British troops at St. Denis on the twenty-third, but the next day government artillery smashed a rebel fort at St. Charles. Within minutes, fifty-six Patriots were killed and thirty taken prisoner. At the rebel village of St. Eustace the next month, government troops trapped eighty insurgents inside a church; a fire started by British soldiers killed many of them, and those who tried to escape were shot, including some who were trying to surrender. Government troops returning to Montreal by way of St. Benoit met a delegation of citizens offering to surrender, but, after the regulars left, undisciplined loyalist volunteers pillaged and burned the town. Defeat intensified anti-British feeling. From all over Lower Canada, rebels made their way across the border into Vermont and New York, where their lasting bitterness would nurture problems along the Canadian-American border.[22]

The rebellion in Upper Canada was also unsuccessful. In July 1837 radicals adopted a Declaration of Grievances that established committees of vigilance and called for a convention of reformers. Mackenzie, the "agent and corresponding secretary" of the committees, plotted to seize Toronto City Hall, capture Lieutenant Governor Head and his advisers, and proclaim a provisional government. On December 1 Head ordered the arrest of Mackenzie and called out two regiments of militia. Mackenzie asked his followers to concentrate at Montgomery's Tavern, on the outskirts of Toronto. Ninety rebels reached the tavern but found no weapons as Mackenzie had promised, and no food. Over the next few days, their numbers increased to about five hundred, but arms and food remained in short supply.

The Upper Canadian rebels, mostly unarmed, marched on Toronto the morning of December 6. As they approached, a squad of pickets fired, driving them back to the tavern. The next day, government forces moved against them. Leaving Toronto in a blare of military music, to the enthusiastic shouts of the men, women, and children of the city, eleven hundred progovernment volunteers took the field. By this time, the ranks of Mackenzie's force had been depleted by a sudden loss of interest in martial life, precipitated by lack of supplies and also suspicion that Mackenzie, who now spent much of his time shouting at subordinates, was unbalanced. Government troops announced their arrival by sending rounds of cannon shot into the tavern. Many defenders fled into the woods, while the remainder briefly engaged the loyalists before escaping in twos and threes.[23]

Upper Canadian rebels who fled to the United States after the defeat at Montgomery's Tavern found their American neighbors sympathetic. After several narrow escapes, the exhausted Mackenzie arrived in Buffalo on December 11 and received a hero's welcome. That night, his supporters filled the Buffalo Coffee House, where they heard his plan for a triumphant return to Canada. Speaking before another crowd at the Coffee House the next evening, the rebel leader called for recruits, arms, and ammunition. The following day, twenty-four volunteers marched out of Buffalo and occupied Navy Island, on the British side of the Niagara. Mackenzie called for more volunteers, promising each man three hundred acres and a hundred silver dollars once he took charge of the government. Recruits at Navy Island increased to about one hundred fifty, mostly Americans.[24] The rebels' occupation of a British island and their determination to continue the failed rebellion with American aid would expand their importance far beyond their actual numbers.

Navy Island provided the rebels with an imposing position, for it lay several hundred yards from the Canadian shore, off Chippewa landing, and approximately three miles above Niagara Falls. The river was swift and treacherous, and attackers had to be careful to avoid being pulled into the falls. The sides of the island were steep, the interior heavily wooded, and a landing would be all the more difficult because the Patriots had fortified the shoreline. They also acquired cannon and opened fire on Chippewa, putting holes in several houses and killing a horse.[25]

Lieutenant Governor Head responded by sending twenty-five hundred militiamen to Chippewa under the command of Allan MacNab, a lawyer from Hamilton and Speaker of the Upper Canadian assembly. A high tory and a favorite of the governor, MacNab was Mackenzie's enemy. During the rebellion, he had assumed a militia colonelcy and despite lack of experience had frequently assumed command over veteran officers. Arriving in Chippewa, he carried orders not to return fire from the island or to attempt any effort to storm the Patriots' position. Nevertheless, while his soldiers chafed at inaction, he began preparations for a naval assault on the island.[26]

In faraway Washington, events along the northern border caused anxiety for President Martin Van Buren. Known as the "Red Fox" and the "Little Magician" for his political slyness, he had served as governor of New York, United States senator, and secretary of state under President Andrew Jackson. Ever adroit, he had survived the "Eaton malaria," a Democratic party brouhaha in Jackson's time that pitted him against Vice-President John C. Calhoun. Van Buren was appointed minister to Britain in 1831, and when the Senate denied confirmation he returned to become Jackson's vice-president and heir apparent. When he took the oath as president on March 4, 1837, he was fifty-five, had achieved the prestigious place he had desired, and was not about to put it in jeopardy.[27]

From the beginning, Van Buren committed his administration to peace in foreign affairs and limited government at home. In his inaugural address, he declared that relations with other nations were predicated on commercial reciprocity, open diplomacy, and friendship with all but alliance with none. The United States, he announced, disavowed any claim "to meddle in disputes, whether internal or foreign, that may molest other countries." His principles concerning domestic affairs were as circumspect as his foreign policy. He believed the Founding Fathers had set for the nation a permanent course. In establishing government for a country with diverse interests and a people jealous of their prerogatives, the founders had limited federal authority in favor of the states. For Van Buren, the settled rule of domestic policy would be "strict adherence to the letter and spirit of the Constitution as it was designed by those who framed it."[28]

During the Canadian troubles, Van Buren's principles posed problems for his administration. He wanted to maintain neutrality, but his political views precluded decisive federal action. Early in December 1837, as the seriousness of the Canadian rebellions increased, Secretary of State John Forsyth instructed United States district attorneys in Vermont, New York, and Michigan to be vigilant in prosecution of those violating neutrality laws. It was, he said, the "fixed determination of the President" to prevent meddling in "domestic disputes of other nations." Forsyth also asked state governors to watch for violations.[29]

On December 19, 1837, Treasury Secretary Levi Woodbury ordered customs collectors to help maintain peace along the border, and two days later Forsyth instructed the United States district attorney for northern New York, Nathaniel S. Benton, to inquire about the activities of Mackenzie and other Patriots.[30] Many Americans along the northern frontier openly supported them. As Benton prepared to leave his home in Little Falls for Buffalo, he complained to Secretary of State Forsyth that he did not expect his effort to accomplish anything. According to reports he had received from customs officials and the United States marshal for the district, there were eight hundred Patriots on Navy Island, heavily armed with stolen rifles and field pieces. Most of them appeared to be Americans. Benton advised the government to send an armed force to the frontier if it wished to prevent them from seizing arms stored at Fort Niagara. From Buffalo, the United States marshal for northern New York, Nathaniel Garrow, also warned that the whole frontier was "in commotion." He advised President Van Buren that only an armed force along the Niagara border could stop the continued supply of Patriots on Navy Island.[31]

The increase in Patriot activities also disturbed MacNab, commander of Canadian forces at Chippewa. On December 28 the Navy Island rebels hired the forty-six-ton steamer *Caroline* from William Wells, of Buffalo. Though the vessel was locked in the ice, men worked to free it, and Gilman Appleby, a Great Lakes sailor known as the Patriots' "Admiral of Lake Erie," became its captain. Virtually everyone in Buffalo knew the unusual winter activity was connected with the Patriots, but the collector of the port gave clearance for the *Caroline's* departure. It began working the river from Buffalo to Fort Schlosser, the rebel depot on the New York side, and to Navy Island, carrying recruits, guns, and supplies.[32]

MacNab heard about the Patriots' acquisition of the *Caroline*, and two of his men volunteered to scout Navy Island: Andrew Drew, of the Royal Navy, then in charge of preparing an assault on the island; and Alexander McLeod, a grocer and deputy sheriff from Kingston. McLeod, a veteran of the 12th Royal Lancers who had emigrated from Scotland in 1825, was a fervent loyalist. He had been conspicuous in the action at Montgomery's Tavern and afterward made several trips into the United States. On one of those missions, a Buffalo mob had recognized him, and he had barely escaped.[33]

The reconnaissance proved highly successful. On the night of December 28, Drew and McLeod rowed around Navy Island in a skiff, drawing musket fire from the shore. They spotted the *Caroline*, berthed on the eastern side. When they returned to Chippewa, Drew met with MacNab. By the end of their talk, MacNab had decided that the *Caroline* posed great danger to his forces and resolved to destroy it.[34]

On the next evening, December 29, 1837, the expedition got under way. Volunteers gathered at Chippewa landing, on the Niagara, opposite Navy Island. They were uncertain of their mission, but naval officer Drew had called for "a few fellows with cutlasses who would follow him to the Devil." When preparations were complete, seven rowboats, eight men in each, pushed off. On the river, Drew announced the mission: Colonel MacNab had ordered him to destroy the American steamboat *Caroline*, which they believed was berthed at Navy Island, on the Canadian side of the Niagara.

After a hard struggle against the current, the little force reached the island, but the *Caroline* was not there. Drew then made a fateful decision: instead of turning back, he and his party continued across the Niagara toward the boat's other likely anchorage, Fort Schlosser, on the American side. Partway, the men in two of the boats found the effort too much and went back to Chippewa, but, just before midnight, those in the remaining five saw the lights of the *Caroline* at Fort Schlosser. They rested briefly in a fairway upriver, then reentered the stream, which took them swiftly toward the wharf where the steamboat lay docked for the night.

Having found their quarry, Drew's men moved quickly. On board the *Caroline*, most of the passengers and crew were sleeping, but when the attackers were within twenty yards a watch called out:

"Boat ahoy! Who comes there?"
"A friend," answered Drew.
"Give us the countersign," replied the sentry.
"I will give you the countersign when I get on board,"
was the response.

An instant later, the British and Canadians were on the *Caroline*, Drew leading the way. Five men confronted him, and he attacked with his cutlass. One fired a musket into his face, but the ball missed. Drew slashed him and then another man who also tried to shoot him.

Chaos reigned on the *Caroline*. The raiding party made their way below, where their victims were trying to escape up ladders or out portholes. The steamboat's captain, Gilman Appleby, tried to climb on deck from inside the boat, but was pushed back. While hiding in the engine room, he saw a passenger, Amos Durfee, taken prisoner. One attacker started a fire with coals from the steamer's furnace. Flames spread. Americans heard the shout, "Damn them—give no quarters—kill every man—fire, fire!"

Freeing the *Caroline* from the dock, the raiders towed it into the river and, giving three cheers, released it to the current. By this time, crowds of spectators, roused by the shouting of the combatants and the noise of battle, watched the flaming steamboat race ever faster toward Niagara Falls. Before reaching the precipice, it suddenly broke up and sank, though watchers on the American side thought they saw it go over the falls. A poem commemorated the event:

As over the shelving rocks she broke,
And plunged in her turbulent grave,
The slumbering genius of freedom broke
Baptized in Niagara's wave.

Their mission completed, the Canadian volunteers returned to Chippewa, where they were greeted as heroes.[35]

At Fort Schlosser, the victims of the assault hid in the village until daylight. When they emerged, they found the body of Durfee, the man Captain Appleby had seen taken prisoner the night before. He apparently had been executed, shot in the head at such close range that his cap bore powder burns.

Confusion gripped the frontier. Although Durfee's was the only known death, other men were unaccounted for. Rumor had it that some had been on the *Caroline* when it was cut away from the dock. Commander Drew later denied that anyone remained on board, but in his early accounts he claimed his men had killed five or six of the "enemy." In Albany, Governor William L. Marcy heard that twelve had been killed, and, as news traveled, the calculations of dead and wounded soared. According to the first word received at the Buffalo *Commercial-Advertiser*, twenty-two died. *Niles' National Register* noted the loss of nearly thirty. By the time word reached New York City, forty unarmed American citizens had been massacred in their sleep.[36]

Along the whole northern frontier, the population was incensed. In Rochester the courthouse bell and drums summoned people to a meeting, where they heard rousing speeches and

passed a resolution to defend American soil against all invaders.
At Albany, six thousand listened to addresses by the mayor and
other worthies. Citizens at Ogdensburg drafted a letter to President Van Buren denouncing the raid as an "outrage unparalleled
in its atrocity."[37]

Turmoil prevailed at Buffalo, the town nearest Fort Schlosser.
Despite an appeal from the mayor, one newspaper correspondent reported that "excitement here is beyond any thing you can
possibly imagine." Two days after the raid, three thousand
armed men were in the city and more were arriving every hour.
Public agitation reached its peak with the public funeral of Amos
Durfee. For several hours after his body had been found, he had
been left where he fell, on the dock, as a public spectacle. The
next afternoon, his grisly remains—his "pale forehead, mangled
by the pistol ball, and his locks matted with his blood!"—were
taken to Buffalo for display at the Eagle Hotel. The following
day, three thousand people jammed the area around city hall
for his funeral obsequies, a solemn occasion marked by a veri-
table orgy of patriotic expression.[38]

Shortly after the attack, one angry New Yorker sent a scur-
rilous note on the *Caroline* to the recently appointed governor-
general of Canada, Lord Durham:

> Durham!!
> how do you like to have your Steam Boat Burnt Drew or MacNab
> will git a Bowie knife in thair damd Hart when thay little think
> of such a thing
> What is the reason that navy Island was not taken if they was
> so fast for fighting no thay took good care to keep clear of that
> you would have had a small tast of New Orleans the[re] is a
> scrap brewing in Newyork with your damd steam ships next thing
> thay will be Burnt
> God Dam the Queen[39]

His Lordship's reaction is not recorded.

President Van Buren learned of the attack on January 4, 1838,
shortly before a formal dinner at the Executive Mansion. Guests
watched the appointed hour pass without his appearance, and

at length they learned that he was meeting with his cabinet. At last, he entered the drawing room and passed straight to the towering figure of General Winfield Scott, a hero of the War of 1812 and the leading military man of the era. "Blood has been shed," he told the general. "You must go with all speed to the Niagara frontier." Secretary of War Joel Poinsett was already preparing his instructions.[40]

2

NEUTRALITY
FALLS SHORT

As was his wont, the "Red Fox of Kinderhook" adopted a circumspect policy toward the unpleasantness in New York state. Besides sending Scott to the frontier, the president promptly issued a neutrality proclamation, encouraged Congress to pass a more effective neutrality statute, and opened discussions with the British minister in Washington. His actions were proper, but unfortunately events and individuals beyond his control undermined his efforts and caused the British—and some Americans—to doubt his sincerity.

Scott's mission well illustrated the president's good intentions and the difficulties the government faced. In 1837 most of the United States Army's force of eight thousand men were engaged against the Seminoles in Florida or stationed on the western frontier. To assist the general, Van Buren called on the governors of New York and Vermont to place their militias under his command, but warned that, given frontier excitement, troops called out should come from areas "distant from the theatre of action."[1]

Van Buren's strict constitutional principles also hindered the general. Given federal statutes, the president questioned the government's legal authority to enforce neutrality. The best Secretary of War Poinsett could offer Scott, in his order issued January 5, 1838, was to use his personal influence in the troubled region. The general, declared the New York *Herald*, had been sent on a "fool's errand."[2]

The same day he ordered Scott to the northern border, Van Buren issued a proclamation condemning the "dangerous excitement" on the frontier. The president warned that Americans who interfered in Canadian affairs not only violated neutrality laws but also forfeited claims to American protection if captured in Canada. He also sent a message to Congress complaining about current neutrality laws, which had been enacted in 1817 and 1818 to deal with Americans who outfitted Latin American rebel privateers. The laws seemed inadequate during the Canadian troubles, for, though they specified penalties for offenses, they gave the government no authority to prevent violations of neutrality. Van Buren asked Congress for revisions that would give preventive power to the executive branch.[3]

Diplomatically, the administration also adopted a quiet approach toward the *Caroline* affair. Secretary of State John Forsyth sent two notes to the British minister in Washington, Henry S. Fox, on January 5. The first, responding to a British complaint about the occupation of Navy Island by the Patriots, made only veiled reference to the *Caroline*. Forsyth informed Fox that the American government would make every effort to prevent its citizens from interfering in Canadian disturbances. Writing as if he had received no word of the *Caroline* raid, Forsyth said the president was confident the countries could avoid a larger crisis unless "insurmountable obstacles" were thrown in the way by reckless British subjects. The tone of Forsyth's second note, specifically about the *Caroline*, was more contentious. Calling the incident an "extraordinary outrage," he denounced the invasion of territory and the destruction of lives as well as property. He requested Fox to obtain a full explanation from Canadian authorities and advised him that the occurrence would "necessarily form the subject of a demand for redress." In the meantime, the American government assumed the aggressors would be punished.[4]

In retrospect, it seems that an opportunity to move the *Caroline* issue toward early settlement now passed. Van Buren was open to discussion. At this point, the range of disagreement on the issue probably could have been narrowed if the British government had responded to Forsyth's notes with an expression of regret about the raid (not necessarily an apology) and if Congress had promptly voted more effective neutrality legislation. Instead, for a number of reasons, the two nations watched a relatively minor fracas evolve into a major embroilment.

The atmosphere along the northern frontier assuredly contributed to this unfortunate transformation. By the time the president learned of the *Caroline* affair, Americans all along the northern border were up in arms. The collector of customs at Cleveland warned that the raid on the boat had infuriated the people, making it impossible to enforce the law in his district. The week before, he reported, a hundred men, "comprising all the thieves, blacklegs, and scoundrels" in the city, had left to join Patriot forces gathering in Detroit.[5]

In fact, the president had no sooner delivered his neutrality proclamation than Patriots undertook an invasion of Canada from Detroit. On January 8, 1838, the schooner *Anne*, commanded by a well-known rebel, Edward A. Theller, moved against the Canadian fortress at Amherstville, on the Detroit River. Unfortunately, he and his crew knew little about sailing, and while they experimented the boat drifted. After several hours, they managed a run along the shoreline and fired several ineffective cannon shots into the village. The schooner came back the next day, but this time the Canadians returned fire, blasting away its sails and killing several of the crew, including the helmsman. The *Anne* drifted helplessly to the Canadian shore, where authorities arrested the survivors. The next day, Michigan's governor, Stephens T. Mason, persuaded the men still at rebel headquarters to disperse, but the captive crew of the *Anne* had already provided another subject of diplomatic negotiation.[6]

The most volatile portion of the frontier remained the Niagara area, where an angry American population was matched by an equally irritated Canadian citizenry. The Patriots still held Navy Island, while a large force of Canadian militia remained posted at Chippewa. There could be no peace so long as Patriots stood on Canadian soil. Arriving at Albany, Scott convinced Governor Marcy to accompany him to Buffalo, where they met with the

Patriot commander of Navy Island, Rensselaer Van Rensselaer, son of Revolutionary War General Solomon Van Rensselaer. Scott warned him that his position was hopeless because he lacked supplies and his men were undisciplined. If the Navy Island Patriots managed an attack against Canada, Scott thought they would be cut to pieces. Marcy seemed mainly interested in getting the Patriots out of New York. According to Van Rensselaer, when he and the governor were alone, Marcy told him that, as long as Navy Island were evacuated, *"he* knew of *no law* that could prevent my marching a body of *armed* men through the country." Van Rensselaer interpreted this commentary as a hint that Marcy would not interfere with plans to transfer Patriot headquarters westward to Detroit.[7]

The combination of Scott's threats and Marcy's coaxing did convince the Patriot leader to evacuate Navy Island. The Patriots knew that the ice buildup in the river would soon cut off the island from its Buffalo base. On the night of January 14, they left Navy Island, and the next day British troops reoccupied the coveted territory. Federal authorities arrested Van Rensselaer at Buffalo for violating the neutrality laws, but he was quickly bailed out.[8]

Scott fortunately remained on the frontier in case the Patriots attempted other movements, and shortly thereafter he averted another armed clash. The Patriots had arranged for use of another steamboat, the *Barcelona,* but, before they could raise sufficient funds, Scott undercut their efforts by chartering the boat for government service. Unaware of this action, the British decided to sink the steamer. Andrew Drew, leader of the expedition against the *Caroline,* positioned three armed schooners on the American side of the Niagara and readied shore batteries. Scott sent the Canadians a note protesting the presence of armed vessels in American waters and warning them against taking action. The next day, as the *Barcelona* proceeded upriver, he established his own batteries at Black Rock, opposite the schooners. As cannoneers on both sides of the river held their matches at the ready, the *Barcelona* came into view and passed the schooners without incident. The British had decided not to test Scott.[9]

Meanwhile, Scott sought to calm his American compatriots.

His blustering was probably intentional. He knew that feeling along the Niagara frontier remained high partly because the *Caroline* raid had touched American pride. By upholding national prestige at Black Rock, he fostered peace by soothing injured feelings. New Yorkers, too, knew him and were willing to listen to him, for many remembered his leadership during the War of 1812 and especially his victory against the British at the Battle of Lundy's Lane. Throughout the winter, he toured the frontier—a tall, imposing figure, usually resplendent in a blue uniform heavily trimmed with gold—reminding crowds of their duties as citizens. The *Caroline* raid was an outrage, he conceded, but obtaining redress was solely the responsibility of the national government. The pace of his peace-keeping mission nearly wore him out. He traveled at night, sleeping in his coach or sleigh while bumping over the roads. A month of trips, from the frontier to Albany, to New York City, back to Buffalo, and from there to the Michigan frontier and Cleveland, proved almost too much. Back in Albany in early March, he spent a week in bed recuperating.[10] Although his efforts probably had a calming effect on law-abiding citizens along the border, time would prove he had not subdued the Patriots.

Another problem in resolving the *Caroline* affair was that the individuals most involved in officially discussing it—British Minister Fox and Secretary of State Forsyth—were both unequal to the task of resolving such a critical and sensitive disagreement. Fox, son of a British general and nephew of the famous Charles James Fox, was a competent but ordinary diplomat. Like his illustrious relative, he was a gambler and had early lost a fortune. After proposing to several heiresses, he was shipped off to Buenos Aires in 1830 as secretary to the legation. Two years later, he was rewarded with the legation at Rio de Janeiro. According to one interesting story, not altogether improbable, Foreign Secretary Palmerston selected him as minister to Washington because he was the only Briton ever sent to American assignments who never complained about the heat.[11]

In the United States, Fox made friends among the gambling set but drew animosity from other acquaintances. The New York merchant Philip Hone detested him and made him the subject of more than one venomous entry in his diary. Remarking on his slovenly appearance and resemblance to his animal namesake, Hone declared Fox looked more like "a little shriveled Frenchman" than an Englishman. "The sooner we get rid of him, the better . . . he sleeps all day and sits up all night; returns no visits; gives no entertainments; and does not pay his gambling debts." On one occasion, a mob of unfriendly creditors surrounded his house and demanded that he name a time when he would pay his debts. He appeared at a window and carefully announced that he had in mind a time, pausing before intoning, "The Day of Judgment."[12]

Perhaps understandably, Fox did not especially like Americans and had little respect for their political system. Lacking contacts in their government, and unfriendly to it anyway, he limited his efforts on the *Caroline* affair to strictly official measures at a time when adept personal diplomacy would have been invaluable.

On the American side, Secretary Forsyth was an individual with a long but uneven record in political and foreign affairs. Virginia-born, Georgia-bred, Princeton-educated, he had managed to propel himself from a Georgia law practice into a larger orbit. He had found his income insufficient to maintain him in a style he desired. Besides, his Northern wife, Clara Meigs, hated the humidity of Georgia and especially life in the town of Louisville—then the state capital—which she referred to as an "odious hole." Forsyth promised her that he would seek a position in the North, and in 1812 their goals were realized when he was elected to the United States House of Representatives.[13]

Congressman Forsyth gained experience in foreign relations as chairman of the Committee on Foreign Affairs, where his record was marked by a strong sense of nationalism and by strict construction of the Constitution. He urged the government to send the navy against Algerian pirates who harassed American merchant shipping in the Mediterranean and recommended economic retaliation against the British for their restrictions on American trade in the West Indies. His conservative constitutional principles became clear when, after ratification of the Treaty of Commerce of 1815 with Britain, he argued that carrying out the agreement required legislative as well as executive action.

Forsyth, in 1819, briefly entered the Senate but resigned when named as minister to Spain. It was an unfortunate appointment, memorable for a series of undiplomatic altercations with his hosts, including an episode in which he caned a Spanish soldier who brushed against him on a Madrid street.[14] His sojourn as minister was a low point in his career, and, when he was re-elected to the House of Representatives in 1823, he and the Spanish gladly took leave of one another.

Forsyth served in Congress until 1827, when he was elected as governor of Georgia. Two years later, he went back to Washington, this time to the Senate, where he remained until President Andrew Jackson appointed him to succeed Louis McLane as secretary of state. When Van Buren became president, Forsyth stayed on. He was an able administrator but lacked the sensibilities necessary for complex diplomatic problems.

Instead of trying to resolve the *Caroline* issue, Fox and Forsyth engaged in useless argument. Forsyth pressed a demand for redress on January 19, 1838, when he sent Fox a follow-up to his note of the fifth, enclosing several affidavits as evidence of the "extra-ordinary outrage" at Fort Schlosser. Fox responded with his own collection of depositions, pointing out the "piratical character" of the *Caroline* and the inability of the United States to enforce its own laws on the frontier. British subjects hence had been forced to "consult their own security," and a "necessity of self defence and self preservation" had given them the right to destroy the *Caroline* wherever they found it. On February 13 Forsyth addressed a curt reply to Fox, disputing this version of the incident. In any case, he said, there was no justification for aggression upon United States territory. The government in Washington was acting to prevent interference in the Canadian insurrection, but Britain had created an obstacle by arousing American resentment. This was enough for Fox. He informed the secretary of state that he wished to avoid controversy with him on the subject. Henceforth, discussion of the case would take place between the American minister and Her Majesty's government in England.[15]

Fox had spoken without instructions, but he had correctly anticipated his government. When news of the *Caroline* reached London in February 1838, officials submitted the facts to the law officers of the Crown. They tendentiously decided that, because the *Caroline* had acted as a belligerent vessel, Fort Schlosser was not "justly entitled to the privileges of a neutral territory." British forces, "with a view of self-preservation, were fully justified" in attacking the vessel wherever they located it.[16]

The doctrine of intervention in other states for reasons of self-defense and self-preservation was one of the most troublesome notions in international law. Early writers on the law of nations, including Hugo Grotius, Samuel Pufendorf, and Emerich de Vattel, recognized intervention in principle. Vattel had written in his *Law of Nations*, published in 1758, that a nation was obligated to preserve itself and had "a right to every thing that can secure it from such a threatening danger, and to keep at a distance whatever is capable of causing its ruin."[17]

In practice, strong nations had used the doctrine to justify aggression against weaker ones. In 1807, when Foreign Minister George Canning suspected that Napoleon intended to use Denmark's navy against England, British forces bombarded Copenhagen and seized the Danish fleet. Critics in Parliament denounced the action as an outrage, but the government asserted it had been necessary for the nation's preservation.[18]

The United States had also justified invasion of foreign territory in the name of self-defense. In 1817 the collapse of Spanish power in America created unique problems and opportunities along the country's southern frontier. One of the problems involved a rebel privateering base at Amelia Island, in the St. Mary's River between American Georgia and Spanish Florida. The privateers professed hostilities only against Spanish vessels, but many of them were freebooters who cared little what flag a ship carried. In his first annual message of December 2, 1817, President James Monroe declared that a "just regard for the rights and the interests of the United States" required suppression of the rebel outpost and informed Congress he had issued orders to accomplish that end. Shortly thereafter, American forces occupied Spain's Amelia Island. Monroe reported the takeover in a special message to the House and Senate, justifying the action because, he said, in failing to maintain authority over the island, Spain had surrendered its jurisdiction.[19]

A few months later, the United States again forcibly entered Spanish territory. General Andrew Jackson, ordered to terminate the depredations by the Seminole Indians, invaded Florida and executed two Englishmen—Alexander Arbuthnot and Robert Ambrister—who had encouraged them. He also captured the Spanish towns of St. Marks and Pensacola. News of his deeds created an international uproar. The Spanish minister to the United States, Luis de Onís, denounced Jackson's course as an outrage that had "filled even the people of this Union with wonder and surprise." Jackson came under fire in Monroe's cabinet, where everyone except Secretary of State John Quincy Adams stood against him. After five days of argument that left him physically and emotionally drained, Adams brought the president and the whole cabinet around: Jackson's actions were justified by the need for strong action at the moment.[20]

The Florida affair was an interesting business. The secretary of state defended Jackson on grounds of international law. Adams concluded that Spain had shown itself incapable of maintaining its authority in the region. Jackson had occupied St. Marks because of "imminent danger" that the Seminoles were about to seize the fort; it was an act forced on him "by the necessities of self-defence." Jackson captured Pensacola in self-defense because he faced hostilities from the Spanish commandant there.[21]

Adams had wrested a principle of international law from the rash and embarrassing action of an ambitious and impetuous general: the invasion of foreign territory was justifiable if the other nation failed to exercise authority and endangered its neighbor. The Florida episode reveals as much about international law at the time as about the individuals involved. In the nineteenth century, the act came first; then the diplomats searched for justification.

Congressional politics also left its imprint on the *Caroline* case. In the Senate, Van Buren's policy of neutrality and his mild reaction to the *Caroline* raid fared well. Despite political differences on other issues, two senior statesmen in the Senate, Henry Clay and John C. Calhoun, concurred with the neutrality proclamation of January 5, 1838, and the request of the same day for a revised neutrality law. John Davis, of Massachusetts, criticized the administration for not acting sooner but said he was "glad at last the executive had waked up."[22] The president's request went to the Foreign Relations Committee, which immediately took up the problem.

House reaction to the Canadian troubles foretold more difficulty. Van Buren sent a message on January 8 informing Congress that the government had called out the frontier militia and had demanded reparations through the British minister. The message and correspondence included with it caused a sensation. South Carolina's Waddy Thompson charged that the secretary of state's note of January 5 was "altogether too tame for the occasion" and argued that the "murderers should have been at once demanded by our government" and held for trial. A Kentucky Whig, Richard H. Menefee, urged calm because the *Caroline* affair represented "no great principle" such as search on the high seas or impressment. "Great God!" Thompson exclaimed. "Were they to be told on that floor that American citizens, within the lines of American jurisdiction, might be murdered in their sleep by foreign mercenaries, and yet no principle involved?"[23]

While the House argued, the Senate acted. Foreign Relations Committee Chairman James Buchanan reported a neutrality bill on January 9, and on the 15th the Senate passed it with little discussion. The bill substantially increased the power of the national government to enforce neutrality. Written with the Canadian difficulties in mind, it authorized federal officials to seize "vessels or vehicles" about to pass over the border into a neighboring state for hostile purposes, empowered the government to disarm men entering the United States, and authorized the president to use the army and navy to prevent violations of the nation's neutrality.[24]

The Senate bill met a turbulent reception in the House. Proponents declared that neutrality was an American tradition, and failure to stop Anglo-American conflict along the northern border would lead to war.[25] Menefee, who earlier had seen no violation of principle in the *Caroline* raid, now denounced the idea of neutrality as an attempt to sustain royal power in Canada. Some members of Van Buren's own party objected to the bill on constitutional grounds. A Democrat from upstate New York, where the neutrality law would have the strongest effect, complained that it gave federal officials power to seize property without due process. Maine Democrat Francis O. J. Smith blasted the legislation as an attempt to disarm American citizens. Virginia Whig Henry A. Wise, who opposed any extension of the 1818 law, thought the new bill was an attempt to bestow the same "arbitrary power upon the President and upon his minions" as the alien and sedition laws had done in earlier times.[26]

As discussion dragged on, impatience in the House grew. A vote on February 24 saw the bill fail, 76 for and 88 against.[27] On March 1, after the Foreign Affairs Committee changed its wording, the House wearied of the protracted effort and passed the bill. A week later, the Senate approved, and Van Buren signed it on March 10.

The new measure extended the reach of the law beyond privateers and warships to include any vessels engaged in hostilities and, unlike the legislation of 1818, specifically referred to the use of other vehicles, meaning wagons and sleds. It also authorized prevention: federal officials could seize vessels and vehicles without warrants if they had probable cause to believe they were intended for military expeditions. Continued detention of property required a subsequent federal court warrant, but, if a judge approved, the property would remain in custody. The act also gave the national government the significant option of using the army, navy, and state militias to prevent violation of neutrality.[28] The effect of the act remained to be seen, but it was a substantial improvement over existing legislation and no doubt the best obtainable under the circumstances.

As soon as the act passed Congress, Minister Fox wrote the lieutenant governor of Upper Canada, Sir Francis Bond Head (who had been ordered home because of his ineffective handling of the rebellion), that passage of the law had averted immediate danger of war but had done little to settle accounts between the countries. If disturbances in Canada resumed, Fox believed there was "no power within the United States capable of restraining the people from rushing in mass across the frontier." He warned Head that Americans were determined to avenge the *Caroline* and advised him to return to England by the longer and less convenient Halifax route rather than through the United States because the border people might through a "pretence of legal process" bring charges against him for the *Caroline*. A man of remarkable stubbornness, Head traveled incognito through the United States, but he was recognized at one point and had to run for his life.[29]

Head's successor, Sir George Arthur, hardly helped matters. He immediately formed an unfavorable opinion of the United States. A soldier for thirty-four years, he had served as superintendent of British Honduras, where he had suppressed a slave revolt, and as lieutenant governor of the rugged British penal colony in Van Diemen's Land. His selection as chief officer of Upper Canada foretold strong measures against the insurgents and their American supporters. En route to Canada through the United States, he talked with General Scott and Governor Marcy at Albany. Despite their assurances that all was tranquil, he felt distrust. Marcy made the "worst impression." Arthur was sure that, if New York authorities were not involved in the border ✓ disturbances, they had done little to prevent them.[30]

Meanwhile, many Americans were concerned about Arthur's intentions toward United States citizens captured in Canada with the rebels. Despite Van Buren's declaration that they had forfeited their right to protection under American law, friends and relatives of men from Theller's *Anne* expedition petitioned the federal government for assistance. George Johnson, of Maryland, informed his congressman that his son had foolishly joined the crew of the *Anne* and was in a Toronto jail. A relative of W. W. Dodge, one of Theller's officers, wrote Forsyth that Dodge had lost an eye, which the family considered enough punishment. Some sought aid on behalf of Theller, who had been sentenced to hang. Writing the president, his wife asked how a United States citizen could be tried and condemned by a British court. Lending support to her petition were the Democratic governor of Michigan, Stephens T. Mason, and the United States marshal for the Michigan district, Conrad Ten Eyck, both suspected by the British of involvement with the Patriots.[31]

One of the particularly difficult cases was that of Thomas Jefferson Sutherland, an enterprising New York lawyer who had been an early participant in the Upper Canadian rebellion; he had been at Navy Island and after the *Caroline* raid was given command of Patriot forces at Detroit. Early in March, he was sleighing on the Lake Erie ice when he was spotted by a Canadian militia officer, arrested, and taken back to Canada. The incident aroused objection on two grounds. First, an American who witnessed the arrest stated that Sutherland was captured on the American side of the lake, a contention the arresting officer denied. The other objection was that Sutherland was tried before a militia tribunal rather than a civil court. Even Lieutenant Governor Arthur found the proceedings distasteful, but Sutherland was convicted and ordered transported to Van Diemen's Land for life. In the end, Sutherland and Theller both prevented additional diplomatic furors by escaping, but their cases were only the most prominent of many that raised similar difficulties.[32]

Responding to public concern, Van Buren decided to send a trusted veteran diplomat, Aaron Vail, to investigate claims that Americans were being held in Canada without evidence of guilt. Vail was urbane and competent, a good choice for the mission. Born in France, where his father was an American commercial agent, he had served as a clerk in the United States legation at Paris and in the State Department at Washington. As secretary of legation at London in 1831, he had become chargé d'affaires when the Senate denied Van Buren's nomination as minister to England. In December 1836 he returned to the United States and resumed his post as a State Department clerk.[33]

Early in April 1838, Secretary Forsyth informed Fox of Vail's mission. Fox reluctantly gave Vail a letter of introduction to Canadian authorities, and Vail set out from Washington the next day. According to his instructions, if he found prisoners entitled to American protection, he was to advise the authorities and attempt to obtain their release. The whole effort at first disturbed Governor Arthur, who believed that Vail's "strange mission" was evidence of official American sympathy for the rebels. Van Buren, he believed, was "playing a deep game," and he wondered why Fox had agreed to it.[34]

Arthur's suspicions were groundless, for from the British perspective Vail proved to be a perfect guest. Arriving in Montreal on April 9, he reported that the jails of the city were opened to him, and after searching every cell he found no Americans entitled to intervention. At Kingston, eight were in jail, but solid charges were pending against three, and the others were likely to be released. In Toronto, he found thirty-five prisoners who claimed United States citizenship—seventeen from the *Anne* and others arrested in Canada on various charges. Because the latter group had already pled guilty to charges of treason against Britain in exchange for clemency, Vail decided that this was a "renunciation of American citizenship" that ended their claim to protection; he never considered whether or not they had freely chosen to renounce their citizenship. He decided not to intervene for prisoners who had violated American neutrality laws, but he believed they would be "dealt with in the mildest manner consistent with the demands of justice and the nature of their offense." To Arthur, he privately referred to those involved with the Patriots as the "scum" of the frontier.[35]

Vail's mission had a salutary effect. His friendly attitude and lack of sympathy for Americans involved with the Patriots eased Arthur's suspicion. In any event, Fox assured the governor that Vail's mission did not represent a "deep game." Arthur's courtesies in turn pleased Vail, who informed the American government that the prisoners had no just grounds for complaint. Perhaps as a result of Vail's mission (but at least partly because their jails were overflowing), Canadian authorities released the *Anne* prisoners to American custody, with the expectation that, when they returned home, they would be prosecuted for violating neutrality laws.[36]

The issue of the *Anne* could be settled quickly, if not wholly satisfactorily. The Michigan official who received the men con-gratulated them for serving the cause of liberty and let them go. The *Caroline* did not yield to such resolution. The *Anne*, handled as a local issue between Canadian and American officials, was settled in a matter of weeks, but the *Caroline* had become a major dispute between the governments of two sovereign nations and was destined to drag on for years.✓

3

Van Buren Caves In

As soon as he learned of the *Caroline* affair, the American minister to the Court of St. James, Andrew Stevenson, returned to London from a Paris vacation, but in the absence of instructions from Washington he delivered no protest. Nobody was sure what course the British government would adopt, but, after private conversation with Palmerston, Stevenson thought it would justify the attack. His suspicions were correct. Indeed, the law officers of the Crown had already decided that, in accordance with the law of nations, the rule of self-preservation justified the invasion of American territory.[1]

In the United States, diplomatic discussion of the *Caroline* had closed unsatisfactorily when Fox informed the secretary of state that he could make no settlement of the issue. Forsyth sent Stevenson stiff instructions on the affair on March 12. The note was unfortunate because it presented as fact some highly colored testimony by victims of the raid. Forsyth's argument introduced a hardly credible presumption of American innocence when compared to the facts of the *Caroline*'s operations. He charged that the attackers had "slaughtered" several of the defenseless crew and passengers after the vessel had surrendered. Although Durfee was the only confirmed death, the secretary of state alleged others were unaccounted for, and rumor held that murdered and wounded left on board had gone over the falls to "a watery grave in the cataract." Forsyth contended that, even if

British accounts were true, and the attackers had taken care that no one was left on board, the invasion of United States territory was wrong. Canadian efforts to justify the raid were so preposterous that he presumed, he said, the British government would not sustain them.[2]

Probably the abrasive tone of this note came from the secretary of state rather than the president. Despite public pressure to demand satisfaction for the *Caroline*, Van Buren remained committed to resolving border problems as quickly as possible. About the same time Forsyth instructed Stevenson to demand reparations, Van Buren sent his son, John, to see Foreign Secretary Palmerston with a much different message. Young Van Buren carried a private letter from his father, expressing regret at the "embarrassments in our national relations" and assuring Palmerston that the feelings of the administration were against those who caused difficulties. If the "wishes of the men in power in both countries were alone to be consulted," Van Buren felt certain they could settle disagreements.[3]

Although skeptical about Americans in general, even Minister Fox now became convinced of Van Buren's sincerity. Writing to his government, Fox observed that the president had convinced him "beyond a doubt, of his sincere personal wish in favor of peace." His good feelings about Van Buren continued, and a few months later he told Palmerston that, of all politicians in America, the president most desired peace. If war were averted, it would be due "more to his individual character and conduct" than to anyone else in the United States. The secretary of state, however, continued to arouse Fox's distrust. Forsyth, he thought, was unfriendly to Britain and not "upon very cordial terms with the President."[4]

After receiving Forsyth's instructions, Stevenson, on May 22, sent an official protest on the *Caroline* to Palmerston. As a Virginian and slave owner, Stevenson usually adopted a strident tone on such questions as the slave trade, but his *Caroline* note, though firm, lent sophistication to Forsyth's demand for reparations by adding well-constructed arguments from international law. Opening with a condemnation of the "signal and extraordinary outrage," Stevenson denied the British view that the *Caro-*

line was piratical and that the ship and crew were, according to international law, subject to destruction wherever found. If the men on board had taken part in the rebellion, they were subject to punishment in Canada, but Britain had no right forcibly to enter another "sovereign and independent state." Stevenson knew a nation could justify such an invasion on grounds of necessity, but he objected to England's claim in this case. Writers on international law, he said, agreed that "the necessity must be imminent, and extreme, and involving impending destruction."[5]

Stevenson's arguments were excellent. Hugo Grotius had averred in 1625 that war in self-defense was permissible, but only when danger was "immediate and imminent." Working from earlier texts himself, he had argued that the most awful wrongs had been committed by those who feared harm from others without reason. He had opposed preemptive violence even when it was known that an enemy planned an attack, if delay afforded opportunity to apply other remedies. Samuel Pufendorf, too, had urged caution. He accepted the principle of inflicting injury on another in self-defense, but proposed rules for exercising the right. Mere suspicion of another's intentions could not justify an attack. In his view, the "beginning of the time at which a man may, without fear of punishment, kill another in self-defence, is when the aggressor, showing clearly his desire to take my life, and equipped with the capacity and the weapons for his purpose, has gotten into the position where he can in fact hurt me, the space being also reckoned as that which is necessary, if I wish to attack him rather than to be attacked by him."[6]

It is clear today that proper circumstances for intervention did not exist when British forces attacked the *Caroline*, and that, according to the law of nations at the time, Britain did not have justification. No necessity impelled MacNab's order to attack the *Caroline* or Drew's decision to continue across the Niagara into United States territory when he did not find the steamer at Navy Island. Canadian authorities had observed it for hours before the raid and carefully prepared for an assault. If MacNab had considered the circumstances, he would have realized that the

Caroline was not an immediate threat. There was no indication that occupants of Navy Island intended the steamboat for any purpose except carrying supplies and a few recruits. If the Patriots, who numbered only about one hundred fifty, had attempted an invasion with the vessel, the twenty-five hundred Canadians at Chippewa would have repelled them, a fact General Scott had pointed out to Van Rensselaer at their first meeting. Impatience and political feeling, not overriding necessity, had inspired the Canadian forces, despite British insistence that they had acted for self-preservation.

While diplomats argued points of international law, the Van Buren administration again found itself embarrassed by the activities of the Patriots. In the spring of 1838, devastated by military defeats and harassed by federal officials, they transformed themselves from a public organization into secret societies generally called Patriot Hunters' Lodges. Nobody knew the number of lodges, but the collector of customs at Oswego believed there was no "city, village, or port upon the lake frontier" where they did not exist. He estimated their numbers at twenty to forty thousand and thought they made "use of secret obligations and of secret signs and means of communication derived from the institution of Masonry." These societies, an informant told Van Buren, had spread all along the frontier.[7]

Estimates about the extent and organization of the Patriots were exaggerated. A number of groups had vested interests in creating the appearance of large and well-organized secret societies. The British felt no need to belittle reports of Patriot plans, partly because it seemed risky to ignore them and partly because they hoped to prod the American government into action against the movement. At the same time, lower-level federal officials in the United States probably used Patriot activity to display diligence to superiors. So it is no surprise that stories about the Patriots strained credulity. The same accounts that had forty thousand of them in towns and villages along the frontier claimed Patriot Hunters' lodges were organized in mysterious orders—Snowshoes, Beavers, Grand Hunters, and Patriot Hunters—whose members recognized each other by secret signs.[8]

Then came the incident of the *Sir Robert Peel*. The Patriots so concerned Lieutenant Governor Arthur that, in May 1838, he urged Fox to press the American government about the growth of secret organizations on the American frontier. Arthur believed border miscreants would not rest until they had revenge for the *Caroline*, and his suspicions were soon confirmed. On May 29 the Canadian steam packet *Sir Robert Peel*, bound from Prescott to Kingston, on Lake Ontario, stopped for fuel at Wells Island. On board were thirty Canadian lumbermen, other passengers, including women and children, and, as part of the freight, a package containing twelve thousand dollars from the Bank of Upper Canada. That night, fifty men, dressed and painted as Indians, attacked the *Peel*. Their leader, incongruously wearing Indian warpaint as well as a false beard and armed with six pistols, a sword, and a rifle, bullied the men and "wantonly and brutally" insulted the women. The attackers drove everybody ashore, then towed the vessel into the lake. Shouting "Remember the *Caroline!*" they then burned it. Afterward, some of the lumbermen could not be found, and one witness said he heard voices calling for help from the burning vessel.

The leader of the raid was Bill Johnston, a well-known renegade of the Thousand Islands region and bitter enemy of the regime in Canada. Canadian by birth, he had been imprisoned for several months during the War of 1812 as an American sympathizer. After his release, he left the country and for the rest of the war was an agent for the United States. The British seized his property and retained a hearty dislike for him. Even before the *Peel* affair, he was generally recognized as a river pirate, and Canadian authorities had already offered a reward for his capture.[9]

As soon as he learned about the *Peel* episode, Governor Marcy offered a reward for the arrest of Johnston and the others involved. He called out two companies of state militia but urged Secretary of War Joel Poinsett to replace them with regulars as soon as possible, primarily because he suspected the frontier militia still sympathized with the Patriot movement. The governor traveled from Albany to Watertown to investigate the *Peel* case personally and informed Poinsett that twelve participants had been apprehended, but Johnston and several others had holed up in the Thousand Islands over a twenty-five-mile stretch of the river. The islands had steep sides and dense coverings of trees and brush. According to Marcy, it was "scarcely possible to conceive of a place better formed by nature to afford a safe retreat for freebooters." He thought it would take an army of five hundred to clear the islands of the "desperate men who are concealed among them."[10]

Despite Lieutenant Governor Arthur's appeals that they not respond with similar acts of lawless violence, Canadians sought to retaliate. On June 2 an American steamboat, the *Telegraph*, was met by an unruly crowd at the Canadian port of Brockville. When the captain pulled away from the dock, two militiamen ordered him to halt. "Go to hell!" he answered. The guards opened fire, three rounds striking the boat and three falling short, as the skipper stubbornly continued up the river.[11]

In Washington, the administration remained unruffled. Following Governor Marcy's suggestion, Van Buren sent Major General Alexander Macomb to Sackett's Harbor, New York, to post regular troops at ferries and lake ports to protect British vessels from further Patriot outrages. When Congress called for information, the president advised the House that, instead of demanding redress from each other, the governments had agreed to regard the *Peel* and *Telegraph* incidents as offenses subject to state and provincial tribunals. The United States, he said, would make every effort to spoil the plans of Canadian refugees and the "few reckless persons" on the frontier who wished to embroil Britain and the United States in war.[12] The message seemed intended to reassure the British as much as Congress.

The Patriot Hunters nonetheless attempted to invade Canada. The district attorney for northern New York, Nathaniel S. Benton, informed Van Buren that the "whole frontier is filled with people . . . who appear to be ready at a moment's warning for any movement upon or acts of violence" against Canada. On June 20, 1838, between two hundred and four hundred men crossed the Niagara to Short Hills and briefly fought with British forces before being driven back to American soil. In September the collector of customs at Oswego informed Treasury Secretary

Levi Woodbury that he had received information about a major
Patriot convention planned for Cleveland. Among those who
would attend was Gilman Appleby, captain of the *Caroline.*
Woodbury issued a treasury circular warning collectors to exercise utmost vigilance, and the State Department's chief clerk,
Aaron Vail, passed the information on to the British minister.
Fox forwarded the reports to Lieutenant Governor Arthur, adding that, though exaggerated, there was a good deal of truth in
them. As rumors about a Patriot invasion continued into October, Fox worried that the mischief was more extensive and
imminent than he had at first thought. The presence of "vast
hordes of banditti and assassins" in the United States, he told
Arthur, posed great danger to peace between the countries.[13]

The attempt to invade Canada took place in November. For
several weeks, bands of Patriots had been gathering at towns
along the St. Lawrence, and on November 11 the steamer *United
States* left Sackett's Harbor with Patriots on board. Proceeding
downriver, it picked up more men and was joined by two armed
schooners. The next day, one of the schooners, captained by a
Polish refugee living in the United States, Niles Gustav von
Schoultz, reached the Canadian shore and briefly tied up to the
wharf at Prescott before moving downriver, where men from
the boat occupied a stone windmill. The other schooner, commanded by the raffish Bill Johnston, meanwhile had grounded
on a mud bar in the river and was attacked by a British gunboat.
Although the vessel regained headway, United States Marshal
Nathaniel Garrow seized both schooners and two Patriot steamboats. This action doomed the expedition, for it cut off the Patriots at the windmill from their supplies and prevented their
escape. While British steamers attacked from the river, troops
surrounded the windmill and opened fire with artillery. On November 16 the Patriots surrendered. Between twenty and forty
men on each side had been killed. Of the one hundred forty
Patriots taken prisoner, almost all were American citizens.[14]

Unaware of events at Prescott, Forsyth was responding to a
note Fox had written him about Patriot plans. The United States,
Forsyth said, regarded rumors about the Patriots as "highly exaggerated," but he assured the minister that the federal gov-

ernment would arrest those involved in filibustering. Of course, he related, the British had to be aware of the impracticality of placing a thousand-mile frontier in a "military attitude suffi-ciently imposing and effective to prevent such enterprises." When details of the Prescott affair did reach Washington, Van Buren issued a proclamation on November 21 condemning the invasion and warning "misguided or deluded persons" that cap-tured Americans could not expect protection from the United States government. Colonial authorities took Van Buren at his word. The Americans captured at the windmill were tried by the Canadian government and many were sentenced to hang. Nine were executed. Most had their sentences commuted to transportation to the British penal colony at Van Diemen's Land.[15]

The last attempt to take Upper Canada occurred in December 1838. After the Battle of the Windmill, the Patriots began gath-ering recruits for an invasion from Detroit. By December they had assembled five hundred men under General Lucius Verrus Bierce, a well-known Ohio Democrat. He had warned Van Buren in July that enforcement of neutrality would destroy the admin-istration. On December 3 he commandeered a steamer and landed one hundred and thirty-five men at the military barracks near Windsor. After he made a speech promising liberation for the Canadian people, his men set fire to the barracks and shot some of the occupants as they ran out. Moving toward Windsor, they burned the steamer *Thames* in revenge for the *Caroline* and, according to one report, murdered two civilians. By this time, the militia, commanded by Colonel John Prince, had assembled and, inflicting a withering fire, killed twenty-one of the Patriots. The rest, including Bierce, broke ranks. Twenty-four were taken prisoner. Prince ordered four executed on the spot. Those who escaped to the United States were honored with a reception at Detroit's city hall, where a thousand-dollar reward was offered for Prince's capture. The crowd by acclamation passed a set of resolutions condemning Congress for passing the Neutrality Act of March 10, 1838, and the president for enforcing the law. The closing resolution denounced the British government for the "unwarranted and inhuman massacre of American citizens on board the steamer *Caroline*."[16]

The military defeats the Patriots suffered during 1838 ended their effort to invade Canada but did not stop their dedication to overthrowing British rule. They turned instead to a policy of border provocations, similar to the *Peel* affair, designed to provoke a war between Britain and the United States. They nearly succeeded.

For much of 1838, American military leadership seemed unable to stop the Patriots. Although Scott, as President Van Buren's representative, had exerted a calming influence, the same could not be said for the general-in-chief of the army, Alexander Macomb, who seemed oblivious to Patriot activities. In September, just before the Battle of the Windmill, reports reached Washington that he was unaware of Patriot preparations. By the president's direction, the general was advised not to leave the frontier "without express authority from the proper quarter." But a British officer sent to New York to gather information reported that a week before the Battle of the Windmill Macomb saw "little cause for serious alarm" and insisted that reports about large-scale Patriot movements originated "either with men anxious for employment as spies, or with men in subordinate offices, anxious to shew their zeal and activity."[17]

After Macomb's failure to anticipate the Prescott invasion, Scott was recalled from the South, where he had been directing removal of the Cherokees. Arriving in Cleveland just as news of the Windsor invasion reached the city, he began arranging for volunteers and for assistance from federal attorneys, marshals, and customs collectors. As in the previous winter, he made a highly visible tour of the frontier and convinced many to abandon the Patriot cause. In April he issued a confidential circular authorizing local commanders to employ agents to obtain information about the Patriots and ordering them to share their knowledge with British officials, who had been skeptical about the American army in general and Macomb in particular. Fox informed Lieutenant Governor Arthur that he believed Macomb and other ranking officers in the army were honest, but their means were "wholly inadequate to repress the lawless propensities of their fellow citizens." Arthur was less charitable; he viewed Macomb as weak, unreliable, and "easily duped by the Patriots." Scott, however, inspired confidence. Fox advised Arthur that he was "punctilious and incredibly vain," but honest and more able than Macomb.[18]

Related to military difficulties of maintaining peace on the frontier were problems within the executive branch of the government. The Van Buren administration found itself hindered by insufficient personnel, by officials who narrowly construed their duties, and by some who were actually in collusion with Patriots to violate the neutrality laws.

Some officials, to be sure, were able and industrious. Nathaniel S. Benton, the federal district attorney for northern New York, spent a good deal of time tracking Patriots. Appearing before a grand jury in the summer of 1838, he obtained fourteen indictments against well-known Patriots, including Mackenzie, Van Rensselaer, and Johnston. The same grand jury, he informed Secretary Forsyth, ignored twelve other indictments he tried to present. In October, Benton advised the secretary of state that two participants in the *Peel* affair were living in Massillon, Ohio, and he hoped to go there to arrest them. Another dedicated official on the northern frontier was United States Marshal Garrow, who had seized Patriot boats at the Battle of the Windmill.[19]

Unfortunately, not all federal officials were as diligent. Although the Treasury Department had instructed customs collectors in April 1838 to assist District Attorney Benton in gathering testimony for the summer grand jury session, he later informed the president that only two had "rendered or preferred any assistance whatever." Marshal Garrow learned in advance about Patriot plans to attack Prescott but could find no volunteers for deputies and received no help from the customs collector at Ogdensburg, who brashly told him, "We are all Patriots here." Characteristic of the problem was the United States marshal at Detroit, Conrad Ten Eyck, who was generally considered to be a Patriot, or at least a sympathizer, despite his occasional vehement protests to the contrary. After the *Anne* expedition, he had signed a petition to the president on behalf of Theller, and he once stopped his deputies from firing on a Patriot steamboat. Reportedly he even supplied the Patriots with guns from the government inventory in his charge.

Ten Eyck was apt to become surly when his attitude came into question. In response to a State Department query, he sullenly reminded Forsyth that his district extended 140 miles along the Canadian border with "Citys & Towns every 5, 10, & 20 miles, and all of them contain Patriot feeling & action." When Scott complained about his performance, one of his supporters, Judge Ross Wilkins (also suspected of involvement with the Patriots) informed Van Buren that the criticism resulted from Scott's personal animosity toward Ten Eyck.[20]

To make things worse, District Attorney Benton and Marshal Garrow, the two most conscientious federal officials on the New York frontier, fell into personal bickering. Their problems began when Garrow arrested several men for taking part in the Prescott invasion, including two Patriot leaders, Johnston and John W. Birge. Benton wanted them held at the county jail, but Garrow, suspecting the guards, ordered them watched by his deputies at the town hotel. During the night, to Garrow's "surprise and deep mortification," the two men escaped. This so angered Benton that he not only upbraided the marshal but also wrote the president criticizing his laxness. After Secretary Forsyth sent the marshal a copy of Benton's remarks, Garrow responded, complaining that he had never received cooperation from the district attorney. From the beginning of his official relationship with Benton, he said, he had "received from him no other than the most uncurteous and disrespectful treatment," which he attributed to the marshal's "highly reprehensible temper."[21] Relations between the two may have mended when Johnston and Birge were recaptured, but the dispute between such dedicated officials probably disrupted government efforts as much as inattention to duty by others.

Political difficulties also hampered efforts to control the Patriots. Sympathy for the movement and a corresponding antagonism toward Britain ran both broad and deep in the northern states, and anti-Patriot measures carried political risks. When

Lieutenant Governor Arthur sent an emissary to the American army a week before the Prescott invasion, he was led to understand that no action could be taken against the Patriots until after the New York state election for governor on November 7. From Washington, the British minister informed Arthur that he had not even bothered to address notes about the Patriots to the American government until after the election, "during which time it was vain to hope that they would move hand or foot, in any thing that might endanger the vote of the lowest ruffian or patriot in that State." In the contest between Marcy and Seward, the issues were chiefly economic, growing out of the depression, but the Democrats' efforts to maintain neutrality on the border cost Marcy support in the frontier countries, and he lost to Seward by ten thousand votes.[22]

After losing New York to the Whigs, Van Buren's political adviser, state Comptroller Azariah Flagg, cautioned the president to choose words carefully for his annual message of December 3, 1838. Although it was important to preserve neutrality, Flagg reminded him that "thousands of our own people" considered the Canadian rebellion "identical with the cause of liberty for which our fathers contended, against the same tyrannical government." Similar warning came from prominent Democrat Edwin Croswell, editor of the Albany *Argus*, who advised Van Buren that the Canadian troubles could bring further political injury. Van Buren adopted a course consistent with neutrality but of doubtful political expediency. Replying to Flagg, he contended that it was "utterly impossible to prevent the young . . . from embarking in those enterprises, so long as their conduct is indirectly applauded by public expressions of sympathy." In his annual message of 1838, he took a firm stand against interference in Canadian affairs. "Criminal assaults" on Canada by U.S. citizens, he said, had proven "fatally destructive to the misguided or deluded persons engaged in them." Although Americans were entitled to their opinion regarding the rebellion, they had no right to violate the "peace and order of a neighboring Country," or the honor and laws of their own. When his message reached New York, the president heard more grumbling. Sentiment for the Patriots, he was warned, was "almost universal among our mechanics, farmers, and laborers," and growing stronger every day.[23]

Discussion of Canadian affairs soon revived congressional interest in the subject. Representative Caleb Cushing, on January 29, 1839, presented a series of resolutions asking for information on relations with Britain, the number and status of American citizens held in Canada, and progress in negotiations on the *Caroline*. Over the next few weeks, State Department clerks prepared reports on these issues. Meanwhile, in response to disturbances along the disputed northeastern boundary, between Maine and New Brunswick, Congress began discussing measures to defend the United States in case of invasion. On March 2, just before adjourning, it passed a bill authorizing the president to call up a provisional military force of fifty thousand volunteers and appropriated ten thousand dollars for defense.[24]

Perhaps the most difficult political problem Van Buren faced was the effort to win a presidential pardon for William Lyon Mackenzie, the Canadian who had been sentenced to eighteen months in prison for violating American neutrality laws. The difficulty was that, if Van Buren pardoned Mackenzie, his protestations in favor of neutrality would seem insincere. Yet, he faced increasing pressure for Mackenzie's release. ▬

Mackenzie displayed a marked disinclination for the hardships that usually accompany revolutionary causes. Tried and convicted in federal court at Canandaigua in June 1839, he informed Judge Smith Thompson that he should receive a mild sentence because, he claimed, he had not been involved in any Patriot activities since the previous June. Reminding the court that he had a "large and helpless family," he suggested a fine of one dollar and twenty-four hours in jail. Thompson fined him ten dollars but sentenced him to eighteen months. In Washington, Fox thought the jail term was too mild but expressed satisfaction that Mackenzie had been convicted.[25]

Mackenzie immediately began seeking a pardon. When his first appeal to United States Attorney General Felix Grundy received no reply, he sent a memorial directly to Van Buren complaining about his treatment. If the president left him in prison he would not live through half his sentence. He had heard, he said, that Van Buren did not want to pardon him because Britain might see it as approval of the Canadian rebellions. If that were the case, he would move anywhere Van Buren named, even be "banished to Texas." He hoped the president would at least issue orders allowing him to visit his home once a day or give him parole within the Rochester city limits.[26]

Van Buren had little sympathy for the Canadian. In his annual message of December 1839, he said that misguided individuals could not violate American neutrality "without encountering public indignation, in addition to the severest penalties of the law." But Mackenzie's supporters were persistent. John Norvell, Democratic senator from Michigan, sent Forsyth a letter he had received protesting imprisonment of "an old and tride friend of freedom." The senator had received similar letters from others and wondered what answer he should give. Congressman George M. Keim, of Pennsylvania, visited the president to seek a pardon for Mackenzie but was informed that it would be improper.[27]

When Mackenzie read the president's annual message and learned of Keim's lack of success, he sent the president an extraordinary letter. With some heat, he reminded Van Buren of previous unanswered letters, which showed in his view how one "supposed to be without political influence" was treated in America.[28] He then appealed to Governor Seward, who recognized an opportunity to discomfit the Democratic president. Seward replied that, because Mackenzie had violated a federal law, he could not alleviate his sentence. But he believed that, given the political nature of the offense, it ought to be treated differently. Both the Patriot leader and Seward sent Van Buren copies of the letter, to which Mackenzie added a note saying he had petitioned the "humane and considerate" governor once he saw that the president would pay no attention to his complaints.[29]

By this time, the chants for Mackenzie's freedom were deafening. In February 1840 a Democratic party leader from northern Ohio warned the state central committee that naturalized immigrants resented Mackenzie's imprisonment. "I have never seen a stronger tide of public feeling on any subject than there is here relative to this matter," he said. If Van Buren did not release Mackenzie, the state would go against him in the next election. In the Senate the following month, Michigan Senator Norvell presented a memorial for Mackenzie's release; in April Senator Richard M. Young, of Illinois, did likewise, and yet another petition arrived from Michigan. At the end of April, Norvell submitted a series of resolutions requesting the president to pardon Mackenzie.[30]

Van Buren at last caved in and ordered Mackenzie's release. Concern for Britain's opinion apparently had given way to the realities of American politics. The neutrality law of March 10, 1838, the center of Van Buren's effort to keep peace on the northern frontier, could not surmount three persistent problems: weak military forces, the federal government's inadequate administrative apparatus, and domestic political necessity. As Van Buren groped, the British thought the United States increasingly incapable of, or uninterested in, controlling the frontier population and preserving neutrality. Feeling grew among decision-makers in London that a policy of toughness was the only way to deal with the Americans.

4

BRITAIN DRAWS
THE LINE

In the years preceding the Civil War, many leaders
of British opinion viewed Americans both as worthy bearers of their English heritage and as demagogues and
mountebanks. Nassau Senior, the political economist, once declared that outside Britain no country had political and social
institutions equal to those in the United States, but he decried
the frenzy of the presidential elections, which he regarded as a
"disgrace to the Anglo-Saxon race."[1] Especially during the
depression of the 1830s, when many states defaulted on debts
to British creditors, and during the Canadian border troubles,
Britons turned increasingly skeptical about American credentials
for membership in the family of civilized nations.

Official policy toward the United States mirrored this am-
bivalence. The foreign secretary from 1830 to 1841, except for a
brief period out of power in 1834–35, was the volatile Lord Palmerston. He had been friendly with Martin Van Buren when
the latter was minister to Britain, and he had a pleasant enough
relationship with Van Buren's successor in the legation, Andrew
Stevenson, whom he entertained for a week at Broadlands in
January 1837. Palmerston accepted Americans as united by common blood, language, tradition, and values, but he regarded the
United States with a large measure of distrust. Its people, he
believed, were shrewd, devious, and jealous of their parent
country. He felt that the young nation was always searching for

opportunities to encroach. Van Buren's administration was too weak to carry out open aggression, but Palmerston was convinced that only firmness would keep the Yankees from following their natural inclinations.[2]

The principal agents of British policy in North America shared Palmerston's suspicions but did not complicate their attitudes with any favorable opinion of American character. Just before his recall to England, Lieutenant Governor Sir Francis Bond Head proudly informed Colonial Secretary Lord Glenelg that the hatred of loyal Canadians for Americans was "incurable." If Upper Canada were firmly governed, he believed the "barbarous tyranny of mob government in America would eventually collapse." In his opinion, President Van Buren gave the appearance of seeking good relations with Britain, but his administration failed to take actions essential to ending frontier problems. The British minister in Washington, Fox, informed Canada's Sir John Colborne that, though outwardly the president had done all that could be expected, the United States government had "both wished and expected that the Canadian rebellion would succeed." As border troubles continued, British officials increasingly doubted that they could keep peace with the United States unless its people were forced to realize the danger in their irresponsible actions. In an effort to turn America around, these officials adopted stern policies toward the United States.[3] The result was a series of alarums that increased rather than diminished the risk of conflict.

Because the British minister in Washington was antagonistic toward Americans, Canadian and British officials heard little from him to change their opinions. As soon as Van Buren signed the neutrality law of March 10, 1838, Fox informed Head that, though the act had reduced the danger of war, the safety of the provinces ultimately had to depend on Canadians themselves because there was "no power within the United States, capable of restraining the people from rushing in mass across the frontier, for the purposes of plunder and devastation," if the opportunity arose. In June, Fox wrote Head's successor, Arthur, in a similar vein, telling him that, if British efforts ever relaxed for a moment, American neutrality would end. Although government officials were sincere in their occasional protestations of goodwill, he said, the people had been "born and bred up in the expectation, that the Canadas were necessarily destined to belong, sooner or later, to them." From the beginning, Arthur himself had been skeptical about Van Buren. Arthur told one confidant he thought Americans planned to take Canada the same way they had Texas: their government would give the appearance of disapproving unneutral proceedings but privately encourage them. Writing to his principal military commander, Sir John Colborne, Arthur said that American leaders could avert the "coming storm" but he did not have the "slightest confidence in them." The Canadian troubles, he maintained, "cannot end without an American war."[4]

If anything, Fox became more pessimistic. After Van Buren's proclamation of November 21, he informed Palmerston that the inadequacy of the neutrality act became more obvious every day. At the end of 1838, he recommended that the government adopt a tougher policy toward the United States. The president's annual message, he said, recognized the lawlessness on the frontier but revealed the ineffectiveness of the government. Instead of taking firm action, Van Buren did "little more than implore and beseech his fellow citizens, to desist from a career of acknowledged and infamous publick crime." Britain, Fox suggested, should declare its intent to defend Canada in a way that would show Americans that their actions would arouse the "vengeance of England, and the ruinous penalty of a national war." Sending a copy of this effusion to Lieutenant Governor Arthur, he added that the administration was "striving, so far as so weak and feeble a Government can be said to strive at any thing,—to fulfill its national duties"; nonetheless, the government's weakness undermined its sincerity. The United States would need to be addressed in a much harsher tone.[5]

Concerned about the deteriorating diplomatic relations, British officials displayed considerable energy. In March 1838 Fox advised the commander of naval forces in North America, Vice Admiral Sir Charles Paget, to position his squadron "as to render it most available in the event of war breaking out, suddenly, between Great Britain and the United States." Palmerston ordered Fox to collect information on American arsenals and naval preparation. Fox directed the British consul at Norfolk to send him confidential reports, particularly regarding the 120-gun warship *Pennsylvania* and the status of ships intended for Captain Charles Wilkes's exploring expedition. Fox sent intelligence about American naval movements on to Paget in May, noting that the situation seemed quieter than it had earlier.[6]

The British also increased their forces in North America and the West Indies. During the Canadian rebellions, only 2,000 regulars were stationed in Canada. During 1838 and 1839, the number was increased to 10,000 and the militia and volunteers raised to 21,000. During the same period, naval forces in American waters were augmented from twenty-seven vessels at the beginning of 1838 to forty-one at the end of the year. In March 1839 British army Colonel William Napier made plans against the United States in the event of war; the navy would blockade it and proclaim liberty for slaves in expectation of causing a "servile war" in America. Later that year, Lord John Russell, secretary for war and the colonies, proposed creating a government committee of military experts to review measures for the defense of the colonies.[7]

The most significant British military preparations took place on the St. Lawrence and the Great Lakes. In an exchange of notes in 1817, acting United States Secretary of State Richard Rush and British minister Charles Bagot had agreed that neither country would maintain armed forces on the Great Lakes. Both governments approved the arrangement, which was subject to cancellation on six months' notice. Nevertheless, Britain sent a Royal Navy officer, Captain Richard Sandom, to Canada in 1838 to supervise a naval buildup. By the end of 1839, he reported that he had increased forces on the Great Lakes by four steamboats, several schooners and gunboats, and more than four hundred men. A Yankeephobe, he declared that "war with the Yankees" was inevitable.[8]

In going beyond the limits of the Rush-Bagot Agreement, Canadian Lieutenant Governor Arthur assumed that his predecessor, Sir Francis Bond Head, had reached an understanding with Washington. But that was not the case. Fox informed Arthur there was no such agreement. Fox had asked for Palmerston's authorization to negotiate one, but Palmerston had never sent him instructions. Still, Fox urged Arthur to "disregard the restrictions stipulated in the Agreement." Given conditions on the border, he did not think the United States would be so "monstrously unreasonable and perverse" as to object. Advising Forsyth of the increases, Fox explained that they were intended only to protect the provinces against the Patriots and would be reduced as soon as possible. Palmerston and Colonial Secretary Lord Glenelg decided that, because the American government had not protested the violation, "it might perhaps be well to let the matter rest as it does."[9]

The British government also decided that, if necessary, their forces would pursue Patriots who invaded Canada back into American territory. Apparently this idea originated with Arthur, who asked Fox to make the necessary arrangements with the United States. Fox agreed that pursuit of rebels would almost inevitably result in violation of American territory, but in a confidential letter to Arthur he said that any agreement to cover such a contingency would be impossible. Infringement of territory would involve risk of collision with American forces and carry the "instant probability of a national war." Despite his misgivings, Fox addressed a note to the State Department remarking that Britain could not allow hordes of "ruffians and brigands . . . again and again, to issue forth from within the jurisdiction of the United States, for the ruin of Her Majesty's subjects." Forsyth's response confirmed Fox's opinion. He told the minister that the United States would never peacefully accept infringement of its territory by British forces.[10]

Fox then informed London that any arrangement for entering American territory was impossible because, even if Van Buren wished one, which was doubtful, "he would not dare to encounter the clamour of his citizens." Even so, Fox believed that support for the Patriot movement in the United States made such retaliation inevitable. The American people would not stop border provocations until they were convinced their actions could incur the risk of war.[11]

Officials in London accepted this view. After conferring with

Lord Melbourne, who had strong reservations about such a policy, Palmerston instructed Fox to say that Britain would regret the necessity to pursue "Bands of Rebels or Pirates" into the United States, but "some little overstepping of the boundary" might occur. Such an event, Fox should assure the American government, would not be to inflict vengeance but to destroy rebels.[12] Thus, policymakers in London accepted the idea, advocated most persistently by Arthur and Fox, that Britain had to deal forcefully with the United States. The government seriously underestimated American sensitivity on subjects that involved the sense of national honor, and the consequence was a series of increasingly dangerous misunderstandings between the nations.

The first of these occurred at the beginning of 1839, in an incident similar to that of Thomas Jefferson Sutherland, the Patriot leader whom Colonel John Prince had arrested, allegedly on the American side of Lake Erie. From Michigan came word that a Detroit resident who had previously lived in Canada, Howland Hastings, had been arrested while visiting there for a crime committed in the United States against a British subject. Hastings was charged with assaulting Samuel Wilcox in Detroit shortly after the Battle of Windsor, an act the British considered an offense "against the peace and dignity of the Queen" even though it had happened in the United States. Wilcox claimed that Hastings had offered him $800 if he would bring in the head of Colonel Prince and $1,000 for Prince alive, in revenge for the four Patriots executed after the Battle of Windsor. After being beaten for refusing to undertake such dastardly deeds, Wilcox escaped to Canada, where he filed charges. When Hastings later ventured into Canada he was arrested.[13]

As soon as he learned of the arrest, Forsyth sent a note to Fox asking for an explanation. The president, he declared, was "utterly unable to persuade himself" that Canadian courts believed they had jurisdiction over offenses committed in the United States. Fox promised to query Arthur about the incident, but in the meantime Hastings had been sentenced to six months' imprisonment. On reviewing the case, Canadian officials decided the provincial government did not have authority to try him for a crime committed in the United States and ordered his release, but Prince immediately filed new charges for threats Hastings made while under arrest. So he remained in custody, not for the original charges, but now held, as Arthur informed Michigan Governor Stephens T. Mason, until he could give security for "future good behavior." Mason asked the Detroit collector of customs, John McDonell, who knew Canadian officials, to help procure Hastings's release, and on February 21, he returned to the United States, having spent time in a Canadian jail on highly questionable charges. McDonell believed the second charge was without foundation and reported that, when he had secured Hastings's release, Prince denounced him in a "strain of vulgar abuse." In England, Stevenson protested the affair to Palmerston, but the foreign secretary replied that, because Hastings had been released, he considered the matter settled.[14] The incident had ended satisfactorily, but the detention of Hastings on such questionable grounds demonstrated British antagonism.

One reason British authorities considered, and in the Hastings case, resorted to unusual means was a well-founded concern that in the United States neither state nor federal officials would carry out justice. Part of the problem lay in the federal system itself, for in the nineteenth century the division between state and federal authority on extradition was not fully settled. In several cases, criminals went free because of confusion in the law. As far as the British were concerned, however, the problem was not legal technicality but American perfidy. The two countries had reached an extradition agreement in article 27 of the Jay Treaty of 1794, but the article had expired in 1807. The surrender of mutineer Jonathan Robbins (alias Thomas Nash) to the British navy in 1799 had resulted in widespread American prejudice against any new accord of extradition.[15]

It was difficult to predict American cooperation with the British over extradition because of the absence of an extradition treaty. In 1822 New York passed a law that allowed the governor to surrender fugitives. But other states were more cautious. When Canada requested two fugitives from Vermont in 1825, Governor Cornelius P. Van Ness replied that extradition was a national question over which he had no authority. He referred the case to Secretary of State Henry Clay, who contended the national government lacked the power to surrender fugitives ✓without a treaty. Extradition again became an issue during the Canadian rebellions when Lieutenant Governor Head requested the surrender of Mackenzie from New York on charges of murder, arson, and robbery. New York Governor William L. Marcy decided the charges were political rather than criminal, and refused.[16] In subsequent cases, American authorities refused to extradite notorious outlaws.

To Canadians, who were more interested in return of criminals for punishment than in American constitutional theory, the confusion between state and national authority on extradition seemed sophistic and the release of felons treacherous. In January 1839 the military governor of Lower Canada, Sir John Colborne, asked Vermont's chief executive, Silas H. Jenison, to surrender some men who had crossed into Canada and committed arson. The perpetrators of the outrages were the James Grogans—elder and younger—then residents of Alburgh, Vermont, but for nearly twenty years previously farmers in Lower Canada. During the rebellion in the province, they had been turned out of the area and their property seized because they refused to take an oath of allegiance. They swore revenge, and on the night of December 30, 1838, they and a dozen accomplices crossed into Canada. At about three in the morning, they reached the farm of John Gibson, who claimed he heard them banging on the door and calling out, "We are murderers and robbers." The parents and five children jumped out a rear window in their nightclothes, and the Grogans burned their house and barn. Before returning to the United States, they set the torch to three more farms. A few weeks later, a similar outrage was committed against another Canadian farmer, Abraham Vosburgh, by unidentified culprits from Alburgh. Vosburgh and his son were bound and jabbed several times with bayonets. Their barn was burned to the ground, but neighbors managed to save their house.[17]

Canadian authorities demanded extradition of the Grogans and the nameless Vosburgh offenders, but Governor Jenison decided that the state had no authority to surrender fugitives.

He told Colborne he was against "lawless and vindictive violence" on the frontier, but because American law and the Constitution were silent on extradition, he needed time to reflect. He soon decided that extradition of fugitives was the exclusive concern of the national government because it involved foreign relations. In Washington, Fox asked for the arrest of the Grogans, but the government took no action.[18]⇀

Although the Grogan case could be considered political, the extradition issue arose again in 1839 over a crime clearly unconnected with politics. George Holmes, born in New Hampshire, but at the time a physician in Quebec, was the paramour of another man's wife. When the husband discovered the affair, Holmes murdered him and fled across the border to Vermont. General Colborne requested his extradition, and state officials arrested him in Burlington. But, given the unclear disposition of the Grogan case, they were unsure what to do. They ordered him held pending a decision from the national government.[19]

The Van Buren administration again disappointed the British. In answer to Fox's request for Holmes's surrender, Forsyth conveyed the president's "regret and abhorrence" at the crime but said that in view of the expiration of the extradition article of the 1794 treaty, there was not a thing to do except express repugnance at the crime. The British already had heard in the Grogan case that a state lacked power to give over fugitives because extradition was the concern of the national government; now they were told the federal government did not have the power either. Where did power to extradite lie? It turned out that, in the absence of treaty provisions, it rested nowhere. Holmes, who under the circumstances had no burning desire to return to Canada, applied to the Vermont Supreme Court for a writ of habeas corpus, which it denied. The United States Supreme Court divided four to four (one justice was absent) on the question. Chief Justice Roger B. Taney, with the concurrence of three justices, ruled that the federal government held exclusive jurisdiction over foreign affairs; Vermont had no authority to deal with the Canadians. The other justices felt the Court lacked jurisdiction or believed Vermont had authority to extradite. The case was remanded to the Vermont Supreme Court which, after studying this welter of the higher body's opinion, decided the state had no power to surrender Holmes and declared him free. Again, the British believed, a criminal had escaped justice because of defects in the American political system.[20]

The most provoking case from the British point of view was an effort to extradite the frontier outlaw Benjamin Lett, whose hatred for the British seemed unquenchable. He had been with the Patriots at Navy Island in the winter of 1837 and reportedly accompanied Bill Johnston at the burning of the *Sir Robert Peel*. On other occasions, he had murdered a British officer, blown up a monument dedicated to General Isaac Brock in Queenston, and demolished several locks on the Welland Canal. In January 1839 he tried to set fire to British warships at Kingston.

Lett was beyond doubt a dangerous and unpredictable character, but the American government seemed oblivious to the menace he presented. Perhaps it was because his activities had a way of raising political issues. When the Canadians in 1839 asked New York to extradite him, Governor William H. Seward saw an opportunity both to serve justice and annoy President Van Buren. At Seward's direction, New York's secretary of state, John C. Spencer, informed the State Department of the British request and served notice that, even though New York had a law authorizing the governor to surrender fugitives, Seward believed anything associated with foreign relations was "exclusively under the control of the General Government."[21]

Seward's willingness to send Lett's problem to Washington was an astute move by a New York Whig against a New York Democrat. The chief clerk of the State Department, Aaron Vail, answered Seward that, in the absence of specific treaty provisions, the administration believed the federal government lacked authority to extradite. Vail believed Seward's objection to state extradition raised a constitutional question; he therefore suggested that New York initiate proceedings against Lett so the issue could be brought before the United States Supreme Court. Vail's note gave Seward an opportunity to occupy high ground while consigning the Democratic administration to the unprincipled swamps below. Lett's case, the governor maintained, was a clear instance of "atrocious guilt," and he deplored the president's refusal to act. Seward said he remained convinced that foreign relations were the concern of the national government, and he had no interest in acting unconstitutionally 'for the sake of trying experiments."

Both Seward and Van Buren stood by their principles, and Lett remained free, a continuing irritant to Anglo-American relations. Eventually he overstepped himself, for in June 1840 he was caught attempting to blow up a British steamer at Oswego. Sentenced by a New York court to seven years' confinement, he escaped on the way to the state prison by a daring leap from a moving train.[22]

As understanding declined between Americans and Canadians, incidents increased along the frontier. From Rouses Point, New York, in March 1839 came news that Canadian troops, taking revenge for acts of arson, had entered the United States to set fires. During the same month, some soldiers' barracks were burned, purportedly by British militia from Odletown, and one witness heard them say as they passed his farm that the whole area would be set afire. Guards gathered around farms, but the militiamen struck again on March 18, when they burned a barn. A light snow had fallen, and Americans followed tracks to the border, where they were shot at from the Canadian side. Five nights later, arsonists—perhaps the Odletown volunteers—torched another barn. Seward informed Van Buren of the outrages and issued a proclamation against such "evil disposed persons."[23]

In April another disturbance occurred when the steamboat *United States* left Ogdensburg, New York, for a trip up the St. Lawrence. The captain had been warned that some Canadians intended to fire on the boat, but he nonetheless decided to continue. As it made its way past Prescott, three Canadian officers and a soldier stepped onto the wharf. One of the officers ordered the soldier to fire. Six shots passed over the steamer, which was carrying about eighty passengers. Americans reporting the episode were particularly annoyed because a crowd gathered on the Prescott wharf had "huzzaed and exulted."[24]

In May a fracas nearly resulted in a clash between British and

American forces. On May 16 the schooner *G. S. Weeks*, of Oswego, New York, arrived at the Upper Canadian town of Brockville carrying cargo for that port and other destinations. Included in the bill of lading was a six-pound cannon consigned to A. B. James, of Ogdensburg. British authorities suspected that this man, captain of a state militia artillery unit, was a Patriot who had supplied state arms to rebel forces at the Battle of the Windmill the previous December. When townspeople learned about the cannon, a menacing crowd gathered, and someone sent for the British customs collector from nearby Prescott. To the delight of the Canadians, he seized the vessel and its cargo. The cannon was taken to the village square, where it was discharged several times to the "loud and repeated cheers" of the crowd.[25]

In a short time, news of the event reached Colonel William J. Worth, of the United States Army, then patrolling in the St. Lawrence aboard the *Oneida*, and he decided that the British had committed an outrage against the national honor. Steaming into Brockville harbor, he demanded, in the name of the United States, that the collector release the *Weeks*, "unjustifiably seized and held by your authority, and especially the restitution of the gun." After two hours without a response, the colonel pulled the *Oneida* alongside the Prescott wharf and advised the captain of the *Weeks* to abandon the vessel because it might come in the line of fire. Recognizing that Worth was spoiling for a fight, the collector decided the seizure had been a mistake and returned the *Weeks*, with its gun, to the captain. Escorted by the *Oneida*, the vessel returned to the United States, where Worth's superior, General Abraham Eustis, expressed satisfaction with the colonel's "prompt and energetic course."[26]

If the Americans had reason to be satisfied with these proceedings, the British did not. Arthur asked the province's legal advisers if seizure of the *Weeks* had been justified. He was informed, to his distress, that in their opinion it was not. Arthur became angry with everyone involved: the collector, he felt, had been "popularity-hunting." He had erred in seizing the vessel and the gun, but having done so, he should have not given in to the threat of force. Arthur felt Worth's behavior was "worse than anything" that had happened so far between the countries.

Arthur vented his frustration on the citizens of Brockville, whose actions, he told them, had placed him in the "humiliating position" of having to admit British wrong while complaining to the United States about Colonel Worth.[27]

In a review of the case, provincial authorities found a way for Arthur to justify both the detention of the *Weeks* and its release. The seizure, they now found, had been legal because British law forbade importation of gunpowder, arms and ammunition, or "utensils of war" into Canada. The captain's presentation of a bill of lading, which proved the gun was consigned to Captain James in the United States, justified the release.[28] The British saw no grounds for the United States government to complain but believed that the behavior of Colonel Worth gave them ample reason to protest. The American view, of course, was the opposite.

Both sides would have been well advised to let the matter rest, but, acting on instructions from Secretary of State Forsyth, Minister Stevenson protested the *Weeks* affair to Palmerston in an angry note that widened an already complicated and unnecessary dispute. In his account, the Americans had been victims of a "disgraceful, insulting and riotous" mob and the unfriendly attitude of the collector. The illegally seized property had been returned, but Stevenson thought it important to call the inappropriate conduct of the collector to the British government's attention. Stevenson significantly omitted any mention of Colonel Worth's actions.[29]

Palmerston's reply attacked not only Stevenson's *Weeks* protest, but also the whole attitude of Americans toward border problems. He informed Stevenson that, after yet another examination of the circumstances, the Crown's lawyers in England had decided that the collector had been correct in seizing the *Weeks* and there had been no obligation to return it. The law required the master of any ship entering a British port to present a manifest of his cargo with a list of the consignees, but the captain of the *Weeks* had not done so until after the seizure. Because the penalty for violation was forfeiture of vessel and cargo, their return by the collector was an indulgence. Worth's behavior particularly irritated Palmerston. The colonel, without seeking explanation, had entered British territory with force to demand redress. Palmerston warned that any American officer who so conducted himself in the future would bear responsibility for the resulting clash of arms.[30]

In the same note, Palmerston brought up another matter of displeasure: the release, with congratulations from the judge, of the seventeen *Anne* prisoners who had been returned to the United States in expectation that American authorities would punish them. Told that neither the federal government nor the states had authority to extradite criminals who congregated in the United States, British leaders now saw that, even when felons were handed over to American justice, they were praised rather than jailed. Palmerston reacted with a threat of military force: if the United States did not take measures "to prevent or to punish such delinquencies," Britain would consider itself "obliged to have recourse to such measures as may appear called for."[31]

Obviously, the foreign secretary's remarks were not only complaints about Worth and the *Anne* prisoners, but also a statement of policy toward the United States, particularly regarding the possibility of future cases like the *Caroline*. If the nation could not control its populace or its officials, Britain reserved the right to enter its territory forcibly.

Stevenson replied without waiting for instructions from Washington. Worth's actions, he felt, were unexceptionable under the circumstances. He conceded Britain's grounds for objection regarding the *Anne* prisoners but reminded the foreign secretary that in the American federal system the national government had no authority over state officials. He also objected to Palmerston's threat of force. Discussion of an issue of such "deep and vital importance to the Peace and Tranquility" of the countries, he remarked, more properly belonged to another case: the *Caroline*.[32]

In Washington, Fox conveyed Palmerston's sentiments to the American government. President Van Buren expressed regret at "reprehensible declarations" by the Michigan magistrate who received the crew from the *Anne* and assured Fox that his government had made great efforts to prevent violations of neutrality on the frontier. Still, Britain had to understand the difficulty of policing a "sparsely settled frontier of some thousand miles in extent" against acts of refugees determined on revolution; furthermore, the United States would not tolerate another invasion of its territory. Fox, however, still failed to understand the abhorrence with which Americans regarded British views on that subject. He informed his government that the United States still maintained an "unreasonable, unjust and inadmissible position" that insisted on the sanctity of "Territory of the Republick."[33]

Diplomatically, neither country had done credit to itself by pressing a case both could view as undeserving. Palmerston had every reason to fault Worth's behavior in the affair, but his own gyrations on the legal issues were contrived to make the British appear in the right, despite the facts of the case. Once the captain of the *Weeks* had proved the gun was destined for an officer in the New York state militia, the matter should have ended. Instead, the foreign minister unwisely complicated circumstances by linking the *Weeks* affair with the unrelated issue of forcible entry of American territory, and thus, by indirection, the *Caroline* question. But the problems were not confined to the British ministry. The most dangerous part of the occurrences had been the ill-considered actions by both sides at Brockville. The Canadian collector of customs had surrendered his sense of duty to an unruly crowd, and Worth's threat to obtain release of the *Weeks* and its gun was inappropriate and perilous for relations between the countries. There were a number of remedies, but Colonel Worth chose the worst. His superiors should have censured him instead of praising him, and it is surprising that the American government went to such lengths to defend him. In sum, the affair began needlessly, ended inconclusively, and left neither side satisfied with the result.

Thus, despite Van Buren's best efforts, difficulties along the Canadian border continued to disturb Anglo-American relations. In adopting an abrasive policy toward the border problems, the British made a mistake. Their frustrations with the American government were frequently legitimate, but their reactions were unrealistic. Rather than providing a calming effect, their policy irritated the frontier population and many of the country's political leaders. In an atmosphere of suspicion and hostility, petty issues took on an importance they did not deserve, and, in their responses to such incidents, the two countries unnecessarily surrendered their ability to compromise more serious differences. Up to the time of the *Weeks* affair, they had faced no difficulties that required skills beyond ordinary diplomacy, which was especially fortunate because their handling of the issues seemed ordinary indeed. The arrest of Alexander McLeod for murder and arson in connection with the *Caroline* raid changed all that.

Admiral Andrew Drew by H. Holmes (Courtesy of the Public Archives of Canada/C-25729)

"The Capture of the *Caroline*" by Alfred Sandham from Sir Francis B. Head, *A Narrative*, London, 1839 (Courtesy of the Public Archives of Canada/C-272)

"The Cutting-out of the *Caroline*" by Alfred Sandham from Henry J. Morgan, *Sketches of Celebrated Canadians*, Quebec, 1862 (Courtesy of the Public Archives of Canada/C-4787)

"The Destruction of the *Caroline*" by George Tattersall (Courtesy of the Public Archives of Canada/C-4788)

William Henry Seward by J. C. Buttre after Henry Inman (Courtesy of William Henry Seward Papers, Department of Rare Books and Special Collections, Rush Rhees Library, University of Rochester)

Daniel Webster, attributed to Bass Otis (Courtesy of the White House Collection)

John Tyler by George Peter Alexander Healy (In the Collection of the Corcoran Gallery of Art, Museum Purchase, Gallery Fund, 1879)

5

THE ARREST OF ALEXANDER MCLEOD

The cauldron of frontier troubles boiled over in November 1840, when Alexander McLeod, a Canadian deputy sheriff from Niagara, was arrested in New York on charges of arson and murder connected with the *Caroline* affair. Britain and the United States had complained of one another's behavior in that event for almost three years, but their arguments were not constrained by any need for resolution. Each side seemed ready to argue indefinitely that the other deserved almost exclusive blame. When McLeod was arrested, the matter took on a new immediacy; not only national honor but a man's life was suddenly at stake.

McLeod was a fitting catalyst for this renewed crisis, for both his patriotism and his personality stirred controversy. On both sides of the border, the Scottish-born veteran of the Royal Lancers was known as a man of courage and uncompromising loyalty to the Crown. In the engagement against the Patriots at Montgomery's Tavern, shortly before the *Caroline* affair, he had recklessly charged ahead of the main force into the rebel ranks. Later, he entered the United States as an agent and made several reports to Lieutenant Governor Arthur about Patriot plans; on one occasion, he had to flee from a mob in Buffalo. It was he who first brought British leaders information about the *Caroline*. Such dedication and industry had won Arthur's praise, but it had also gained McLeod the undying hatred of the Patriots and their American sympathizers.[1]

Although nobody would deny his bravery, McLeod also made enemies with his reputation for sharp practice. Among his duties as deputy sheriff, he executed writs involving transfers of money. Before the *Caroline* affair, a complaint had been made about his probity. The British consul in New York, James Buchanan, charged that the deputy had collected sixty pounds on behalf of the consul's family but offered to turn over only forty.[2] Because McLeod's duties frequently took him to the United States, his foolhardiness and avarice eventually put him on trial for his life and embroiled the United States and Britain in a seemingly impossible dispute.

McLeod was first arrested in Manchester, New York, on September 2, 1840, on charges arising from the *Caroline* raid. He was quickly released for want of evidence, but not before shouting to a crowd outside the jail that, if he had been on the raid, he would be among the last to deny it. He was no sooner set free than he was again taken into custody and spirited to Niagara to face the same charges from another indictment issued in Niagara County. Once more, he was released because that indictment was issued against Angus rather than Alexander McLeod. During these proceedings, McLeod was also named a defendant in a civil suit filed by a New Yorker, Hezekiah Davis, who said McLeod had sold some of his Canadian property for the execution of a writ and kept the money. McLeod was returning to Canada from the United States, where he had gone to gather evidence for his defense in that case, when he was arrested a third time, on November 12, 1840, at the Frontier House inn in Lewistown, New York. This time, the charges stuck because new key witnesses, who had not come forward in the earlier proceedings, now testified against him: J. C. Davis, brother of Hezekiah, who owned the inn where McLeod was arrested; Philo Smith, brother-in-law of J. C.; and Charles Parke, an employee at the inn. All swore they had heard McLeod boast of his exploits on the *Caroline*. Based on their testimony, he was jailed at Lockport.[3]

McLeod lost no time in seeking assistance. He engaged two

local attorneys, Hiram Gardner and Alvin C. Bradley, and appealed to Civil Secretary of Canada Samuel B. Harrison. When word of his arrest reached Canada, more than a hundred residents of the Niagara district sent a memorial to Lieutenant Governor Arthur testifying that he had not been a member of the *Caroline* party. After consulting Harrison and his attorney general, William H. Draper, Arthur sent a Niagara solicitor to assist McLeod.[4]

At first, British officials underestimated the seriousness of the situation at Lockport, an understandable reaction because Canadians had been harassed in this manner before. In March 1838 Francis Dawson had crossed into New York to get married, only to be arrested on *Caroline* charges and held three weeks. In August of that year, Buffalo authorities had seized another Canadian, John Christie, and held him until he established an alibi for the night of the *Caroline* raid. Canadian sailors had informed Arthur that they feared entering American ports because steamboats had been searched by mobs looking for participants in the affair.

Arthur told the governor-general of Canada, Lord Sydenham, that he had written the minister in Washington, Fox, asking him to help obtain McLeod's release. Arthur told Sydenham that he had no reason to disbelieve McLeod's assertion that he was not on the raid, but added that, if the man had been at Chippewa that night, he was the "most probable man I know to have been one of the Party." The incident aroused ardent military feelings in Sir Richard Jackson, head of forces in Canada, who wrote Arthur early in January 1841 that, if the Americans hanged McLeod, Canadians should procure his skin for a drum to raise the troops for vengeance.[5]

Official esteem for the prisoner began to decline when Arthur heard disturbing reports that McLeod had invited his own arrest by boasting about his participation in the raid. Allegations about his financial misconduct also disturbed Arthur. Although still believing the Scot had not taken part in the raid, Arthur informed confidants that McLeod, whom he described as "altogether a scheming kind of gentleman," probably had encouraged the excitement to gain attention and perhaps money. He began to regard McLeod as one of those on both sides of the frontier who stood to gain from trouble, and he thought the man might be willing to undergo some difficulty to bring it about. General Jackson quickly adopted Arthur's views, referring sarcastically in his correspondence to McLeod as "that illustrious martyr."[6]

The arrest could hardly have occurred at a worse time for relations between Britain and the United States. Border incidents had raised a shrill dialogue between the governments and reduced their flexibility. To further frustrate an early conclusion to McLeod's case, Van Buren lost his bid for reelection in 1840 to the Whig candidate, William Henry Harrison. Although always chary about American politicians, Fox had assured his government only the year before that Van Buren was the one most dedicated to peace. If war between the two countries could be averted, Fox believed it would be due mainly to Van Buren's character and effort, and he judged it fortunate that each day increased the president's chances for reelection. But, when the nation went to the polls, Van Buren met defeat. The British minister despondently informed his government that the election signaled the "complete overthrow and prostration" of Van Buren's government. In a reversal of his earlier views, Fox now believed that neither the president nor the secretary of state would be interested in resolving the difficult questions facing the countries because they would not receive credit for their efforts.[7]

Still, when Fox learned about McLeod's arrest, he protested to Secretary of State Forsyth on two counts. First, he wrote, it was well known that McLeod had not participated in the *Caroline* raid and that the charges rested on the perjured testimony of outlaws. Second, and more important, the raid was a "publick act of persons in Her Majesty's service," for which an individual obeying orders of superiors could not be held personally responsible. The issue was properly between the national governments, not subject to proceedings within the states, especially when the *Caroline* affair was under discussion between Britain and the United States. In reminding Forsyth that the subject of the *Caroline* was pending, Fox touched a nerve, for Palmerston had not yet replied to Stevenson's protest note of May 22, 1838.[8] Even though the American minister had anticipated that Britian would justify the raid, Fox's note of December 13, 1840, was the first official acknowledgment by one of its officials, in Britain or America, that it was regarded as an act of state.

British failure to advance negotiations on the *Caroline* was partly attributable to the nature of the Foreign Office and partly to the personality of its minister in charge of foreign affairs. To manage the international relations of the most powerful nation in the world, Palmerston relied on a staff of thirty-nine under-secretaries and clerks. He drafted the texts of most dispatches himself and frequently attended to such routine duties as writing articles and policy directives for the press. Besides his administrative tasks, there were interviews with ambassadors, cabinet meetings, and sessions to attend in the House of Commons.

Overworked, Palmerston acquired a reputation for lack of punctuality and no shortage of irritability. He frequently kept representatives of other nations waiting in his offices for hours. Examination of his correspondence reveals the same tendency; he took months, sometimes years, to reply to communications. Yet he could be punctual when he wanted. He managed to be on time for parliamentary debates, and despite his workload attended many social functions and kept three mistresses. His dilatory habits came from arrogance and lack of consideration for others. In the case of the *Caroline*, he saw little reason to be prompt. Because he regarded the Van Buren administration as weak and pacific, he allowed issues between the two countries to accumulate. Relations with America, in his view, were much less important than those with France or the eastern Mediterranean.[9]

In the *Caroline* case, Palmerston's delay assuredly complicated the problem. Both governments initially assumed that the Fort Schlosser raid was a public act, but, when Palmerston failed to reply to the American protest, he missed an opportunity to settle the affair. If he had promptly acknowleged the raid as an act of state, the federal government could have claimed control over the crisis as a foreign relations incident, and McLeod would not have been arrested. By taking no diplomatic stand, Palmerston left the door open for the small community of Lockport to take control of the matter.

In his reply to Fox's note, Forsyth made clear that the American attitude toward McLeod's case was closely associated with resentment over the way the British had handled the *Caroline* issue. Forsyth's note undoubtedly reminded them of their difficulties in dealing with the federal system of his country. In rejecting Fox's demand that the national government secure McLeod's release, he lectured the minister on the dual nature of American government. A state's jurisdiction over crimes within its borders was independent of the national government's, he wrote, and neither the Constitution nor the country's laws permitted interference in such cases. Fox had argued that New York could not hold McLeod accountable because the case was the subject of discussion between the national governments, but, in Forsyth's view, the two means of redress—state prosecution and diplomatic negotiation—were independent of each other.

Forsyth took the opportunity to express anger over British policy on the *Caroline*. He informed Fox that, even if the national government had power to interfere, the president would refuse to exercise it because, aside from the invasion of territory, the case involved destruction of private property and the murder of an undetermined number of American citizens. In the opinion of the United States, no principle of logic or international law entitled criminals to immunity because they had obeyed orders from superiors or because acts had become subjects of negotiation. New York was as entitled to seek redress for wrongs against the state as the federal government was to vindicate the national honor by whatever means it chose. In closing, the secretary fastened on Fox's announcement that the *Caroline* raid had been a public act of the British government, a fact, he said, that had never been officially communicated to the United States. Forsyth expressed hope that, seeing the consequences, England would "perceive the importance of no longer leaving the Government of the United States uninformed of its views and intentions."[10]

The tone and sentiment of Forsyth's reply vexed but did not

surprise Fox, who informed Palmerston it was what he had expected. The arguments, like those advanced in extradition questions, he judged to be specious. The American government had resorted to a familiar justification based on its uniqueness as a federal republic, yet other countries could deal only with the national government. Britain had to decide, Fox thought, how often it was willing to allow Americans to attribute inactivity to their "peculiar institutions." The case was exasperating. Fox believed that McLeod had not been a member of the *Caroline* raid, but he had heard that "border outlaws" were prepared to swear whatever was necessary to convict him.[11]

Unwilling to let Forsyth's remarks pass, Fox challenged the secretary of state. McLeod's unjust imprisonment, he said, was an "extraordinary proceeding," bound to have serious consequences. In his note, however, he did not address Forsyth's main point. As far as Fox was concerned, the issue was simply the *Caroline* raid. Once the United States admitted the justice and necessity of that event, Britain's failure to respond to its protests would become less important, and by logical extension the Americans would have to concede that they could not hold McLeod. Fox insisted that Forsyth's view of the affair resulted from failure to examine the facts carefully. The *Caroline*, the minister said, was a "hostile vessel, engaged in piratical war" against his people. It had been destroyed in United States territory, but at the time the New York frontier was a lawless region. The raid was an act of "self-defence, rendered absolutely necessary by the circumstances of the occasion." Forsyth retorted waspishly that the minister would hardly have made such statements if he had read the testimony already presented to his government.[12] Once more, the two men showed the mutual distrust and absence of tact that hindered a settlement, for each remained firm in his own interpretation of events and made no effort to understand the other.

After receiving Forsyth's rebuff, Fox sent a long dispatch to London. The assertion upholding New York's right of jurisdiction in the McLeod case was not sincere, he thought, but was contrived to make the issue more difficult for political reasons. Pointing out that Van Buren would leave office the following

March, he speculated that the Democrats were "well pleased to leave the question as one of extreme and alarming difficulty to their successors." While in charge, Van Buren had worked to maintain peaceful relations with Britain; now that he had been repudiated, Fox worried that he would not "scruple or regret to bequeath a war to Messrs Harrison, Clay, and Webster." Besides, Fox observed, New York Governor Seward was an implacable enemy of Van Buren, and any effort to free McLeod through federal intervention might worsen the situation. If he were executed, Fox did not see what could save the two countries from a "war of the most hateful and terrible kind, a war to avenge the shedding of innocent blood." What, he asked, should he do if the Canadian were put to death?[13]

It should be kept in mind that during the McLeod controversy the right of the United States to try a foreigner for a criminal act was never an issue. International law held that foreigners were both protected by and subject to laws of the nations they visited. At the time McLeod was held, one hundred twenty-five foreigners were under arrest in New York, all but thirteen British subjects, yet no others were the subject of diplomatic discussion.[14] The question in the McLeod case was whether a state could assume jurisdiction in a case involving the foreign relations of the United States. If he had been on the raid, the British held, he had not acted as an individual but on behalf of his country, and that act was being discussed by the two governments.

Fox assumed the protests about New York's right of jurisdiction were insincere, and yet the United States was acting according to long-established practice. In several instances, reaching back to the formative years of government, state courts had exercised jurisdiction over representatives of foreign states. In 1794 the governor of French Guadeloupe, Charles Collot, was arrested in Philadelphia on charges arising from an official act: seizure and condemnation of an American-owned vessel. He at first refused to answer the charges and asked the French minister in the United States to obtain his release because of his official position. The argument was referred to Attorney General William Bradford, who ruled that the governor was not exempt from arrest. In Bradford's opinion, the fact that the vessel had been seized as an official act was a defense, but once the case was before a court its discharge had to come by judicial process, not by executive action. After the plaintiff dropped the suit, Secretary of State Timothy Pickering informed the French representative that, though the United States accepted the principle that an official of another nation was not accountable for injuries resulting from exercise of his lawful power, he could still be held personally responsible for wrongs committed in a private capacity.[15]

Later the same year, a similar case arose involving a British naval officer. During the American Revolution, he had taken an escaped slave on board his ship at Charleston. The American who claimed ownership of the slave later brought suit against him, whereupon Britain asked the United States government to quash it. As in the Collot case, the attorney general refused: any foreigner within the jurisdiction of American courts, except a diplomatic minister, was subject to legal process.[16]

These were civil rather than criminal cases, but they involved points that were significant to McLeod's case. First, the representative of a foreign nation in the United States was not accountable for actions undertaken in public capacity. Second, the agent of a nation could be held responsible for wrongs committed in a private capacity. In McLeod's case, the indictment was brought against him as an individual because New York did not view the *Caroline* raid as an official act but as a personal wrong. Britain could deny this view in court, but, once the indictment was filed, the federal government had no power to interfere. As Jefferson had informed Citizen Genêt in 1793, courts in the United States were sovereign—"liable neither to control nor to opposition from any other branch of the Government."[17]

The exchange between Fox and Forsyth caused a flurry in Congress. On December 21, 1840, Millard Fillmore, a Whig congressman from Buffalo, presented a resolution asking the president to provide correspondence between the United States and Britain on the *Caroline* and McLeod cases. Van Buren sent the House the correspondence, which included Fox's demand for McLeod's release and Forsyth's reply that the case was a matter of state jurisdiction. A few days later, Van Buren sent subsequent notes between Forsyth and Fox.[18]

The correspondence provoked a debate. Fillmore made a hardly credible argument that the *Caroline* had never been connected with the Patriot movement. The death of Durfee, in his view, was murder and exclusively in the state's jurisdiction. House Foreign Affairs Committee Chairman Francis W. Pickens, of South Carolina, called for publication of the correspondence to test the nation's "virtue, and patriotism, and intelligence." If Americans objected to the spirit of Forsyth's remarks, he declared, "then we are no longer an independent people." The House voted for publication and ordered copies sent to the Foreign Affairs Committee, which was directed to consider the question of federal versus state jurisdiction as well as Britain's arguments on international law.[19]

While Congress considered these matters and McLeod's detention continued, British officials formulated their strategy. Earlier, Fox had proposed a simple solution: Britain should pay the man's bail but never return him for trial. Arthur had no compunction about jumping bail but wanted to avoid any action that might give an appearance of legality to the New York proceedings, and he worried that forfeiting bail might seem like paying ransom. If arresting British subjects became lucrative, he believed, the practice would spread. If the case went to trial, he favored a defense upholding the *Caroline* affair as an act of state, even though McLeod was not on the raid, to protect those who had been involved from future prosecution.[20]

McLeod's two Lockport attorneys suggested a strategy of delay. Gardner and Bradley proposed seeking a change of venue for the trial from the volatile western region to a court farther east. That required a request to the state supreme court, which would not sit until May, and the next date a trial could take place would be summer or even fall. Meanwhile, the lawyers suggested sending a commission, created by the New York court, to Canada to gather testimony, which would allow those who had been on the *Caroline* raid to give statements without danger of arrest.[21]

The lawyers settled on a procedure outlined by Governor-

General Lord Sydenham. Like Arthur, he did not wish to legitimize events in New York by open participation in the case, but he felt the British government should post McLeod's bail, even though it amounted to partial recognition of the proceedings. Sydenham disliked the dubious ethic of intentionally forfeiting bail, but concluded such action might be necessary because it was "impossible to act with the Americans as you would do with a civilized people." He felt the best course would be to delay trial and thereby gain time to settle the *Caroline* question. If that issue were concluded, he assumed, the reason for action against McLeod would disappear. If the question were not settled, he would not return to face trial.[22]

From the Lockport jail, McLeod gloomily warned that if anyone intended to help him obtain bail, it had to be done speedily. So far, he was being held on charges from a general indictment that permitted bail, but the county court would meet the first week in February, and if it brought a true bill of indictment against him, he would no longer be eligible. Besides, he complained, he was confined in the "worst prison in the United States" and suffered from fever and other troubles. He felt he would never survive the summer in the place.[23]

The plan to bail out McLeod went well, up to a point. Two local residents agreed to provide sureties, and late on the afternoon of January 28, 1841, a Lockport magistrate ordered his release. Then, despite efforts to keep the news quiet, word spread before the judge's order could be delivered to the sheriff, and men marched through the town beating drums to alert the populace. McLeod considered a dash for the border, but the gathering crowd around the jail prevented it. A committee demanded to see if he was still in custody, and their eyewitness report that he was still behind bars aroused loud cheers. Another committee met with the judge, the district attorney, the bail providers, and McLeod's lawyers. In the evening, fires were lit, and the mob found two cannons, which they aimed at McLeod's cell window. All through the night, they fired blank charges from the guns and threw stones in the direction of the cell. The next afternoon, the two citizens withdrew their offer to secure McLeod's bail; he would remain in prison.[24]

The bail incident revealed one disturbing course the McLeod affair could assume. Arthur's agent at Lockport advised his government that he had seen the "many headed monster," American democracy, in its most savage form. Arthur agreed that the episode indicated its downward trend, but he thought the unseemly outbreak of popular violence would serve Britain well in any future discussion of the case. He speculated that reproaches from the rest of the world might cause decent citizens of Lockport to let McLeod slip away.

As soon as news reached Washington, Fox asked the State Department whether or not the report on the bail incident were true and what the United States government intended to do. Fox, in fact, had already learned the details, but wanted the Americans formally to acknowledge such a "manifest outrage upon law and order." Surely the government would not try to justify it. Forsyth, however, would not be pulled into the trap of recognizing the incident as a government responsibility. The only information the State Department had of the affair came, he said, from the same newspaper accounts Fox had seen.[25]

The bail incident aroused concern in Britain as well as America. In London, the *Times* gave the episode prominent coverage, calling it a "triumph of the mob" over law and threatening "retributive justice" over the "hotbrained democracy of the northern states." Many Americans reluctantly agreed with the *Times*, though in less vehement language. The Buffalo *Commercial Advertiser* castigated McLeod for the "muss that has been raised on his account" but deplored the violence at Lockport. New York Whig Congressman Richard P. Marvin informed Governor Seward that the incident had caused alarm in Washington. Fearing such incidents could provoke war, Marvin suggested that Seward consider executive action in the McLeod case. The governor expressed regret about the mob's influence, but made no promises regarding McLeod.[26]

Clearly, Seward was aware of the potential for political gain offered by the affair, and he was determined to proceed with the trial. He argued to Forsyth that McLeod had never been legally bailed out. The judge had ordered his release because citizens had agreed to assure his appearance, but, when they cancelled their surety, as they had a right to do, the order became invalid. Seward neglected to mention the mob outside the jail or the committee that had convinced the bondsmen to withdraw. In the governor's view, the cause of the trouble at Lockport was the judge's ill-advised action in bailing out a murder suspect.

Soon after the incident, during the first week in February 1841, a Lockport grand jury issued a true bill of indictment against McLeod. There was no longer any chance of avoiding trial, but Gardner and Bradley informed Arthur's agent in Lockport that the case, which depended on the testimony of known Patriots, was weak, and they were confident of acquittal.[27]

The excitement at Lockport coincided with renewed congressional turmoil over Anglo-American relations. On February 13, 1841, the House Foreign Affairs Committee issued a report on the correspondence between Fox and Forsyth.[28] Congress had instructed the committee to consider whether Britain could justify the *Caroline* raid by international law and whether New York could claim jurisdiction in the McLeod case. Drafted by the fiery committee chairman, South Carolina's Francis W. Pickens, the report addressed those questions but presumed a mandate to carry the discussion far beyond them.

Britain's characterization of the *Caroline* as a pirate vessel offended Pickens, for pirates were "freebooters, enemies of the human race" who had "no flag and no home." The *Caroline* had been a respectable ferryboat engaged in trade between Buffalo and Navy Island. If it had carried contraband, it was subject to seizure, but that did not give Britain excuse to invade another nation. Yet, declared the Anglophobic Pickens, that country had decided to pass beyond Navy Island, its own territory occupied by Canadian rebels, and "in the plenitude of its power to cast the aegis of British jurisdiction over American soil." Whatever the *Caroline's* character, once it entered the United States it came under American jurisdiction; therefore, the British assault against it at Fort Schlosser was a national outrage. If Britain had first expressed its concern about the conduct of the *Caroline* to state or federal authorities, it would at least have shown some "respect for our sovereignty and independence, and a disposition to treat us as an equal." But, in dealing with the United

States, Pickens charged, Britain always acted in a manner "revolting to the pride and spirit" of a free people. He had expressed what many Americans considered the principal reason for difficulties in Anglo-American relations: British contempt for America.

A congressman moved to oratory was difficult to halt. Turning to the McLeod case, Pickens observed that, if the United States and Britain had been at war, the *Caroline* affair would fall under "rules and regulations of war," and McLeod could not be held personally accountable. But he was charged with a criminal act committed during peacetime within the state of New York. Fox had alleged that McLeod was not part of the *Caroline* party, but his guilt or innocence, said Pickens, was the "very point upon which an American jury alone have a right to decide." Federal interference was impossible in the system of sovereign and independent states.

These points made, Pickens could have closed his report, but he continued in a manner that reveals much about Anglo-American animosity. He charged that, in claiming the right to search American vessels on the high seas on the pretext of suppressing the slave trade, Britain was endeavoring to "sweep our commerce from the coast of Africa." Britain dominated the world: a growing presence in the West Indies that threatened the United States; bases in the Mediterranean (Gibraltar, Malta, the Ionian Islands, St. Jean d'Acre) that controlled the sea and the Levant; St. Helena and the Cape of Good Hope, which gave dominance over the African coast; Bombay, Calcutta, points in the East Indies and China Seas; the Falkland Islands, which controlled Cape Horn. All over the world, Britain was building up military strength, using resources, skills, and capital beyond estimate and moving "steadily upon her objects with an ambition that knows no bounds."

One reason Pickens and many other Americans had become so concerned about this power was the recent success of British forces in several parts of the globe. In 1839 they invaded Afghanistan and established a savage despot under their tutelage. Later that year, hostilities broke out between British and Chinese forces, the first phase of the Opium War, resulting in the cession of Hong Kong. The most impressive example of military strength occurred in November 1840, when the British navy defeated the forces of Egyptian Pasha Mehemet Ali at the Syrian fortress of St. Jean d'Acre. The victory resulted from clever strategy and accurate British gunnery, but what seized the public imagination was that four steam warships, mounted with heavier guns than sailing vessels, took part in the bombardment. It seemed that a new and terrifying era in warfare had suddenly arisen. Pickens referred to the dreadful possibilities in his report: "Steam power," he said, "has recently brought us so near together, that in the event of any future conflict, *war with its effects* will be precipitated upon with much more rapidity than formerly."[29]

The report agitated the House. A New York Whig on the Foreign Affairs Committee, Francis Granger, said its adoption by the House might have nearly the same consequence as a declaration of war. He charged that, though the Foreign Affairs Committee had been instructed to investigate only the *Caroline* and McLeod cases, the report ranged over the globe in its concerns, made no recommendations, and failed to come to any conclusion. Given the excitement provoked by McLeod's bail, it might endanger the Canadian's life. Its discussion ought to be postponed until after his trial: if McLeod were executed, the whole nation would unite in patriotic feeling, but Congress meantime should not inflame the public. In rebuttal, Pickens held that his report was simply a clear expression of American rights. If the world knew the nation were prepared to assert itself, the danger of conflict would diminish. Speaking plainly and fearlessly would prevent war, not cause one. Nor did Pickens fear the report would provoke excitement on the frontier. He thought it would produce quiet by assuring people in the region that the national government would protect their rights.

Members of the House urged Pickens to return the report to committee. John Quincy Adams thought it should be rewritten, leaving out reference to the "grasping spirit of Britain." Edward Everett maintained that because the *Caroline* affair and McLeod case were in negotiation action ought to be left to the executive branch; with the Democrats about to leave office and the Whigs about to enter, the report seemed intended to embarrass the new administration. Fillmore believed the report might further excite feelings on the frontier, possibly causing violence. Such an event could result in injustice to McLeod, who was entitled to a fair trial, and might compromise the national government in its negotiations. The committee, Fillmore said, should reconsider its report and confine itself to the issue. Despite the protests, Pickens stood firm.

Although offended by the report, British minister Fox was hardly likely to consider it a declaration of war, as Granger had feared. He described it as "so weak and extravagant in the execution as to be quite undeserving of resentment." Nonetheless, he remained concerned about McLeod's detention because neither the government in Washington nor the public seemed "aware of the serious and desperate nature of the issue" between the countries. The Americans, he said, again seemed to have deluded themselves that their peculiar belief in states' rights would answer whatever disagreements they might have with foreign nations.[30]

In England, too, excitement arose as transatlantic steamers brought accounts of the congressional debate. The London *Morning Herald* declared that McLeod's release was "indispensable" to British honor. The *Times* called Pickens's report "menacing and insulting," and declared that, if Americans committed an act so "atrocious and disgusting" as the execution of McLeod, there would not be "three Englishmen living" who would not insist on war. In that event, the *Times* argued, the navy of the United States would prove too feeble to offer resistance to the British fleet; the nation's coastal towns lacked adequate defenses, and its trade would be swept from the seas within a few weeks.[31]

On February 8 and 9, 1841, both houses of Parliament discussed the McLeod crisis. In the House of Lords, Earl Mountcashell asked Prime Minister Lord Melbourne why, despite newspaper reports, the government had not given Parliament information. The case involved the country's honor, and he hoped the government would not "suffer the national character to sink into contempt." If Britain did not stand up to the United States, its subjects would be victimized wherever they went. Melbourne assured him that the government would take measures necessary to ensure McLeod's safety and vindicate national honor. The McLeod issue came before the Commons the same evening. Lord Stanley pointed out that a British subject was in jeopardy simply because he had acted for his country, and Parliament wished to know what steps had been taken to assist him. Palmerston replied that the government was taking action, but he preferred not to discuss it at the moment.[32]

Palmerston was prepared to use a firm tone with the United States. In January, responding to news of McLeod's arrest, he had ordered Fox to express England's "confident expectation" that the American government would do whatever was necessary to free the man and prevent similar recurrences. On February 9 Palmerston instructed Fox to send a note to the secretary of state "formally repeating in the name of the British government, a demand for the immediate release of McLeod." Britain was not prepared to accept the American argument that the national government could not interfere in matters of state jurisdiction. The peculiar nature of the federal system was of no concern to other nations, which could only deal with the central government of the country.[33]

After the discussion in Parliament, Palmerston summoned Stevenson for a talk. Referring to the public agitation, Palmerston warned the American minister that measures against McLeod would lead to a collision and repeated that the Caroline question was a matter between national governments, not appropriate for any action by New York. Confidentially, he asked Stevenson to urge presidential interposition in the case. During the meeting, Stevenson held to his country's official position, pointing out that the raid was an outrage against the national honor, and defending the jurisdiction of New York. But the talk with Palmerston worried him, and, in a confidential report to Van Buren, he pointed out that the execution of McLeod would mean "immediate war!"[34]

Was Palmerston simply blustering to frighten the United States into releasing McLeod? Evidence indicates that the foreign secretary was trying to intimidate the Americans, but he was prepared to back up his words. In a dispatch to Fox, he said that, if McLeod were executed, the minister was "forthwith to quit Washington and to return to England," giving notice to Canadian authorities and British naval officers at the Halifax and West Indian stations. The substance of these orders he was to communicate unofficially and confidentially to the president. Separately, the Admiralty Office ordered the British naval commander at Bermuda, Sir Thomas Harvey, to stay in touch with Fox and Governor-General Sydenham and to conform as much as possible to their wishes. In a private letter to his brother, Palmerston said he did not believe that the Americans intended to execute McLeod, but, if they did, "we could not stand it, and war would be the inevitable result."[35]

Such actions, as has been pointed out elsewhere, were part of Palmerston's general approach toward the United States, a "diplomacy of menace" based on the premise that the Van Buren administration desperately wished peace. Palmerston's unflinching posture toward the former colony worked well in British politics. Parliament was generally uninterested in foreign affairs, but issues involving national honor could arouse enthusiastic support across political lines. Even Sir Robert Peel, leader of the Conservative opposition, supported Palmerston's pronouncements on McLeod.[36]

As the Democrats prepared to surrender the government to the Whigs, relations between the two countries stood at a dangerous pass. Melbourne's promise to vindicate British honor, if necessary, seemed to demand retaliation if McLeod were executed. Palmerston did not believe that would happen, but his optimism did not take into account American politics in the United States. According to widely held opinion there, the federal government had no grounds to interfere in a criminal case within a state's jurisdiction. As governor, Seward did have the power to pardon McLeod if he were convicted, or even to direct that the case not be prosecuted—a *nolle prosequi*—if he chose, but that course carried political risks that the Whig governor would not assume for the Democrats, especially for an old political foe like Van Buren. At the same time, as Fox had informed his government, the outgoing president hardly seemed likely to work toward settlement of the issue in the brief remainder of his administration. The Democrats would be happy to leave such a difficult and alarming issue for the Whigs—even, Fox asserted, if it meant war. In Canada, Governor-General Sydenham believed that Forsyth's communications on the case were not really directed to the British government, but against the new administration, "a patriotic course which these Republicans seem to think a *matter* of course."[37]

Increasingly, it seemed that the best hope for resolving the *Caroline* and McLeod affairs depended on the new Whig government. Philip Hone defined the difficulty: "If McLeod is convicted they will hang him out of spite, and if he is pardoned by Govr. Seward they will almost hang *him* and if the genl Government would liberate him after the ground they have taken it will have the appearance of pussilanimity. The only chance of a settlement is that a new administration will soon come in, uncommitted on this subject." British officials reached the same conclusion. Sydenham found republican government offensive but was hopeful that the incoming administration would exhibit more "good sense" than the old one. Fox heard that President Harrison intended to send a special mission to England to settle the dangerous issues between the countries and informed London that he expected the new government to prove "more reasonable and satisfactory."[38] So, for the moment, with McLeod's trial postponed, American and British leaders were content to let the cauldron bubble, in the hope that the Whigs could settle the differences between the nations.

6

TIPPECANOE AND TYLER, TOO

One distinguishing feature of the McLeod controversy was the way in which the possibility of its settlement seemed to draw near and then recede. This was especially evident in the period from March through May 1841. As anticipated, the new Whig administration in Washington intended to conclude the matter as soon as possible, but hopes for its quick end vanished when the new president died, throwing the nation into confusion and bringing John Tyler into office.

William Henry Harrison, a former Indian fighter and territorial governor of Indiana, was the oldest man ever elected as president of the United States. It is true that from the start few expected greatness from the old hero. Writing to a friend, John C. Calhoun described him as "quite unconscious" of the duties and responsibilities before him and possessing neither the physical nor mental powers to handle them. In the absence of a strong president, Calhoun and many others thought it likely that Harrison's tenure would be marred by a continuing struggle between Daniel Webster and Henry Clay for control of the Whig party. Webster, named as secretary of state, initially seemed about to pull ahead in the contest. Richard M. Blatchford, a New York lawyer, wrote Seward that Harrison had "thrown himself almost entirely into Webster's hands." Webster only had to suggest Thomas Ewing for the Treasury Department: "'So let it be,' said Harrison—no more words than that did it—& it did not consume 20 seconds."[1]

Webster, widely regarded as one of the country's ablest lawyers and politicians, was fifty-nine in March 1841. For years, he had harbored presidential ambitions. However, several terms in the House of Representatives—first from his native New Hampshire, then from Massachusetts—and experience in the Senate failed to bring the coveted prize. In 1836 and 1840, he competed to no avail for the Whig nomination. When Harrison offered the office of secretary of state, the presidency again seemed within reach. Perhaps the State Department would become the stepping-stone to a higher place, provided he could become the dominant figure in the new government.

But even Webster was not likely to have had the upper hand over Harrison. The president-elect had a penchant for ostentatious references to Greek and Roman history and was reluctant to let Webster edit his inaugural address. Webster finally prevailed and labored on it for several hours. When he returned that evening to the home of William W. Seaton, editor of the Washington *National Intelligencer*, where he was staying, Mrs. Seaton commented on how tired he appeared. She hoped, she said, nothing bad had happened. Webster replied, "You would think that something had happened if you knew what I have done. I have killed *seventeen Roman procounsuls* as dead as smelts, every one of them!"[2] In the end, Harrison apparently delivered the speech as he had written it, an excruciating two-hour address filled with references to long-dead Roman statesmen. British minister Fox, accustomed to a higher caliber of pomp and circumstance, was particularly unimpressed. Harrison's remarks, he said, were long and vague and evidently disappointing to those who had hoped to suppress "some part of the diffuse and rather childish rhetoric with which the address abounds." The whole inaugural, he concluded, was uninteresting, probably because the "habits and the institutions of this country have the effect of banishing from such a ceremony every thing that is grand or striking, or even decorous."[3]

The most important business for the new government was, of course, the McLeod issue, and in this arena the new president and secretary of state promptly charted a policy far different from Van Buren's. Secretary Forsyth had taken a states'-rights position and advised the British that the president lacked the power or, he bluntly informed Fox, inclination to interfere in McLeod's case.[4] As soon as Harrison was sworn in, Webster entered into long and confidential conferences with Fox, assuring him that he and the president intended a course entirely different. Fox believed that, whereas the Americans earlier had not considered the McLeod affair serious, they were now "thoroughly alarmed," even "terrified," by the excitement the case had produced in England. Talks with Webster convinced Fox that McLeod would be released, but whether it would take place in a "bold straitforward manner, as it ought . . . or whether it will be procured by legal management and fiction" he could not determine; nor did he believe the new administration yet knew what it would do. Meantime, he promised Webster he would delay a demand for McLeod's release until after the new cabinet met.[5]

The secretary of state was eager to end the affair, which he regarded as an obstacle to a durable and general Anglo-American settlement. Webster was an Anglophile, and he had witnessed deteriorating relations between the countries with distress. When trouble broke out along the unresolved northeastern boundary in 1839, he had drawn up a detailed proposal for negotiating an end to the dispute, hoping President Van Buren would send him on a special mission to England.[6] As secretary of state, Webster also wanted to restore Anglo-American investments and credit, which had been badly damaged after the Panic of 1837. Some states had defaulted on British debts, wreaking havoc in the international financial community. When British creditors turned skittish about advancing more money across the Atlantic, Webster, as American counsel for the House of Baring in London, was called on to affirm that the states were responsible for their debts. Indeed, he replied, debts were moral as well as legal obligations, dischargeable only by payment, which upheld the "plighted faith of the state, as a political community."[7] Such questions disrupted good relations between the two countries, which Webster believed essential for the prosperity of the United States.[8] The McLeod case was another serious obstacle to restoring harmony, and the secretary of state hoped to bring a quick end to it.

In his talks with Fox, Webster apparently intimated that New Yorkers justified McLeod's arrest and detention because the British government had not accepted responsibility for the *Caroline* raid, Palmerston having never officially answered Minister Stevenson's note of May 22, 1838.[9] In Webster's opinion, British avowal of the raid would elevate the dispute from a state criminal case to a matter involving foreign relations, which came under the exclusive provenance of the national government. He advised Fox that he thought New York would agree to close the McLeod case on those terms, but, if it did not, the federal government would seek to remove it to the United States Supreme Court.[10] After concluding his meetings with Fox, Webster informed New York's secretary of state, John C. Spencer, that he hourly expected a formal demand for McLeod's release. When he received it, he said, he would write again.[11] Webster expected no problems from New York.

Fox presented the avowal and demand on March 12, 1841. Destruction of the *Caroline*, he said, was a public transaction of the British state. Holding a participant personally responsible for the act would be contrary to the practice of the civilized world, and his government did not believe the United States intended to "set an example so fraught with evil to the community of nations." He argued that the raid may have been, as Britain contended, a justifiable use of force to defend its territory from rebels and pirates, or, as the United States maintained, a wrongful invasion of American soil, but in either instance it was "a question essentially of a political and international kind, which can be discussed and settled only between the two governments." Other nations were not concerned with the character of the American federal union, a subject of particular irritation to Fox, but dealt only with the national government. Hence, he demanded "from the government of the United States, formally, in the name of the British government, the immediate release of Mr. Alexander McLeod."[12]

Webster took immediate steps. He sent Scott and Attorney

General John J. Crittenden to the frontier with orders to preserve tranquillity. Secretary of War John Bell informed Scott that British subjects might attempt to rescue McLeod. Scott was to repel invasion and prevent any retaliation by American citizens. He should confer with Seward and could call out the state militia if necessary.[13] But Scott ran into difficulty. Stepping out of a scow onto an ice hummock at the Albany crossing, he slipped and fell. With great effort, he walked to a hotel, where he corresponded with Seward from his bed. Only after several days of rest could Scott resume his peripatetic habits of visiting the border towns and calming the public.[14]

Webster provided Crittenden with more politically controversial instructions that were intended to bring about McLeod's release. Because the British government had acknowledged the *Caroline* raid as a public act, the president thought that relieved McLeod of personal responsibility. The principle that an individual was not answerable for an act on behalf of his government was "sanctioned by the usages of all civilized nations," and the administration saw it as a question between national governments. Webster was aware that Seward, in a letter to Forsyth, had committed New York to legal action against McLeod, and he took pains not to embarrass the governor. The national government, he advised the attorney general, had no power to intervene in New York proceedings, but Seward should be informed that, if the case were pending in a federal court, the president would have issued a *nolle prosequi*—an order not to prosecute the case—upon receiving the British avowal. Despite his protestations, Webster was involving the national government. Besides virtually outlining the rationale upon which McLeod's release could be justified, he ordered the attorney general to Lockport to consult with McLeod's counsel. If judgment came against McLeod, Crittenden was to take steps toward removing the case to the United States Supreme Court.[15]

Grumbling because a trip to New York would interrupt plans for a visit to Kentucky, Crittenden set off.[16] In Albany, he and Seward met, and the attorney general assured the governor he was present not to interfere in a state process but because the British avowal of the *Caroline* and demand for McLeod's release had made the case a matter of national importance. Seward explained his views: he was not willing to direct a *nolle prosequi*; he had no power to do so even if he wished. A *nolle prosequi*, he declared, could be entered only through consent of the court. Crittenden suggested that Seward pardon McLeod before trial, a course the governor not surprisingly found unacceptable. The man had to stand trial; New Yorkers would consider a pardon beforehand as an "ignoble submission." He had entered New York's jurisdiction and, Seward asserted, boasted of his part in an outrage against the state and nation. Public sentiment demanded that the law follow its course. Seward assured the attorney general that, even if the Canadian were convicted, a trial must take place; on that point, Seward was firm.[17] He opposed any "extraordinary proceedings" by the national government.[18]

Despite Seward's care to present his position clearly and the administration's desire to conciliate him, a misunderstanding arose between Albany and Washington. On March 17 Webster confidentially wrote the governor that the president had learned "by means of a letter from a friend" that Seward was disposed to enter a *nolle prosequi* in the McLeod case. The president thanked the governor for that intention, which he considered proper and likely to conclude an embarrassing and dangerous situation.[19] Seward responded with both public and private letters. In an official letter, he informed Webster that, despite the British avowal of the *Caroline* affair, his views regarding McLeod had not changed since his letter of February 27 to Forsyth: the case was of "judicial cognizance" and could be settled no other way, either by the federal or the state government. In a private letter, Seward told Webster that he had never considered the possibility of a *nolle prosequi*. The president's unidentified correspondent had misapprehended his views.[20]

The name of Harrison's "friend" has never been determined, but evidence points to an ambitious and conniving New York writer, Simeon DeWitt Bloodgood, who was seeking to advance himself by exploiting his tenuous connections with Seward. Bloodgood, who had headed a Young Men's Whig Association in Utica, had asked for and received from Seward a letter of introduction to Webster.[21] Just before Harrison's inauguration,

Bloodgood was in Washington, apparently passing himself off as Seward's emissary to the government and writing conspiratorial letters to the governor. He had discovered a "political secret," he informed Seward: "*You hold* the most important position of any individual in the US." If Seward refused to allow a change of venue in McLeod's case, the Canadian would certainly be convicted, and, if he refused to prevent McLeod's execution, war would probably result. The administration, Bloodgood concluded, "*will be in your hands.*"[22] A few days later, he sent Seward another letter reporting an interview with Webster in which he had advised the secretary of state that the governor's goodwill was "worthy of consideration & conciliation at this crisis."[23]

To his credit, Webster was never willing to deal on the level Bloodgood suggested, and in a letter to the New Yorker the secretary asserted that he presumed Seward would do his duty. Bloodgood replied that, if McLeod were convicted, Seward's duty would be to execute him, the worst event possible for the administration.[24]

In a meeting with his cabinet, President Harrison assailed the governor for using McLeod's case to achieve influence over the administration. Webster, too, told his friend Edward Curtis that Seward had made a dishonorable proposition in the McLeod affair. Months later, after Harrison's death, Seward learned about the remarks to the cabinet and wrote President Tyler forswearing personal motives and denouncing Bloodgood. Seward had never intended Bloodgood to represent him and had merely sent him as a bearer of congratulations to Harrison. When Seward received Bloodgood's letters about his talks with the president and Webster, he left them unanswered, he said, because he regarded such conduct as mortifying, though unlikely to produce injury. Interestingly, it appears that he never sent that letter to Tyler. Instead, he sent an amended copy to New York Congressman Christopher Morgan, whom he asked to set the matter straight with the president if the opportunity arose. Whether Morgan ever discussed Seward's letter with Tyler is doubtful; there is no extant reply from Tyler or subsequent reference to one in Seward's correspondence.[25]

The Bloodgood matter left a lasting impression on Harrison and Webster, who as a result had reason to think they would have to settle the McLeod case without Seward's cooperation and perhaps over his opposition. Seward, unaware of the animosity Bloodgood's threats had produced, confidently assumed that the national government would respect the views he had presented to Crittenden. The way was prepared for disagreement between state and federal authority more awkward than anything that had occurred in the McLeod case so far.

Meanwhile, the dispute was causing excitement in England. Newspapers began printing bellicose editorials. The London *Sun* warned that Britain had "ample means of terribly avenging any outrage of our rights" and said that, if conflict broke out, internal discord in the United States would make the "utter disruption of the Union a matter of very little difficulty." The *Times* of London said that McLeod must be released or avenged.[26] Patriotic interest in his fate went beyond the chauvinism typical of newspapers of that day. Even such level-headed observers as Egerton V. Harcourt, a Yankeephile who had become Webster's friend during a visit to the United States, wrote that, however ruinous a break, if McLeod were executed, "we must throw away the scabbard at once."[27]

The American minister, Stevenson, found himself caught up in the agitation. He wrote the commander of the Mediterranean squadron, Commodore Isaac Hull, that the United States might be "forced into war with Great Britain." Fearful that if hostilities broke out American ships in the Mediterranean would be trapped, he suggested that Hull move his vessels closer to home.[28] Pleased with his prescience, Stevenson informed Webster of his letter to Hull, adding that the commander would "in all probability return immediately to the U. States." Opinion in Britain, he said, regarded war as inevitable, and the United States government should place the country in a state of defense.[29] Stevenson later sent the secretary of state another dispatch advising him that the British press and people were deeply excited over the McLeod controversy and that the government was engaged in military preparation. The purpose of the martial activity had not been made public, but Stevenson had no doubt it concerned the United States. Recent events in the Levant, where British steamers had assisted in the capture of St. Jean d'Acre, gave Britain the "means of giving to any war, a character of great activity & extent."[30] Three weeks later, Stevenson was still disturbed: military measures were continuing at dockyards and arsenals, and he understood a notice had been posted at Lloyd's inviting shipowners to submit bids for transporting troops to Canada.[31]

Stevenson's note and another alarming report from London reached Hull at Minorca, with significant consequences. Summoning his commanders to the flagship, *Ohio*, on March 24, he read the letters and asked their views. All agreed that the best course would be to get outside the British-controlled Strait of Gibraltar. The next day, Hull ordered his squadron out of the Mediterranean. If his commanders learned the two countries were at war, they should cruise the Atlantic as long as possible, making every effort "to annoy the enemy" before heading for the United States.[32]

Two of the ships, *Preble* and *Ohio*, remained close by Gibraltar—the best place for information regarding Anglo-American relations—but the third, the *Brandywine*, under William C. Bolton, left its companions behind and sailed for the United States. Arriving at Long Island, Bolton, no doubt anticipating a hero's welcome, presented his ship and crew for the defense of the country. The public response to his return was far different. Democratic organs, such as the Washington *Globe* and the Albany *Argus*, approved the *Brandywine*'s return, but Whig journals, such as the New York *American*, demanded Stevenson's recall, and the Boston *Courier*, to whom the episode revealed the minister's lack of sense, mocked Bolton's theatrics as evidence of his "strong desire to get home." The navy relieved him of command and sent the *Brandywine* back to the Mediterranean.[33]

At the time, though, conditions seemed serious to many people in Europe. The American minister to France, Lewis Cass, sent Webster a private letter about British naval movements, warning that the victory at Acre had opened "all eyes here to the surpassing effect of steam." These new engines of destruction, Cass felt, had rendered permanent batteries obsolete because they fired heavier shells than most wooden ships and could move beyond reach of shore guns, even in the absence of wind.[34] Ten days later, Cass wrote Webster in a more anxious vein. He had seen Louis Philippe four times during the week, and the king was concerned about the quarrelsome relations between the United States and Britain. Louis feared that, if they went to war, France would be dragged in because hostilities would "excite some of those pretensions, which England arrogates to herself upon the Ocean."[35]

The Russian government also worried about the growing problems between the Atlantic nations. In March 1841 Foreign Minister Count Nesselrode sent London and the United States an offer from Czar Nicholas to mediate the McLeod dispute. No doubt the czar thought trouble with the United States might cause an English rapprochement with France that would work against Russian interests. The czar also feared that a collision between the two countries would affect Russia's trade. If the "counsels of an impartial friend" would be of assistance, he would rejoice to be of service. Neither the Americans nor the British, however, pursued arbitration, probably because both distrusted Russian motives.[36]

Through all the turmoil, state and defense attorneys continued to prepare for McLeod's trial. Gardner and Bradley had outlined their strategy to Lieutenant Governor Arthur in February. Changing the venue farther east hopefully would provide a jury less agitated by the *Caroline* question. The lawyers also proposed sending a court-appointed commission to Canada to gather testimony without endangering witnesses who had participated in the raid. Most significant, the lawyers discouraged a defense that justified the *Caroline* attack because such a plea would produce an unfavorable impression on a jury. Instead, McLeod should seek acquittal by establishing an alibi that showed he had not participated in the raid.[37] Arthur approved without enthusiasm, informing Lord Sydenham that, though he doubted McLeod could have a fair trial no matter what measures the counselors adopted, he supposed such things should be left to their discretion.[38] Actually, just as New Yorkers suspected, Arthur was considering a scheme to "facilitate McLeod's escape" by bribing the jailers. The plan collapsed when the American conspirators backed out. But apparently someone indeed attempted a half-baked escape plot. After a visitor left McLeod's cell, guards reportedly discovered a saw, files, and chisels hidden in his bed. Whether such an event actually occurred is questionable, but Arthur's correspondence reveals that American suspicions were by no means unfounded.[39]

Perhaps the person least troubled by the disquiet was Governor Seward, who rebuffed expressions of concern about the case from his political advisers and friends. When New York Whig Peter B. Porter suggested the state should drop the case because the British had avowed the *Caroline* raid, Seward reiterated his determination to see the affair go to trial.[40] Writing the state attorney general, Willis Hall, whom he had instructed to prosecute the case personally, he maintained it was "indispensable to the honor of the country and the dignity of the state that reparation be made by the British government or the prisoner be tried."[41]

Those who hoped for a speedy trial, however, were disappointed when the court clerk mistakenly gave only five days notice for summoning the jury instead of the six required by statute. The judge decided the error would be fatal on challenge, and, because new arrangements had to be made, the trial could not take place for some time.[42] Nevertheless, the court went ahead with the arraignment, and McLeod entered a plea of not guilty. Gardner and Bradley then obtained writs from the judge enabling them to take testimony by commission from Webster and Fox in Washington and from some of the *Caroline* participants in Canada.[43] For the moment, the situation seemed calm. Fox informed his government of the trial's delay, and added his opinion that the clerk had intentionally committed an error to give the government more time. Seward, he said, was a "warm supporter" of the administration but needed some way to escape the political embarrassment that would accompany McLeod's release.[44]

Historians often debate the part accident plays in history, and possibly the death of Harrison and Tyler's succession to the presidency did not alter the outcome of the McLeod case. But that unexpected event certainly complicated the affair. Before President Harrison could make any mark in office, he contracted pneumonia. On April 3 his symptoms became alarming. He suffered through the evening, asking his followers to carry out the "true principles of the government," and died at thirty minutes after midnight, on April 4, 1841.[45] In Williamsburg, Virginia, Vice-President Tyler learned of Harrison's illness from a friend, Richmond lawyer James Lyons. Then, on the morning of April 5, Webster's son, Fletcher, appeared with news of the president's death. Tyler set out at once for Washington, summoned the cabinet, and took over the government.[46]

That Tyler would become leader of the Whigs was ironic. At the beginning of his political life, the aristocratic Virginian had been a Democrat. Like many Southerners, he had broken with Jackson over nullification and the Bank War and had become a states'-rights Whig. In 1840, when he ran for vice-president on Harrison's ticket, few people thought the slave-owning former Democrat would ever occupy the White House. The new president, though not young, had seemed robust. Shortly after the inauguration, Tyler had returned to his home near Williamsburg, probably expecting to remain there for most of the next four years.[47]

The nation was saddened by Harrison's death, but some people were equally uneasy about the qualifications of the new president. John Quincy Adams regarded Tyler as only an "acting president" until another could be chosen and denounced him as a "political sectarian, of the slave-driving, Virginian, Jeffersonian school, principled against all improvement, with all the interests and passions and vices of slavery rooted in his moral and political constitution—with talents not above mediocrity, and a spirit incapable of expansion to the dimensions of the station upon which he has been cast by the hand of Providence."[48] Former Secretary of War Poinsett believed Tyler would become the "ready tool of Mr. Clay."[49]

Among the president's first concerns was the McLeod case. At the first regular cabinet meeting, Webster handed Tyler a copy of Fox's March 12 demand for the prisoner's release. Fox had informed Palmerston that he thought the secretary of state and Tyler had differences about the McLeod case, but the two actually agreed, apparently without difficulty.[50] Webster, showing the final text of a proposed response to Tyler said, "Lord Palmerston, sir, may put that in his pipe and smoke it."[51]

Webster's note of April 24, 1841, was a model of diplomatic craftmanship, and his definition of circumstances necessary for a nation to justify hostilities in the name of self-defense has become a classic in international law.[52] Seeking to move discussion beyond the stasis of charge and countercharge, Webster tried to open the way for settlement by conceding some points and upholding others.

He began with the McLeod affair. Breaking with Van Buren's policy, the secretary of state admitted the British argument that in accordance with the law of nations an individual should not be held personally accountable for acts committed on behalf of a government. Because Britain had avowed the act for which he was held, McLeod ought to be released. Still, Webster pointed out, the executive branch of the United States government could not disrupt New York's state judicial process, but had to operate within legal means. McLeod could obtain freedom by filing for a habeas corpus, arguing exemption from jurisdiction on national grounds, or could offer the same defense at a trial. At that moment, his lawyers were working to bring his case before the New York Supreme Court, seeking a habeas corpus, and Webster held that a tribunal as "eminently distinguished for ability and learning as the Supreme Court of New York, may be safely relied upon, for the just and impartial administration of the law." Immunity from prosecution in such a case, he said, was an accepted principle among civilized nations. Webster was almost assuring the minister that the court would release McLeod.

There remained the *Caroline*. Britain justified the raid as an act of self-defense, a principle Webster admitted was attached to nations as well as individuals. Yet, exercise of the right ought to be judged in view of the "circumstances of each particular case." Britain averred that the raid was justified because the American side of the border had been infested with pirates who openly violated their country's neutrality laws. Pointing out that the northern frontier was a "line long enough to divide the whole of Europe into halves," Webster suggested it was hardly surprising that irregularities should break out against the wishes of both governments. The United States, he asserted, had been the first nation to enforce neutrality by national law, and the government had steadfastly sought to punish violations. In its efforts along the border and through its policy of noninterference, the United States believed it "set an example, not unfit to be followed by others"—an obvious reference to British participation in Latin American revolutions—and that, in its steady adherence to neutrality since its founding, it had "done something to promote peace and good neighborhood among Nations, and to advance the civilization of mankind."

Then, almost as if he were delivering a peroration before the Supreme Court, Webster brought his letter to a dramatic conclusion. Given the invasion of American territory, Britain, not the United States, had to provide explanation. If the raid were justifiable, it had to show that there was "a necessity of self-defense, instant, overwhelming, leaving no choice of means, and no moment for deliberation." Even if the necessity of the moment justified the attack, the aggressor could do nothing unreasonable or excessive. The act had to be "limited by that necessity, and kept clearly within it." According to Webster, Britain had to prove that any remonstrance to those on the *Caroline* would have been impracticable or unavailing; that the British could not wait for daylight but had to attack the sleeping and unarmed men in the darkness; that it was necessary to pull the steamer into the Niagara current, set it on fire, and, "careless to know whether there might not be in her the innocent with the guilty, or the living with the dead, committing her to a fate, which fills the imagination with horror." No wonder, Webster concluded, the public clamored for vindication when McLeod entered the United States and allegedly boasted of his deeds. It was a powerful letter, one the British would not find easy to answer.✓

According to international law, some circumstances could justify the invasion of another country. Classic writers such as Hugo Grotius and Samuel Pufendorf agreed about the necessity of preemptive attack in cases of imminent danger. Emerich de Vattel, whose work was influential in the United States, maintained that the right of self-preservation entitled a nation to do whatever was necessary to protect itself: "If an unknown man takes aim at me in the middle of a forest I am not yet certain that he wishes to kill me; must I allow him time to fire in order to be sure of his intent? Is there any reasonable casuist who would deny me the right to forestall the act?"[53] In his note of April 24, Webster indicated agreement with that reasoning, but it seems unlikely that he anticipated accepting similar arguments in relation to the *Caroline* raid. His own experience as a lawyer probably directed him toward the opposite conclusion: that the British raid was unjustified.

As a student of law forty years earlier, Webster had become thoroughly familiar with the classic authorities, and his practice in admiralty cases frequently dealt with issues of international law.[54] Of particular interest because it parallels arguments in the *Caroline* affair was Webster's defense of the brash young naval officer, Robert F. Stockton, in the case of the *Marianna Flora*. In autumn 1821, just after a squall, Stockton's *Alligator* came upon the *Marianna Flora* flying no flag but signaling for assistance. As the *Alligator* drew near, the other vessel suddenly opened fire. Stockton counterattacked, and, when he drew alongside and fired a broadside, the ship hoisted a Portuguese flag and surrendered. The captain said he thought the *Alligator* had been a pirate. Stockton had reached the same conclusion regarding the *Marianna Flora*, and he dispatched the vessel to Boston with a prize crew.

Eventually, in 1826, the case reached the Supreme Court, where the Portuguese government argued that the American officer had acted unreasonably and illegally. Webster and his friend George Blake represented Stockton. Drawing on doctrines of self-defense expressed by Grotius and Pufendorf, Blake argued that the American had acted properly in repelling the attack. Webster acknowledged that the *Marianna Flora* turned out not to be a pirate, but the important point was what Stockton thought at the time. Interestingly, the decision in his favor combined the arguments of defense counsel. Speaking for the court, Justice Joseph Story held Stockton blameless. The *Marianna Flora* had fired first: for Stockton and the *Alligator*, it was "not a case of mere remote danger, but of imminent, pressing, and present danger." Hesitation invited destruction.[55]

Renowned for his memory, Webster probably had the *Marianna Flora* in mind when he wrote Fox about the *Caroline*. When he declared that to justify the raid the British government had to prove "a necessity of self-defence, instant, overwhelming, leaving no choice of means, and no moment for deliberation," he was describing Stockton, who had to attack the *Marianna Flora* because he was under fire. But the British had not been overwhelmed by such circumstances in the case of the *Caroline*. They had time to deliberate and to seek other means. They could have applied for assistance from American authorities or delayed hostile action until the ship was in British territory, for Navy Island was Canadian soil. Although Webster suggested the rationale that could justify the event, there seems little possibility he would have conceded any necessity for the *Caroline* raid; instead, he was pressing Britain to admit the act was not justified.

The clerk's error, which delayed McLeod's trial, afforded the national government another opportunity to influence the case. Gardner and Bradley's plan to defend their client by claiming he had not been a member of the *Caroline* raid pleased Seward, who wanted the case to go to trial, but annoyed the secretary of state, who thought the Canadian should be discharged on the ground that the *Caroline* affair was an issue between the national governments.[56] At one point, Webster informed Tyler that he considered the alibi defense neither adequate nor proper and remarked that Gardner and Bradley seemed "men of no great force."[57]

About the same time that Webster expressed dissatisfaction with the attorneys, a veteran trial lawyer from Utica, Joshua A. Spencer, joined the defense. He could be savage in court, and Seward once said that he tore witnesses to pieces.[58] Spencer had been involved in Whig politics nearly as long as the governor. For a time, he was a state senator and mayor of Utica. He had been nominated for Congress in 1834, and, after Seward won the governorship, lost a contest for state attorney general to Willis Hall.[59] When Harrison won the presidency, Spencer was rumored to be a likely choice as United States district attorney for northern New York.[60]

There are no records revealing how or when Spencer became involved in the case, but General Scott informed Seward at the end of March that he had been engaged.[61] Whether Webster had a part in bringing him in is uncertain, but the secretary of state went through the formality of asking Fox, early in April, if he could provide the names of McLeod's lawyers.[62] Because Webster supposedly knew nothing about Spencer but was aware that Gardner and Bradley were working for McLeod, it is unclear why he made this query. Possibly he hoped to disassociate himself from any prior connection with Spencer in case he were accused of recruiting the new counsel. On April 16, within a few days of his note to Fox, Webster sent Spencer a confidential letter offering "to carry on with you, directly, any correspondence which may be necessary" regarding McLeod's defense.[63] Three days later, he sent the counselor a commission as United States district attorney, adding that he could continue as McLeod's counsel despite the appointment, and in fact pointing out the president's desire to "see an early disposition made of this matter."[64]

If the secretary of state found nothing objectionable in Spencer's representing both the national government and McLeod against the state of New York, Seward certainly did. Van Buren Democrats in New York had criticized Attorney General Crittenden's mission, and one representative in the state assembly called it unparalleled interference in state affairs. The governor had no intention of leaving himself open to charges that he had neglected the state's honor.[65] He protested to Tyler that the situation presented the "unseemly aspect" of a conflict between the state and the national government.[66]

If Seward thought the president would give in, he misjudged his man. Tyler replied that Spencer had received no orders from the government to represent McLeod and his engagement as the Canadian's attorney preceded his appointment as district attorney. That did not mean, Tyler added, that the federal government denied itself the "right to resort to all constitutional and legitimate means within its power" to carry out its international obligations, if such measures became necessary. Seward, of course, was not ready to give up. Receiving Tyler's reply, he sent another, and more insistent, call for Spencer's removal from the case. Justice, he said, demanded unfettered proceedings, and any federal interference would adversely affect the honor and dignity of New York. By representing McLeod, the district attorney created a suggestion of disharmony between the state and national governments. The governor had no doubt he ought to withdraw as McLeod's counsel.[67] Tyler regarded Seward's demand for Spencer's removal as "most extraordinary" and retorted that he would never require a lawyer to abandon a client, nor deny the district attorney the privilege of taking up cases in which the United States was "no party to the records."[68]

From that point, the correspondence between the men became more unpleasant. Seward responded that the president's decision was harmful to the state. He had learned with "surprise and exceeding regret" that the United States government, which under Van Buren had taken New York's cause as its own, now denied it was a party in the case. Was the state to be abandoned? Seward fumed that, though the district attorney could lay down his duties for a private case, he could never "part with his official character and influence." The case for McLeod was the case for Britain; Spencer thus opposed the interests of the United States as well as New York. The governor was as angry with Spencer as he was with Tyler. He doubted, he said, if any other lawyer in the state would have assumed a public trust and then have embarrassed "himself and the government with a retainer so incongruous and offensive."[69]

The president replied in kind. He regretted that Seward could not understand why he declined to "deprive a man placed upon trial for his life, of the services of his retained counsel" merely because his attorney held a federal commission. The principle that every individual accused of a crime was entitled to a fair trial and counsel of his own choosing was incontestable. As for the charge that the national government had abandoned the state, Tyler claimed that the governor had misrepresented his intent. Indeed, he said, first the governor had urged the federal government to meddle in the case, and, when Tyler refused to remove Spencer, he complained because the president would not *"interfere against the accused."* The national government had neither taken part in the case nor abandoned New York, even though the issue was properly no longer local but national. "Permit me to hope," Tyler said, "that our correspondence on this subject may end here."[70]

Still, Seward could not leave the matter alone. He sent Tyler a long and convoluted letter, answering the president's rebuttal point for point. Spencer's participation in the defense, according to Seward, implicitly stood for Britain's position in the *Caroline* case. By arguing that McLeod was not liable for his action if he had taken part in the raid, the district attorney was admitting "that the transaction was lawful, just, and right."[71] Fortunately, Tyler already had vented sufficient steam, and did not reply.

One may wonder how two intelligent politicians became engaged in such an unproductive dispute. Nonetheless, both of them had valid points. Seward was probably right to suspect that Spencer's appointment as United States attorney was connected to his work in McLeod's defense. Tyler's denials of the link were ingenious. Still, in the Jacksonian era state and national attorneys had frequently carried on concurrent private practices, so Tyler's position was also correct.

Both men had much at stake personally and politically, which was probably the major cause for the level of vehemence in their dispute. Seward especially seemed to feel the pressure, for McLeod's trial was popular among New York Democrats and Whigs alike. As governor, Seward had committed himself on the case when McLeod was arrested during Van Buren's presidency. Backing down when the Whigs were in power might harm him politically. Another factor was his vanity; he believed he should have a voice in forming policy on the *Caroline* and McLeod issues. He complained to Treasury Secretary Thomas Ewing that he had dealt frankly with Attorney General Crittenden and "expected similar confidence to be reposed in us especially as the questions have local bearing and local interest."[72] Seward later complained to a friend, Congressman Christopher Morgan, that the administration had treated him unkindly and unwisely.[73] Finally, he saw himself as highly principled. In his youth, he had been expelled from college when he refused to recite out of turn. He may have learned then the art of holding his ground, for the expulsion ended when the president of the college apologized.[74]

As for Tyler, it is more difficult to explain why he allowed the argument to become so heated. But he too was proud and highly principled. Possibly he regarded the fight with Seward as a test of his presidency. Seward was a nationalist Whig and seemed allied with Henry Clay, Tyler's rival. Perhaps Tyler concluded that loss of face would prove fatal to his administration. In any case, the contest between the governor and the president produced a historical irony: Seward, the champion of nationalism, stood for states' rights; Tyler, the spokesman of Southern particularism, argued for the federal government.

Whatever its causes, the incident produced lasting bitterness. Webster, who managed not to be directly drawn into the affray because he was in New York City, confided to his and Seward's mutual friend Richard M. Blatchford that he was "much annoyed and vexed" at the governor. Webster was, Blatchford told Seward, "in a very bad humor about it all."[75] Writing to his friend Hiram Ketchum, Webster revealed that his feelings went considerably beyond annoyance. "Little Seward," he said, was "a contemptible fellow—& that is the end of it." The United States could yet, he said, have a war on account of "this small piece of political character."[76] Months later, Blatchford reported that the secretary of state was "savage as a meat axe" on the subject of Seward's actions in the McLeod affair.[77]

Seward, too, remained angry. Convinced of his rightness, he resented the national government's lack of support for New York's position. In a scathing letter to Morgan, he wrote that Webster possessed the "most powerful intellect" in the land, but someone with much less wisdom would have known to consult "so important a party as New York" in the McLeod case.[78]

The Whig government's new direction in the case, especially the conflict between Albany and Washington over Spencer's combined duties as United States attorney and counsel for McLeod, was a major political event. For the moment, the national government held the advantage: Spencer would remain both McLeod's lawyer and district attorney. Besides that, Seward had not been able to convince Webster and Tyler that McLeod should go through the ritual of a trial, even though Seward promised to issue a pardon if a conviction occurred. In May, even while the president and the governor engaged in their heated controversy McLeod and his lawyers went to New York City to argue the case for a writ of habeas corpus before the state supreme court.

7

ARGUMENT,
ARGUMENT

Early in May 1841, after failing to conclude his case by executive measures, McLeod and his lawyers traveled to New York City to seek a writ of habeas corpus from the state supreme court. He apparently enjoyed the attention, for one newspaper reported that he was "quite the lion" aboard the boat conveying him to the city, and Philip Hone—who observed that "this fellow has caused more trouble than his deuced neck is worth"—recorded in his diary that, though no pains were taken to prevent his escape, he obviously had no interest in getting away.[1]

Webster meanwhile took up residence in the Astor Hotel, from which he advised McLeod's attorneys. It was important to avoid the appearance that the national government was involved in the case, he wrote his son Fletcher, but he reported that most observers believed McLeod would be discharged.[2]

The principal lawyers, State Attorney General Willis Hall for the prosecution and Joshua A. Spencer leading the defense, came before the supreme court on May 17.[3] McLeod's attorneys maintained that, because destruction of the *Caroline* was "an act of public force, done by the command of the British government," those involved were not personally responsible. In any case, they contended, the United States Constitution granted power over foreign affairs to the federal government, which had officially demanded redress for the act. Interference by New

York was therefore inimical to the Constitution. The state supreme court ought to free McLeod, either by advising the prose-
cuting attorney to enter a *nolle prosequi* or by simply releasing
him on recognizance with the understanding that no prosecution
would ever be pursued.[4]

Prosecutor Hall objected that discharging McLeod would be
an unprecedented infringement on the judicial system. The supreme court, he maintained, had no power to set aside or alter
an indictment issued by a grand jury; it could only decide if the
procedures of the arrest or indictment had been illegal. McLeod's
lawyers were asking the supreme court to decide on the facts of
the case, a task beyond its authority. Innocent men were sometimes arrested, but a decision on their guilt or innocence was a
function of a jury. Beyond technical considerations, Hall made
several substantive points. In the first place, he said, under certain conditions an individual could be held personally responsible for a violent act despite his government's avowal of the
deed. No one, he insisted, was immune to criminal prosecution.
Ambassadors, the invited guests of nations, were subject to indictment for felonies such as murder, and even crimes that were
clearly acts of state could be punished by death. During the
American Revolution, General Washington had hanged two British agents who urged American troops to desert. Besides, was
the killing of Durfee necessary to the success of the British mission or was it excessive violence? Vattel drew a distinction in
international law, but only a jury had the right to decide. Hall
questioned whether McLeod, a civilian, could claim he had per-
formed a military act because, according to his reading of Vattel,
only regular troops had the right to engage in war. Private
citizens who took part were not entitled to the privileges of
soldiers but could be hanged as outlaws. Another issue was
whether the *Caroline* raid was lawful war or mere brigandage.
When a nation was attacked by outlaws, he said, it had no obligation to treat them according to rules of war. The *Caroline*
raiders had gone too far; after taking control of the boat they
had gone ashore and searched for more victims to "satisfy their
insatiable thirst for blood."

Hall concluded his opening remarks with lofty sentiment.

When he read about Roman greatness, he said, it was not pal-
aces, great temples, or power that thrilled him but the excla-
mation, "I am a Roman citizen!"—which had evoked awe even
in the remotest and most barbarous regions of the world. In
modern days, Britons enjoyed "almost an equal passport and
protection." But when would American citizenship have such
merit? Not until the United States decided "with equal scru-
pulousness to protect the lives, liberties and property of the
humblest citizen of our republic," and never so long as Americans remained willing to call on their judiciary to "obey the
irregular and illegal demands of a foreign nation."[5]

The attorney general's technical points—that the supreme
court had no authority to discharge a proper indictment—had
merit, but his arguments on international law were for the most
part weak. True, Vattel proscribed excessive measures in warfare, but he recognized the difficulty of forming "a just estimate
of what the actual situation demands." The distinction between
what was indispensable or barely permissible was a matter of
conscience for the belligerent, a position far removed from Hall's
demand for a judicial determination.[6] The argument that only
regular troops could take part in hostilities was a distortion of
Vattel. The Swiss jurist had said that modern warfare was carried
on by regular armies, leaving the peasantry and townspeople
nothing to fear unless they committed hostilities. Yet, Vattel
meant unorganized noncombatants in territory occupied by an
enemy, whereas McLeod was a member of the Canadian militia.[7]
The prosecutor's other arguments were equally inappropriate.
When Vattel justified execution for brigandage, he meant ma-
rauding ventures rather than state-directed expeditions. Finally,
as Hall pointed out, General Washington had executed British
subjects who attempted to corrupt his men, yet, by longstanding
precedent in international law, agents or spies were commonly
sentenced to death.[8]

Having listened to the state's unconvincing efforts, Spencer
had cause to be optimistic when he took the floor for rebuttal.
He challenged Hall's procedural arguments. According to his
reading of the law, the state supreme court did have power to
look beyond procedural questions in examining all the facts of

the case and could, he believed, order an absolute discharge or direct the attorney general to enter a *nolle prosequi*.[9]

Spencer's strongest arguments rested on international and constitutional law. On the international level, he called the court's attention to conditions in 1837 on the Canadian-American border, where, he said, a state of war existed "in the midst of the peace of nations." Canadian authorities had acted to protect their territory and had called on loyal British subjects for assistance. These subjects, Spencer maintained, had a duty to serve their nation and were not individually responsible for their deeds. He provided a long list of citations from Vattel to support his contention that political societies required authority to regulate public affairs for the common good, and that the people owed their sovereign faithful obedience. Even in doubtful cases, they had to presume the ruler acted justly; if any evil resulted, the state was responsible. "The sovereign," Vattel said, "is the real author of war, which is made in his name at his command." Those who served him were "only instruments in his hands" who carried out "his will and not their own." The law of nations was clear: if a state ratified the act of a citizen, it assumed responsibility for the deed and could be regarded as the source of injury to an affronted party.[10] In terms of international law, Spencer declared, "this whole proceeding is an absurdity."[11]

Spencer argued that McLeod's arrest was illegal because the Constitution gave the president and Senate control over foreign relations. New York's action, the lawyer claimed, interfered with the national government's effort to negotiate the *Caroline* case. Under the Constitution, Congress had the power to declare war, raise armies, and issue letters of marque and reprisal.[12] Having assumed responsibility for resolving the *Caroline* affair, the federal government had exclusive authority because, according to the Supreme Court's ruling in *Gibbons* v. *Ogden*, "two separate independent jurisdictions cannot lawfully act the same time upon the same subject." Nations, the lawyer concluded, were known to each other by their ambassadors, if friends, or by their armies, if enemies. New York had no power to send or receive ambassadors or engage in war. Between the United States and other countries "we are one people possessing one territory,

having one interest, one voice, one duty, one responsibility."
The court should order McLeod's release and leave the case to
the national government.[13]

When the state supreme court hearing closed on the evening
of May 19, 1841, the defense seemed confident. Governor Seward's friend Richard M. Blatchford did not know what impression Hall had made, but he wrote the governor that authorities
in Washington had little doubt of McLeod's release.[14] Webster
informed Minister Fox that he expected that outcome. Fox was
less optimistic. The prevailing feeling, he wrote his government,
was that the defendant would be ordered to trial, for the state's
argument was "much more determined and in earnest than I
had been led to expect."[15]

While lawyers on both sides were working on their cases,
Congress began a discussion of the *Caroline* and McLeod affairs
that eventually dominated half the summer. Everyone in the
House and Senate seemed to have an opinion, and most seemed
determined to have their public say. The debate reveals much
about politics and nationalism in the young republic. Comments
ranged from obvious appeals to voters back home to deep differences about the nation's course in the world.

Secretary Webster, who in a long political and legal career had
made many enemies as well as friends, became the lightning
rod for sharp party and personal division. The matter began on
June 1, when President Tyler provided Congress with copies of
the official correspondence between Webster and Fox.[16] The
head of the Senate Foreign Relations Committee, William C.
Rives, a Tyler Whig, tried to refer the exchanges to committee
quietly, but Democrat James Buchanan requested time for discussion. Denying that he was moved by party feeling, Buchanan
objected strenuously to Webster's course, especially his March
15 instructions to the attorney general and his April 24 note to
the British minister. The secretary, he said, should not have
agreed that British avowal of the act absolved McLeod of personal responsibility. Lawful commands from supervisors protected individuals for hostilities committed during war, but the
United States and Britain had been at peace. McLeod was not a
prisoner of war but a captured marauder. Even if Webster were

correct, Buchanan argued, he should not have taken so strong a position against New York. The McLeod question was pending before the state supreme court and if, as Buchanan expected, the ruling should be against the defendant, Webster would find himself and the country in an awkward situation.

More than anything, though, Buchanan felt that Webster had not responded with sufficient "American spirit" to Britain's arrogant demand for McLeod's immediate release. Fox's note of March 12 was insulting and threatening, but Webster had taken no offense at its tone. Webster's state paper of April 24 was not the real reply to Fox's note at all, according to the senator. The true response, which conceded every point Britain advanced, was in Webster's instructions to Attorney General Crittenden, ordering him to help McLeod obtain counsel and indicating that, if the case were before a federal court, the president would direct the filing of a *nolle prosequi*. The next step, Buchanan concluded sarcastically, would be to bill the government for McLeod's defense.[17]

The most vociferous attack on the secretary of state came from powerful and cantankerous Senator Thomas Hart Benton, of Missouri. He and Webster were bitter antagonists. Benton was comparable to Webster in intelligence, knowledge of the law, and erudition, and nobody could master the old Missourian when it came to political fulmination.[18] It distressed him, Benton said, to see members of the Senate consulting tomes of international law to justify the outrage against their country. It would be better to throw away the books. Jackson had no "musty volumes" of international law when he captured Arbuthnot and Ambrister, but he had an "American heart," which never led him wrong when "the rights, interest, and the honor of his country were at stake." He had executed those malefactors responsible for inciting Indian violence, and, if the "assassins of the *Caroline*" were treated similarly, it would end British outrages along the Canadian frontier. As soon as the Whigs came to power, Benton said, he told his friends McLeod would be released by underhanded means and a letter "cooked up" to justify them.

Soon thereafter, Benton continued, Webster sent the attorney general on an illegal and degrading mission to New York for that purpose, and on April 24 presented the justification, which was "a mere alterpiece—an article for home consumption—a speech for Buncombe, as we say of our addresses to our constituents." The Crittenden instructions were deplorable. They lowered the nation's character in the eyes of the world and took away the respect gained through the last war with England. Benton considered the note to Fox nearly as bad: its views of the law of nations were mistaken, it yielded to threats, it exhibited little patriotism because it took the part of a foreigner against the United States. Its whole aspect was "deficient in manly tone—in American feeling—in nerve—in force."[19]

The Whigs could not permit such criticism of the secretary of state to pass unchallenged, and other senators came to Webster's defense. Rives denied that the instructions to Crittenden interfered with New York's jurisdiction or that the reply to Fox abandoned principles established by Van Buren's administration. British avowal of the raid made the issue a national one, to be redressed by national means, not avenged by persecuting a mere instrument in the affair. Surely, Americans would not have thought of holding the sailors of the *Leopard* personally liable for attacking the *Chesapeake*, even though it was as great an outrage. As Rives finished, Benton quipped from across the aisle, "I would have hanged every one of them."[20]

Making his first Senate speech, Webster's friend from Massachusetts, Rufus Choate, defended Webster's note of April 24 as "worthy of the man, the cause, and the country." Nothing had been conceded except that the law of nations protected a soldier carrying out the orders of his government. What else could Webster have done? Should he have informed Britain that the United States was not "advised exactly whether it may hang prisoners of war?"[21]

Senate Democrats had given Webster a "terrible castigation," Tennessee Congressman Aaron V. Brown reported to James K. Polk. Although the administration's supporters had come to Webster's defense, Minister Fox advised Palmerston that, whereas the Democrats' attack on Webster had been vehement, unmeasured, and delivered by the united force of the opposition, the Whig response was "feeble and timid." Fox concurred with the Democrats that the instructions to Crittenden had been the real answer to the demand for McLeod's release, but, in Fox's opinion, if Webster had insisted on the release in the beginning, the affair would be over and political conflict no worse than it was.[22]

Webster came in for equal criticism in the House. Two Democrats, New York's John G. Floyd and Pennsylvania's Charles J. Ingersoll, joined in a resolution calling for information about the Crittenden and Scott missions and asking whether the secretary of state had informed Fox that he could expect McLeod's release. Floyd was a Utica lawyer and newspaper publisher who apparently had no purpose beyond game participation in the barefisted politics of the day. Bad feeling between Webster and Ingersoll went as far back as the War of 1812. The break occurred in 1826, when Webster, as head of the House Judiciary Committee, investigated charges that Ingersoll, then United States district attorney for Philadelphia, had illegally accepted money from the estate of someone indebted to the government. The committee had taken no action against Ingersoll, but Webster confided to Henry Clay that it had been difficult "to prevent the District Atty from being disgraced." Aside from that, Webster considered Ingersoll's conduct as district attorney ridiculous. Even though his political reputation had been spared, Ingersoll remained bitter and for years afterward missed no opportunity to goad Webster.[23]

Ingersoll charged that the secretary of state had blundered by giving in to Fox's demand for McLeod's release. Unless the American position changed, Ingersoll warned, "oceans of Blood, at perhaps no distant day, will inevitably flow, to wash out the stain of his capitulation."[24] Aaron V. Brown, of Tennessee, agreed and declared that the secretary of state's policy was timid and irresolute. What business had the attorney general traversing the country on behalf of "foreign felons" who had spilled "better blood than ever flowed in English veins"? It was his job to prosecute criminals, not defend them. And what of Scott? Had he been sent to the frontier to obtain the release of McLeod by the sword if Crittenden were unable to do so by the purse?

Could an American heart extend one throb of approbation to the "cold unfeeling diplomacy—to the tame and ready submission of the American Secretary of State?"[25] Another Democrat, Samuel S. Browne, of New York, told the House that Webster's "servile cringing to British power has brought shame and dishonor on our country."[26]

As in the Senate, the Whigs came to Webster's defense. His friend Caleb Cushing, of Massachusetts, charged Ingersoll and the Democrats with attempting to embarrass the administration by stirring war feeling. He regretted seeing party spirit grow for sinister purposes, especially because in making an issue of McLeod's case the Democrats substituted a false concern for the real question of the *Caroline*. Britain had avowed the raid as a public act, and the United States had to seek national redress, not individual retaliation. If the Democrats promoted any other course, they would become "blind instruments of England," which would be glad to distract attention from the *Caroline* and the other great issues between the countries.[27]

Henry A. Wise, of Virginia, deplored Ingersoll's remarks. The secretary of state instead deserved praise for his handling of the negotiations.[28] Hiram P. Hunt, of New York, also had confidence in Webster. The American people, Hunt said, would never need to make allowances for Webster's knowledge of municipal or international law. For a quarter-century, he had "stood out in bold relief, as the great constitutional lawyer of his country," and had been "designated in Europe as the master mind, not of America, but of the age." These assaults, Hunt believed, were not sincere, but only attempts to embarrass the administration and plunge Britain and America into war.[29]

In mid-July, House discussion of the Floyd-Ingersoll resolution came to an inconclusive halt. Its supporters lacked votes to pass the measure, but it served as a useful vehicle to criticize Webster.[30] In September the issue revived, but John Quincy Adams, though no admirer of Webster, used his talents to quash it. The matter, he said, had occupied more of the House's time than it ever should have. Adams sarcastically examined the motives of the resolution's supporters. Floyd had disclaimed partisan feeling: "No party complexion! Oh no!," Adams cried, bringing laughter to the House. "No it was patriotism!—pure patriotism!—patriotism pure and undefiled!" Adams said he was willing to allow anyone credit for patriotism, but "if it had not been for that unqualified profession of patriotism, and no[t] party, which had rung through this House from every gentleman who had supported this resolution, he should have felt bound to believe it the rankest party measure that ever was introduced into the House."

Adams maintained that the resolution's authors erred in making the *Caroline* affair an issue of right or wrong between the United States and England. Americans could talk all they wished about territorial sovereignty and states' rights, but, if the question were given to the leaders of any other nation for judgment, they would cut through abstractions and ask, "Who struck the first blow?" That was the international concern; it went beyond any domestic issue of states' rights. Adams believed Webster's note to Fox of April 24 was "one of the best papers that ever was written," entitling the author to credit rather than reproach. When Adams finished, the House voted to table the resolution.[31]

Adams had provided relief for the besieged Webster, yet the effort on behalf of a man he disliked left an aftertaste. Reviewing proof-slips of his remarks for publication in the Washington *National Intelligencer*, he glumly confided to his diary that the speech had saved the secretary of state from personal ruin and the country from a disastrous war. Webster, he believed, would thank him with "professions of respect and esteem" and then lay "secret and deep-laid intrigues" against him. Such, he concluded, was "human nature, in the gigantic intellect, the envious temper, the ravenous ambition, and the rotten heart of Daniel Webster."[32]

New York's supreme court announced in July that it had reached a decision on McLeod's appeal. His attorney, Joshua A. Spencer, called on the judges on July 6 seeking information, but he reported to Webster that they were careful not to provide any intimation about the judgment. State prosecutor Hall had more success. He had learned, he informed Seward, that his arguments had been upheld.[33] In a long and rambling opinion on July 12, Judge Esek Cowen, speaking for the court, denied

McLeod's request for a writ of habeas corpus. He quickly dispatched the merits of the appeal. The defense could not interpose "extrinsic facts" about the case—evidence that McLeod was not on the raid—in the appeal. Further, he declared, the laws of New York gave the supreme court no authority, specifically or by implication, to discharge McLeod before a trial.[34]

Thus far, the ruling was far from remarkable, but the rest of the opinion revealed that Cowen was attuned to the political arguments. He applied irrelevant points of law. He demonstrated that foreigners residing in the United States were subject to municipal jurisdiction, yet that well-established principle had never been at issue in the McLeod defense. He spent a large portion of his opinion arguing, along the line of Webster's opponents in Congress, that the *Caroline* raid could not be regarded as a legitimate act of state because it had been undertaken without specific authorization of the war-making power, which in England was the queen. The judge maintained that the attack was, despite the subsequent assertion of the British government, an act of private hostility for which the participants could be regarded as pirates. He saw "nothing in the case except a body of men, without color of authority, bearing muskets and doing the deed of arson and death; that it is impossible even for diplomatic ingenuity to make a case of legitimate war."[35]

Cowen's rhetoric was far more appropriate to the political arena than the bench, and he was largely mistaken in his interpretation of public law and precedent. No source in international law maintained that hostilities had to issue directly from the sovereign power, but only from proper authority, such as a military commander. At the same time, Cowen dismissed without examination the question of conflicting powers between the national and state government, arguably the most important issue before the court.

Reaction to the decision depended on one's view of the McLeod issue. Fox, who had never accepted Webster's assurances that the court would release McLeod, revealed the depth of his own confusion about the American federal system when he incredulously reported to Palmerston that the national government found itself in the extraordinary position of being "over-

ruled by an inferior province within one of its own States."
Webster, Fox informed Lord Sydenham, seemed to be struck
"dumb and helpless" by the decision.[36] Seward thought it
showed that he had been right all along and Webster wrong,
and the governor's secretary, Samuel Blatchford, wrote Seward
that the latter's triumph was great.[37]

Cowen's opinion infuriated the secretary of state, who wrote
his old friend Supreme Court Justice Joseph Story, denouncing
it as "hollow, false, & almost dishonest, from beginning to end."
Webster was not ready to accept the opinion passively: he
wanted it critically reviewed, and he insisted that Story lay aside
other duties and "give a day or two, to the subject." Story agreed
with Webster's assessment. The opinion, he wrote back, was
full of truisms that nobody questioned, generalities that admitted of a thousand qualifications, and many "propositions of an
exceedingly questionable nature & character," all the while carefully avoiding the real issues in the case. "In short," he said, "I
never saw so much mere statement with so little reasoning."
But he could not review the opinion; overwhelmed with other
work, he feared his health could not stand the strain.[38] Ultimately, Webster obtained his review, when Judge Daniel B. Tallmadge, of the Superior Court of New York, roundly condemned
Cowen's effort as "deficient in methodical arrangement" and
"unsound in all its parts." Published in a volume of the state
supreme court reports, Tallmadge's review earned him letters
of congratulation from other jurists and from Webster, who informed him that he had "rendered a great service to the *law*."[39]

As soon as the court issued its decision, defense attorney
Spencer sent a letter to Webster outlining the alternatives. They
could, he said, either file a writ of error to bring the case eventually to the United States Supreme Court, or accept the New
York ruling on the habeas corpus and let the case return to circuit
court for a jury trial. If they decided on a trial, he thought the
case would be over by autumn, but, if they sought the writ of
error, it would take the rest of the winter. McLeod, who was
suffering from his confinement, was eager to seek a quick determination.[40] When Webster received Spencer's letter, he con-
ferred with Tyler and then sent formal instructions to the district

attorney. McLeod, the president believed, should decide whether he preferred a trial to another appeal, but, whichever he chose, Spencer should stay with the case. If McLeod decided to present it to a jury, the president directed Spencer to make known his opinion that the issue, involving the foreign relations of the country, properly belonged to the national government.[41]

Once the habeas corpus question was determined against McLeod, Webster came in line with Seward's desire to close the case by trial. Although Tyler preferred an appeal to the United States Supreme Court, Webster wrote Spencer that, though he had no official advice to offer, in his private opinion they should take the case before a jury at the "earliest possible opportunity." Spencer then sought and obtained a change of venue from Niagara, the district of so much excitement, to Oneida County.[42] The trial was scheduled for the fall term, which opened in September. Meanwhile, McLeod would remain in custody.

The decision of the New York supreme court had one consequence as unwelcome to New York officials as it was to Webster: it revived the Patriot Hunters' activities. British rule in Canada could be overturned, they believed, through a war with England if McLeod were convicted and executed. Reports from informants left Webster disturbed—even alarmed, according to Fox—about a Patriot resurgence.[43] The situation, Webster informed the president, was "full of danger," and the "apparent ignorance, or supineness" of New York officials in the face of such reports distressed him. It seemed possible that the Patriots might attempt to murder McLeod during the trial or even after. If he were killed by mob violence, Webster said, war was inevitable.[44]

In August, rumors multiplied about Patriot boldness. From Albany came reports that two cannon had been removed from the state arsenal. Seward heard of a plan to seize McLeod, and Fox received a confidential letter advising that the Patriots intended to surround the jail where he was held and force his surrender. Besides that, Fox's informant continued, the notorious and dangerous outlaw Benjamin Lett was "*openly* and actively" engaging in anti-British activities in Buffalo, and public authorities were making no efforts to apprehend him.[45]

As soon as he received these reports, Seward acted. He ordered state Commissary-General Adoniram Chandler to post guards at state arms depots and called on canal toll collectors to report movements of field pieces. None of the collectors had noticed any unusual traffic. The federal postmaster at Clyde informed Seward that, on the night of July 29, several men had examined the field piece in the town square with the intent of taking it for the Patriots, but they had given up their effort. According to rumor, a canal boat carrying six cannon for the Patriots passed through the canal lock the next day. Chandler at first thought the guns that went through Clyde were some that he had ordered transferred, but a few days later he learned that the pieces, which the collector let by without challenge, were not state property after all.[46] For the time, at least, the Patriots had managed to keep their weapons.

Although Seward professed no alarm, he took steps to ensure McLeod's safety. His secretary, Blatchford, sent a letter to the Oneida County district attorney warning that, as the date drew near for McLeod's trial, "restless persons" might attempt to cause trouble. After receiving, through Webster, an extract of the letter from Fox's informant, the governor told Oneida officials that they should organize a guard of thirty men to watch the jail and form a volunteer force of a hundred men in case of disturbances. Seward advised Webster of his precautions, but soon after assured him that, despite "a thousand rumors," he found no evidence of plans to harm McLeod during or after the trial. Despite Seward's confidence, Blatchford advised him from Utica that New York ought to request federal troops to protect McLeod. If he were acquitted, troops would be necessary to conduct him out of the state, eastward, for "he would not reach her Majesty's dominions alive by way of the frontier."[47]

Seward was much more concerned about the continuing problem with the Canadian outlaw Benjamin Lett, who, Fox's informant had charged, freely roamed the streets of Buffalo. Lett, it will be recalled, was a rabidly anti-British Patriot who had been arrested in 1840 while attempting to blow up a British steamer at Oswego. He had been sentenced to prison but escaped on the way, and Seward had offered a reward for his capture. The charges by Fox's informant angered Seward. He sent a scorching letter to the Oswego County sheriff, Norman Rowe, exclaiming it a "great scandal" that Lett remained at large and, even worse, "that the Sheriff showed such apparent indifference and unconcern on the subject." Seward demanded an explanation and increased the reward for Lett to a thousand dollars. The governor's action brought results: on the morning of September 6, several Buffalo police officers cornered Lett on a steamboat and arrested him.[48]

Lett's recapture by no means signaled the end of trouble with the Patriots, for shortly thereafter some of them broke into the municipal magazine at Lockport and stole sixty-five kegs of gunpowder. After nearly succeeding in blowing up a lock on the Welland Canal, they fired several cannon shots at British steamers anchored in the Niagara River between Navy Island and Chippewa. Webster warned Seward that failure to repress such acts would result in "an inglorious border warfare, of incursion and retaliation."[49]

Tyler and Webster acted vigorously. Following the example of Van Buren, the president issued a proclamation on September 15, 1841, condemning secret associations formed primarily to make "lawless incursions" into neighboring countries, a clear reference to the Patriot Hunters. Tyler reserved his strongest condemnation for traveling agitators from both sides of the border who harangued the lodges and urged them to commit illegal acts while enriching themselves through contributions from their ignorant and credulous supporters. He warned "evil-minded persons" that the laws of the United States would be rigorously enforced, and he exhorted those who had joined lodges to quit them.[50] The same day, the secretary of state sent a confidential circular letter through the Treasury Department warning federal officials on the border that the Patriots were gathering small arms and cannon and storing them for another invasion of Canada, presumably as soon as it became cold enough to allow passage across the ice. In response, Webster received promises of increased vigilance.[51]

But the national government's effort left the British minister unimpressed; as far as Fox was concerned, Tyler's proclamation would accomplish no more than Van Buren's. The McLeod case had given new vitality to the Patriot movement, and Fox believed many state and lower-level federal officials were themselves active in it.[52] After Webster confided to Fox that he might try to remove the McLeod case from New York's jurisdiction by a combination of executive and congressional action, the British minister advised Palmerston that the government wavered "from hour to hour" in attempting to avoid the danger of war and the consequences of unpopular political measures. The secretary of state, he said, was even "more weak and irresolute" than Forsyth when it came to states' rights, and Fox feared that the "indecision and political pusillanimity of Mr. Webster's character" would have a paralyzing effect.[53]

During this period, political events in Britain began to have a favorable impact on Anglo-American relations. In July 1841 Lord Melbourne's government, in which Palmerston was foreign secretary, lost an election. A parliamentary vote of no confidence followed, and in August Palmerston was laboring over issues with the United States as he grudgingly prepared to hand over the Foreign Office to his successor, Lord Aberdeen. The change in ministry forecast better relations with the United States.[54] Palmerston was an advocate of hard-line diplomacy toward the Americans. Aberdeen believed they would respond to generous treatment. A believer in peace, he looked forward to cooperative relations. His pacific intention made good diplomatic sense because it could separate the United States from possible alliance with another troublesome neighbor, France, and improve relations with both countries.[55]

Late in August, as one of his last acts before leaving the Foreign Office, Palmerston sent Minister Stevenson a reply, after a delay of three years and three months, to the *Caroline* protest of May 22, 1838. Buttressing his arguments with supporting documents, Palmerston not only justified the raid, but insisted that the United States government itself had long recognized the affair as an official act of the British government. Because that was the case, there was no excuse for holding McLeod responsible. As for the raid, the foreign secretary said that, if the British had been in the wrong, they would have agreed to reparations, but the facts surrounding the event upheld their view. In December 1837 bands of Canadian malcontents and some Americans had formed a league for the purpose of invading British territory to commit robbery, arson, and murder. Observing the *Caroline* supplying and reinforcing the marauders who occupied British-owned Navy Island, Canadian authorities deemed it necessary to capture the vessel to prevent the threatened invasion.

Having decided to attack, the British commander acted quickly, Palmerston said, for every hour of delay lessened the prospect of success. To avoid, as much as possible, bloodshed on either side, the raiders decided to attack at night and without warning, for if they waited until daylight the occupants of the *Caroline* could prepare for resistance once they sighted the attackers. For the same reason, and to prevent firing on its own men in the dark, the raiding party carried no firearms, only cutlasses and swords. The death of Durfee by a gunshot wound, therefore, necessarily occurred by misadventure from the weapon of one of his own comrades.

It was true that Fort Schlosser was United States territory, but Palmerston contended that the federal government had ceased at that time to "preserve that Neutral and Peaceful character, which every part of the United States was bound to maintain." Either the state of New York had lost control over the border region or had "knowingly and intentionally permitted the band of Invaders to organize and equip themselves within the state, and to arm themselves for War against British Territory, out of the Military Stores of the State." For those reasons, Palmerston believed, the attack on the *Caroline* was justified.

Palmerston could not send the United States a note on the *Caroline* without accounting for the long delay. He had not replied earlier, he informed Stevenson, partly because it seemed that the affair was but a part of a "large account to be settled between the Two Governments," which had to be "adjusted entirely or not at all." The United States had been long aware that Britain regarded the raid as an official act that it would not disavow, and he had thought both governments agreed that "no good could arise from the Communication of a formal Refusal" to American demands.[56]

Stevenson was annoyed that Palmerston had waited so long to reply to his protest, but what irritated him even more was the foreign secretary's implication that the American government already knew Britain regarded the raid as an official act. Stevenson informed both Webster and Palmerston that he had never received any such correspondence or any communication whatever except two *"informal and desultory"* conversations when the first intelligence of the raid reached England. Nor, so far as he was aware, had the British minister in the United States ever expressed anything except his private opinion about the raid.[57]

Despite Stevenson's ire, it was true that the American *Caroline* protests had always assumed British national responsibility, and, if Palmerston had taken his time in answering Stevenson's 1838 protest, it was also true that the American government had not pressed the case. As far back as July 1839, Stevenson had informed Secretary Forsyth he had never received an answer to his note and had asked whether he should press the issue as well as what "degree of urgency" he should adopt. Forsyth had advised him that no further instructions regarding the *Caroline* were necessary because he had frequent conversations with the British minister on the subject.[58] The *Caroline* remained undiscussed as much by American choice as by British.

In the United States, Webster was having his own difficulties with British diplomacy. On receiving Fox's dispatch about the New York decision, Palmerston had instructed him to express his government's "great anxiety for an early settlement of the affair." Fox should inform Webster that, though the British government felt complete confidence in the intention of the federal government, it could not "disguise from Themselves the vast importance of the results which may depend upon the mode of its conclusion."[59] Fox presented his instructions in a tone even more firm than Palmerston seemed to have intended. Pointing out that the New York decision was in "direct contradiction to the formal opinion of the Federal Government," which Webster had expressed in his note of April 24 and his March 15 instructions to the attorney general, Fox said that whether the nations would endure the "heavy calamity of War" depended on the actions of the United States.[60]

Fox's note placed Webster in a difficult position. As the British minister pointed out, the secretary's note of April 24 accepted the British view that the *Caroline* raid was a public act for which an individual should not be responsible, and yet New York had overruled the national government. Webster, who had already been blasted by political foes for supineness regarding Fox's demands, now found it necessary to respond to a blunt reassertion of the British view of the McLeod case.

Webster was so anxious to avoid the dilemma that he took the unusual step of asking the minister to revise his remarks, but Fox felt he could not do so.[61] The secretary had no choice but to reply with as much dignity as possible. It was true, he admitted, that the New York decision contradicted the national government. But it was not final. A writ of error could still be obtained against a state decision and the case carried to the United States Supreme Court. McLeod desired to take his case before a jury in expectation of acquittal. Even if convicted, Webster noted, the defendant could still appeal to the Supreme Court. Webster managed to mitigate some of his concessions by criticizing the British minister's diplomatic manners. The United States, he said, was as eager to reach a settlement of the troublesome affair as Britain, but it seemed hardly necessary to make "allusions to consequences, in diplomatic intercourse, in cases in which both Parties are aware of all the facts." It could be assumed, he continued, that both governments understood their duties as well as their rights and would act accordingly. The American government had provided sufficient evidence of its intention to "uphold the great principles of international law."[62]

Webster's assertions aside, Britain was not about to allow the American government to forget its obligations. If Palmerston's successor at the Foreign Office ever had any intention of moderating his country's stance on the McLeod issue, he had been hemmed in by domestic politics and Palmerston's actions. In August, Palmerston had gone before Parliament to defend his policy on the McLeod case, but Sir Robert Peel, then leading the opposition, had pronounced his explanations unsatisfactory.[63] A few days later, Palmerston sent the *Caroline* note to Stevenson. The new prime minister, Peel, and foreign secretary, Aberdeen, in the manner of Tyler and Webster, found their movements circumscribed by what had been said.

Personally, Aberdeen seemed well intentioned toward the United States and eager to conclude the McLeod affair. At his first reception of the diplomatic corps, he informed Stevenson of his great "interest and anxiety" about the case and asked about the probable course of the United States. Instead of trying to reassure Aberdeen, the American minister replied that, though the national government would take steps if McLeod were convicted, the question of conflicting jurisdiction between the state and national governments was "of a highly delicate and important character, on which different opinions were entertained in the United States." Aberdeen replied that he presumed, if McLeod were convicted, no judgment would be carried out until the issue was resolved between the state and federal governments. Even this Stevenson was unwilling to concede, replying that though in his view no sentence would be carried out so long as the case was pending before the United States Supreme Court, he "was not authorized to give any assurances as to what would be done."[64]

Aberdeen also expressed concern about the McLeod case to the American minister in Sweden and Norway, Christopher Hughes, who was visiting London. Aberdeen, Hughes related to Webster, considered the McLeod case the "gravest matter" in relations between the countries. If it could be concluded, Aberdeen said, he had no doubt all other points of dispute—the northeast and western boundaries, slave-trade questions, and economic relations—could be settled. But the McLeod case caused him the "deepest alarm and apprehension."[65]

Having made advances to American diplomats, Aberdeen turned to martial considerations. In his first dispatch to Fox on September 18, 1841, the foreign secretary renewed the instructions that Palmerston had given Fox the previous February: if the trial of McLeod resulted in conviction, Fox was to report the news and await directions, but, if a guilty verdict were followed by execution, the British minister was to "forthwith quit Washington, and return to his country."[66]

When Fox informed the president of Aberdeen's instructions,

Tyler reacted strangely. He acknowledged that McLeod was held wrongfully, but his detention was against the wishes of the national government, which had done everything in its power to bring about his release. The president conceded that the complicated circumstances resulted in part from what could be described as a defect in the American constitutional system, but Britain had to consider the "peculiar and mixed nature" of his country's federal system. Fox responded that Britain frequently had given consideration to the unusual political system, but it would not sacrifice the life of a subject or submit to a shameful outrage. If McLeod were executed, Fox repeated, he would leave the United States. War would result. Tyler replied that, after much reflection, he had decided that, if the execution occurred, "I shall take upon myself the responsibility of refusing you a Passport, *and shall constrain* you to remain in the United States until your Government shall have had time for reflection." The president, Fox informed Aberdeen, was resolute on the point. Fox at once informed British naval commanders in American waters that, if he remained in the United States after McLeod's execution, they should assume he was detained by force and carry out their orders.[67]

Tyler's declaration caused consternation in London. Prime Minister Peel interpreted his extraordinary statement as apprehension that McLeod would be condemned despite the national government's wishes. Peel informed the queen that, though Tyler's remarks seemed to show a desire for peace, it would be better to comply with Fox's call for his passport coupled with "simultaneous despatch of a special mission to this country conveying whatever explanations or offers of reparation the president may have in contemplation."[68] Peel's information was based on correspondence with Fox, and at the outset the prime minister had no idea of the manner Fox had adopted in his conversation with Tyler. Fox sent his government two notes on the conversation. The first, on October 1, summarized it; the second, on October 17, provided a more detailed account, including his statement to Tyler that by the time he demanded his passport it would be too late to prevent war. Evidently Fox and his home government had different policies toward the United

States, but that was not clear in Washington. London was still relying on the acerbic Fox to make its case in America, and the Tyler administration unfortunately received its understanding of British policy through a man who had complicated the *Caroline* and McLeod matters by his intractability. ⤚

Peel undertook military preparation in case war broke out. In September the government authorized Governor-General Sydenham to maintain two regiments at Halifax but directed him not to initiate hostilities without orders from London. Lord Stanley, the colonial secretary, sought reports on American coastal defenses. From these, the government learned that New York, Boston, and ports in between were poorly prepared. Peel also asked Stanley to investigate British defenses in Bermuda, where he thought the Americans would strike first in event of war, and informed select members of the cabinet that, because war with the United States "may be inevitable," they ought to consider "some immediate and decisive demonstration" as a preventive measure. He proposed sending Lord Sydenham's replacement as governor-general, Sir Charles Bagot, to Halifax in a ship-of-the-line, a convenient way of keeping a powerful vessel in those waters without risk of offense. The decision was also made to station four additional ships at Gibraltar and to begin collecting frigates and steamers at Plymouth.[69]

The United States was likewise concerned about military preparedness, and Webster sent an agent to determine the condition of British defenses in the West Indies. The agent did not report until July 1842, after the McLeod crisis had ended, but the mission illustrated that concern was equally pronounced in both countries. The agent's report included information about ship movements and troop numbers as well as detailed plans of fortresses. The defenses, he indicated, were strong, and work continued on them at a steady pace.[70]

Especially troubling to many Americans was the weakness of their military defenses on the northern frontier and the continuing presence of a large British force on the Great Lakes. Britain, it will be recalled, had increased its fleet on the lakes during the troubles of 1838, in violation of the Rush-Bagot Agreement, but Fox had assured Secretary Forsyth that this had been done only to protect Canada against Patriot invasion and a reduction would occur as soon as possible. As time passed, however, the lakes force was augmented rather than reduced, a circumstance that concerned Americans.[71] In the early months of 1840, the Van Buren administration had received reports that a five-hundred-ton war steamer was under construction at Chippewa and a second one was planned.[72]

By September 1841, when war appeared possible, alarming reports of British naval activity came from the northern frontier. Clark Robinson, United States marshal in Buffalo, informed Seward and Secretary of War John Bell that two large steamers— the *Minos* and the *Toronto*—were at Chippewa. The *Minos*, he said, was a 140-foot sidewheeler with eighteen portholes for guns and a large pivot carriage on the forward deck. Two-foot-thick sides and heavy iron-mesh bars topside made the ship impervious to shot. Robinson had learned less about the *Toronto* but believed it equal to the *Minos*.[73] Seward received another report from a prominent Buffalo Whig, Seth C. Hawley, who heard that British steamers would take up positions opposite Buffalo and warned the governor that, according to well-informed quarters, "we are in danger of a sudden blow from Canada."[74] General Scott, still on the frontier, did not discount such fears. In a report to the secretary of war, he estimated the possibility of war at fifty percent and warned that it was "time to look to the means of taking & holding the command of these Lakes." Scott pointed out that the *Minos* and *Toronto* by themselves could capture the entire merchant fleet on Lake Erie and prevent the United States from constructing ships. He recommended that, to command Lake Erie, the government purchase four steamers exceeding the one-hundred-ton-per-ship limit of the Rush-Bagot Agreement.[75]

Inasmuch as McLeod's trial was about to open, Webster had no wish to press British treaty violations on the lakes. The secretary wrote to Seward, reminding him that the United States had acquiesced to the increased force there during Van Buren's administration. He was more concerned, he indicated, about attacks by American citizens on British boats. His remonstrance to the British minister was equally mild. Because the *Minos* and

Toronto both exceeded Rush-Bagot stipulations, he asked for "explicit assurances to this Government, that these vessels of war, if unhappily it shall be found necessary to use them at all, will be confined to the sole and precise purpose of guarding Her Majesty's Provinces against hostile attacks."[76]

In Congress, objections were more audible. Representative Fillmore introduced a fortifications bill from the Ways and Means Committee, initiating a call for more defense expenditures. In what appears to have been as much an effort at logrolling as real concern, Lewis F. Linn, of Missouri, argued that, if McLeod were hanged, the West would need extra protection against Indians; Levi Woodbury, of New Hampshire, declared that his constituents were as entitled to "equal justice in the distribution of public protection" as St. Augustine or New Bedford; and Richard M. Young, of Illinois, argued that a lighthouse at Chicago was essential to national defense. The $2,226,401 appropriation bill, passed on September 4, 1841, included $160,000 for forts on the lakes and $100,000 for war steamers on Lake Erie.[77]

The weeks between the New York Supreme Court hearing and the outbreak of concern over defenses were wearing and disappointing ones for the secretary of state and the president. In the beginning, Webster had confidently expected the court to release McLeod, but Cowen's opinion dashed his hope. Then, opponents of his policies had vehemently criticized him in Congress. In part the assaults were personal, for he had made many enemies, but the emotion behind the attacks showed that anti-Webster sentiment also reflected diverging views about the nature and future of Anglo-American relations. If Palmerston represented the hard-line school of diplomacy in Britain, Benton was its headmaster in the United States. Speaking against Webster's conciliatory policy, Benton charged that the McLeod case was only one "link in a long chain" of aggressive English behavior. For that country, he declared, war was an occupation, "something like piracy on a vast scale, in which their fleets go forth to capture and destroy, and to return loaded with the spoils of plundered nations."[78] Others agreed with Benton and regarded Webster's policy as the worst approach to relations with Britain. Henry D. Gilpin, of Philadelphia, wrote Van Buren that "it really is hard for me to suppress my gorge when I hear Webster's letter [of April 24, 1841] spoken of without indignation. No such state paper had ever before disgraced the country."[79] Along with these difficulties, the secretary of state faced continuing problems with the Patriot Hunters, who hoped to bring about a war. The situation was indeed grim as the McLeod case proceeded toward trial.

8

TRIAL

As the McLeod case moved inexorably toward trial in September 1841, two events far from Lockport jail added to the problem. In Washington, distrust between Tyler's and Clay's wings of the Whig party led to wholesale resignations from the cabinet. And, in Vermont, British troops seized a former Canadian subject and carried him back across the border, precipitating yet another imbroglio between the countries. Both events complicated an already difficult state of affairs.

In the midst of preparations for McLeod's trial, the fragile understanding that linked Tyler to the Whigs broke apart. The cause was the hoary issue of a national bank, which the new president had opposed since 1819. In May it had seemed likely that the Whigs would reach an accommodation on the bank question. Tyler's states'-rights scruples prevented him from agreeing to the powerful national bank that Clay desired, but he expressed willingness to accept a compromise.

Somehow things went awry. On July 27 the Senate passed the bank bill and Washington was filled with speculation about whether Tyler would accept or reject the measure. Either way, the president seemed the loser: if he signed, he surrendered his principles and political leadership to Clay, yet a veto would isolate him from the Whigs. Senator John M. Clayton, of Delaware, talked with him and thought he intended to sign the measure. If he vetoed it, Clayton believed the cabinet would resign and a resolution of no confidence would be introduced in Congress, with the expectation that Tyler would resign. Andrew Dickinson was not sure what Tyler would do, but he told Seward, "if he vetoes he is a gone coon and I do not know as Salt Peter will save him." But New York Congressman Christopher Morgan never doubted for a moment that the president would reject the bank. "I tell you," he wrote Seward, "Tyler will veto the bill in spite of his cabinet," and there would be the devil to pay.[1]

As Morgan predicted, Tyler vetoed the bank bill. There were desperate attempts to compromise. Tyler seemed close to accepting a plan worked out between cabinet members and legislative leaders, but negotiations collapsed. Even before the second bank bill passed the House on August 27, word spread that the president intended to issue another veto. The political war-horse Thurlow Weed was outraged: "We are betrayed!" Tyler, he said, was a "second Benedict Arnold." Richard M. Blatchford warned Seward that the bill would be vetoed and the cabinet would resign.[2]

The impending veto placed Webster in a position more delicate than that of any other cabinet member. He and Clay were the nation's leading Whig politicians, but Clay seemed about to eclipse him. If Webster sided with Tyler on the veto and remained in the cabinet, he would surrender his position in the party. If he resigned, it implied he was subordinate to Clay. Further, the secretary was committed to bringing about a rapprochement with England and had to ask himself who could perform that task better. On September 9, when Tyler vetoed the second bank bill, all members of the cabinet except Webster and Postmaster General Francis Granger met and decided to resign.

The next day, Webster invited members of the Massachusetts congressional delegation to his home, where he asked whether he too should resign. All agreed he should remain, for the time being at least.[3] Webster wrote Philip Hone, who noted that, if the secretary stayed with Tyler, he would be criticized for an "unworthy desire to retain office," whereas, if he quit when his services as a statesman were so sorely needed, he would be faulted for failure to stand by the country.[4] Despite the show of asking Whig opinion, Webster probably intended all along to remain in the cabinet if he could find a way. He wrote his friend Hiram Ketchum that he had told other members of the cabinet that "they had acted rashly, and that I should consider my own course." For himself, he said, he had to take into account the "great foreign concerns of the country."[5]

Congress was to adjourn on September 13, and the cabinet—except Webster—resigned on the preceding Saturday. Tyler had prepared for the event and promptly submitted the names of replacements to the Senate. Reporting the cabinet breakup to London, Fox declared that Webster remained in office "mainly, if not solely on account of the critical and dangerous" relations between the United States and Britain. He thought Webster would not stay in Tyler's government permanently but would be sent to England as minister.[6]

As if there were not enough difficulties in Washington, late in September a British force crossed the border into Vermont and captured James Grogan the Younger, a refugee whom Canadian authorities regarded as a notorious malefactor. Originally from upstate New York, he had served as a volunteer soldier during the War of 1812 and moved to Alburgh, Vermont, in 1815. Five years later, he purchased a farm in Lower Canada. His life remained uneventful for several years, but, on the outbreak of the rebellion in 1837, he found that his "early education and habits as well perhaps as my natural inclination" rekindled his attachment to republican government while arousing his opposition to the "mischevious and malign influence of monarchial institutions."

Implicated as a participant in the rebellion, Grogan fled in 1838, leaving his wife and eleven children behind. During the spring and summer of that year, he lived in the United States, but, when the Canadian government issued a general amnesty, he returned. He was, he insisted, living quietly at his farm when a British lieutenant ordered him to leave Canada. Troops escorted the family to the border; then, Grogan later learned, some of them returned to his farm and set fire to his house, barn, and outbuildings.[7]

Living as a refugee in Vermont, Grogan had plotted revenge. Late in December 1838, he, his father, and a gang of supporters, had slipped into Canada and burned four farms.[8] Its officials asked Vermont Governor Silas H. Jenison to extradite the culprits, but he responded that, because extradition involved American foreign relations, it was an exclusively national concern. Fox then asked the government in Washington to assist in the case, but the Van Buren administration never took action.[9] ✓

In the fall of 1841, when McLeod was on trial for what Canadians judged to be an act of public service to his state, Grogan filed a civil suit for damages against the leader of the militia who had destroyed his property three years before. This so disturbed a group of dragoons that they determined to capture Grogan and carry him back to Canada for prosecution of his own crimes.

By this time, Grogan was a resident of Lockport, New York, but in September he returned to Vermont to take care of his lawsuit. On the morning of September 19, while staying at an inn in the border village of Alburgh, he met three British soldiers he had known during his days in Canada. They were friendly, and the four of them went to the inn, where they talked and drank for several hours. One of Grogan's American acquaintances, suspicious that the dragoons seemed overly eager for Grogan to drink, warned him that the soldiers might try to carry him across the line into Canada. As soon as he realized the danger, Grogan left the tavern and went to the home of his sister and brother-in-law, Patty and William Brown, five miles south of the border. Carefully avoiding the direct route, which ran along the borderline, he reached their house at eight in the evening. They talked until eleven and retired. Grogan probably considered himself lucky: he had gotten away from the tavern, eluded anybody who might be looking for him, and was safe with relatives several miles from the Canadian line.

His enemies were more determined than he knew. At three in the morning, the door of the house burst open and twenty uniformed British soldiers rushed in. Grogan jumped out of bed. "There he is!" one of them cried. Others shouted, "Shoot him!" "Blow his brains out!" "Put your bayonets into him!" Two men with bayonets rushed Grogan. He tried to parry the thrusts but was stabbed in the groin. Dragged outside, he thought the attackers intended to murder him and made a desperate effort to escape. The men jumped on him, held him down, and beat him nearly senseless. He was thrown into a wagon and driven rapidly toward Canada. Just before daylight, the party arrived at the Canadian town of Clarenceville, where he was placed in a guardhouse. Later that day, he was taken to Montreal, where, he complained, he was held from September 21 until October 4 in a jail with "felons and rogues of the vilest and most debased description" and given no food except bread crusts and water. He was never informed of the charges against him. On October 4 he was taken from his cell, told he would be released, and conveyed to the border. After a long and wearing journey, he arrived back at Alburgh at three in the morning. Within a few days, he addressed a letter to President Tyler, detailing his ordeal, calling for "ample pecuniary compensation" from Britain for his inconvenience and wounds, and asking the government to demand delivery of those responsible so that American authorities could punish them.[10] ▬

Word of the kidnapping set off a familiar train of events on the frontier and in Washington. In Vermont, public meetings denounced Grogan's seizure and called on Washington to demand redress. Vermonters, the citizens of Burlington proclaimed, had had enough of these "repeated insults and aggressions."[11] Writing to the secretary of state about the incident, Governor Jenison reminded Webster that Grogan had been "somewhat notorious" during the Canadian rebellion and that British authorities had requested his extradition at the time. Jenison had decided the charges were political and refused, but, whatever their nature, he told Webster, the invasion of American territory made it necessary to interfere on his behalf.[12]

The same day he wrote Webster, Jenison sent a protest to acting Canadian Governor Sir Richard Jackson, describing the raid as a "brutal attack upon defenceless individuals, and unprovoked aggression upon the sovereignty of a neighboring government." Jenison made no effort to defend Grogan's past but remarked that the "unjustifiable manner of his arrest" demanded his immediate release. The Vermont governor sensibly declined to intrude in the diplomatic issues involved. Following the same course he had taken when the Canadians requested

Grogan's extradition in 1838, he informed Jackson that he would leave it to the government in Washington to take active measures regarding the case.[13]

Webster was not in Washington when news of the incident arrived. Worn out by the cabinet crisis and suffering from the seasonal catarrh that plagued his life, he had gone north late in September, leaving his son, Fletcher, in charge at the State Department. He intended to remain in New York, where he could consult with Spencer until the close of McLeod's trial, then go to his home in Marshfield, Massachusetts, if acquittal occurred.[14] Fletcher meanwhile took over the Grogan case. Acting on the president's instructions, he protested the seizure to Fox on September 28, while Grogan was still in Canadian hands. Infringement of territory and kidnapping of an American citizen, young Webster said, was a "most extraordinary transaction," which had caused the president great anxiety, but the acting secretary did not doubt that the British government upon learning the facts would release Grogan and punish those responsible. Tyler apparently had wanted Webster to take a more insistent tone, but the acting secretary felt that, if the British would not release Grogan without urging, they would "keep him on their own responsibility." Fletcher Webster had no intention of relieving the British of such an embarrassment at the same time they were complaining about America's detention of McLeod, so he evaded Tyler's directions. Fox replied promptly and politely, promising he would inquire of Canadian authorities about the incident, but he reported more candidly to Aberdeen that Grogan was a notorious offender and there was doubt whether he was actually captured on the Vermont side of the line.[15]

Other British officials felt more concern about the affair. In answer to Jenison's letter, Governor Jackson wrote that he had heard of the incident and had started an investigation. He had not yet received a report but assured Jenison that, if the story were true, Grogan would be set free and the governor would take measures to show his disapproval. It was important, he believed, that both governments suppress irritations on the frontier. Later that day, when Jackson learned that the allegations were true, he informed Jenison that, if royal soldiers were involved, he would deal with them with the "utmost rigor."[16]

Officials in London were distressed by the affair, which jeopardized Aberdeen's hope of establishing good relations with the United States. The Duke of Wellington suggested an investigation of those in Canada who were responsible. At Peel's direction, Colonial Secretary Lord Stanley informed the new Canadian governor, Charles Bagot, that issues between the countries were "in themselves sufficiently serious" without additional complications. Stanley hoped reports about Grogan's kidnapping were unfounded or exaggerated, but, if true, he deemed the incident "wholly indefensible." Bagot should disown the act, apologize to Vermont and the national government, and express British government displeasure with the offending military personnel.[17] As soon as he learned of Grogan's release, Aberdeen instructed Fox that Britain would "agree to any reasonable indemnity."[18]

Whether Fox advanced Aberdeen's offer to the American government is uncertain; at least no mention of an indemnity is in Fox's correspondence with the State Department. In fact, throughout the affair, the minister seemed reluctant to admit error on Britain's part. In answer to Fletcher Webster's note about Grogan, Fox assertively pointed out that Governor Jackson had started an investigation even before receiving the American presentation, and, as soon as he ascertained that the arrest had been "improperly effected," the governor had ordered Grogan's release even though he was an "infamous malefactor." In his final note to the American government regarding Grogan, Fox made no mention of reparations, as Aberdeen suggested, but pointed out that Grogan's release was the result of a "prompt and voluntary decision" of the British government, arising from its "own sense of justice" rather than, he seemed to say, from American pressure. Fox probably felt confident in adopting a lofty tone because Webster had steadfastly opposed those who were engaged in trouble on the frontier. The secretary, he informed Aberdeen, did not resent his language regarding Grogan's character but indicated that he hoped public mention of Grogan's character and crimes might restrain border people from giving him undeserved sympathy.[19]

The outcome of the Grogan affair reveals how much leaders in both countries desired an improvement in relations. The *Caroline* had shown that territorial sovereignty was an explosive issue with the United States, and peace or war possibly depended on the result of McLeod's trial. Both governments wanted an end to the embarrassing affair. Everybody felt the McLeod case was already complicated enough.

Despite the distractions—the attacks on Webster in Congress, the cabinet split, and the Grogan affair—the pace of preparation quickened for the McLeod trial at Utica. At the end of August, Seward went there to meet state officials involved in the case, an occurrence, he said, that disturbed the repose of the village while "magnifying Alexander McLeod to the hearts' content" of the secretary of state and Minister Fox in Washington. The meeting bothered Seth C. Hawley, Buffalo attorney and state assemblyman, who was assisting the prosecution. He told Thurlow Weed that he sensed Seward was "harbouring the idea of a pardon for McLeod in case he is convicted." That would be a fatal political move, and he thought it should be left to Tyler, if he dared.[20]

The most pressing matter for both the state and McLeod's defense involved gathering evidence and witnesses. Defense attorneys hoped to prove, by testimony from the leaders of boats engaged in the *Caroline* raid, that McLeod had not belonged to any of the crews. The problem was that those who testified could clear him only by implicating themselves. Spencer avoided endangering witnesses by sending a court-appointed commission to Canada to collect depositions, but even then some of the raiders did not want to give evidence. The head of the expedition, Commander Andrew Drew, refused to take part for reasons of principle. One of the boat captains declined because he feared reprisal. The most important witnesses for the defense—the family of a retired British officer, John W. Morrison, at whose house McLeod later said he had spent the night of the *Caroline* raid—were threatened with violence if they testified but finally agreed to appear at the request of the British government.[21]

As testimony accumulated, Spencer's confidence increased. He wrote Webster that the evidence revealed McLeod had not been involved in the *Caroline* affair. According to general belief in Utica, Spencer said, McLeod would be acquitted. The state had gathered contrary evidence, but the witnesses were all Patriots. "One would think," he told Webster, "that scavengers had been sent out to collect the filth of the Land." Seward's secretary, Blatchford, was in Utica and thought acquittal certain. He had learned, he stated, that evidence was "perfectly conclusive as to the alibi." In fact, acquittal seemed so likely that he had begun arranging safe-conduct for McLeod after the trial.[22] General Scott was less certain, but after talking with Seward he informed the secretary of war that he thought the governor wanted a military escort to conduct McLeod to the Canadian border "no matter what may be the verdict of the jury."[23]

The prosecution seemed confident, but its work was not going well. State Attorney General Willis Hall informed New York Secretary of State John C. Spencer that the "case against the prisoner is strong." Still, as the moment neared for trial, disconcerting problems arose. Without informing anyone of his intentions, one of the state's major witnesses, Gilman Appleby—captain of the *Caroline*—inexplicably jumped aboard a steamboat as it was shoving off the wharf in Buffalo.[24] He was located and returned but seemed irresolute. Besides that, Hawley, who had gone as far as Detroit to find witnesses, found them unwilling or unable to attend the trial unless their expenses were met. He promised compensation. But, once they arrived in Utica, he learned that Spencer was "playing all sorts of monkey shines such as trying to drive away our witnesses by representing to them that they will not be paid." Then, state Chief Justice Samuel Nelson, whom Seward wanted to preside, became ill, and the job fell to Philo Gridley, the circuit judge for the Utica district. The change pleased Spencer, who informed Webster that the judge had no sympathy for Patriots. It annoyed Hawley, who complained to the governor that Gridley was "embarrassing us beyond measure by refusing to order compensation for indigent witnesses."[25]

After months of waiting, the day of the great trial finally arrived on October 4, 1841. Authorities had made some elaborate plans for McLeod's safety. Federal troops were stationed nearby (but at Seward's insistence, not in Utica). A force of sheriff's deputies was sworn in to guard and protect McLeod. Utica officials also organized a corps of civilians to be ready in case of trouble.[26]

A large crowd was on hand. Nearly a century and a half later, Americans can only marvel at how the people of earlier days found such occasions so consuming. Lacking variety and sensation in their hard-working frontier lives, and enamored of law and oratory, spectators flocked to Utica to attend, or perhaps just to be near the scene of such a momentous event. Everything ready, Judge Gridley entered the courtroom a few minutes after nine, followed by the opposing attorneys and the prospective jurors. McLeod, wearing a black suit, entered last. After some haggling over procedure, the jury—consisting of nine farmers, two merchants, and one physician—was sworn in and the indictment against McLeod was read.[27]

Now the oratory began. Hall opened for the state by eliciting the jury's sympathy for the fugitives of the Canadian rebellions "whose houses were burned and property destroyed—and whose wives and children had been forced into the driving snows of a Canadian winter." According to Hall, desperate Canadian rebels, joined by reckless Americans, had congregated on Navy Island, and out of curiosity large numbers of people had gathered near the island at Fort Schlosser. William Wells, of Buffalo, seeing opportunity for profit, had begun ferrying passengers, mainly visitors, and some articles of necessity, to Navy Island. On December 29, 1837, while the *Caroline* was berthed at Schlosser—its "inmates retired to their repose, unsuspicious of danger, as they were unconscious of wrong"—a British force from Chippewa attacked. Hall conjured up images of the assault: shouts, clashing swords, and firing pistols. Some of those on board had hidden below deck. They came out after the attackers left, "only to meet the rushing flames and to hear the roar of Niagara." But those who fled ashore were not safe either. Some took refuge in a warehouse but were pursued. After the attack, Amos Durfee, a Buffalo stage driver, was found dead on the wharf, shot through the back of the head at close range. The issue for the jury, Hall said, was whether or not McLeod took part in the raid. It did not matter if he had fired the fatal shot, for mere participation in the attack made him a principal in the crime.[28] ___

Nonetheless, the state had witnesses who had seen McLeod that night and others who had heard him boast of his exploits aboard the *Caroline*. Among those on board the night of the raid were William Wells, the owner, and his captain, Gilman Appleby. About midnight, it appeared, someone told Wells that four or five boats were approaching. While getting dressed, he had heard a "terrible uproar" and the discharge of firearms. As he and Appleby tried to get on deck, someone called out to give no quarter and kill all the "damned Yankees." Appleby testified that he tried to climb onto the deck, but a man he thought was McLeod swung at him with a sword. The blow cut through his vest and glanced off a metallic button on his trousers. He and Wells had retreated inside the boat and separated. Appleby made his way to the engine room, climbed up to the deck, and hid in a warehouse on the dock until he heard more men come in cursing the "damned Yankees." Jumping into the water, he came to shore under the pier and made his way to safety.

Was Appleby certain, Spencer asked on cross-examination, that the man who swung at him was McLeod? The reply undid the rest of his testimony. Everything happened so fast, Appleby said, that he had not noticed the features of his assailant. At the time, he thought it was McLeod, and that was what he had told a magistrate the day after the raid. Possibly, he admitted, he had been mistaken.[29]

Nor did the testimony of Wells succeed in placing McLeod at the scene. After he and Appleby separated, Wells said, he tried to pass through the boiler room to escape through a forward hatch. He stopped when he saw one of the attackers stoking the fire in the boiler. The man did not see him and Wells froze, but then the man looked up and saw someone else hiding in the boiler room. It was Durfee. The man seized him by the collar and ordered him to the upper deck "or he would blow his brains out." Once the two were gone, Wells made his way to the stern cabin, where he tried to pry open a porthole, but as it began to loosen he noticed two British rowboats with guards in them, tied to the steamer. He went back to the center cabin, planning to act "according to circumstances," but then he felt the *Caroline* move. The attackers were beginning to pull it from the dock. Three men stood at the gangplank, and he walked to them. At first, they ignored him, supposing he was one of them, but then one challenged him. Wells said he was not with the *Caroline*, but the man came toward him. Suddenly there was a pistol shot. His pursuer turned away, and Wells made his way to the inn.[30]

Lodgers at the public house in Fort Schlosser that night had watched the attack in fascinated horror. One took up a musket, ran outside, and shot at the British as they pulled the *Caroline* from the dock. Once it was away, the raiders set it afire. When they reached the middle of the river, they gave three cheers and abandoned it to the current. The *Caroline* drifted some distance and grounded. It burned to the water's edge, broke up, and the pieces swept over the falls. When the situation seemed safe, those at Fort Schlosser began to move about. They found Durfee lying dead on the dock, but not one of them had actually seen the shooting take place.[31]

The state's witnesses who were in Canada rather than at Fort Schlosser testified about the departure or return of the raiding party to the Chippewa landing, and some alleged that afterward McLeod had boasted about his exploits. Invariably these were bitter opponents of British rule. Samuel Drown, then a bartender at Chippewa, said that, after the raid, fires set at the landing guided the return of the boats, and out of curiosity he had watched them come in. One of the men he saw get out of a boat was McLeod, wearing a sword. Some of the raiding party went to a saloon, and Drown saw and heard him talking about the raid. Others confirmed Drown's testimony. Anson Quinby came all the way from Warren County, Pennsylvania, to testify that the morning after the raid he heard someone ask about the affair and McLeod reply that it had gone well. "We killed two of the damned Yankees and destroyed the boat," McLeod said, and he had gotten Yankee blood on his sleeve. Isaac P. Corson, a carpenter, saw McLeod on the saloon steps at Chippewa about sunrise, bragging to a crowd that he had killed "one damned Yankee or two."

One of the strongest testimonies against McLeod came from

Henry Meyer, a blacksmith who had worked in Canada but who left about a week after the burning of the *Caroline*. On his way out of the country, he stopped at a crowded bar in Niagara, and someone called out asking for the man who shot Durfee. McLeod stopped forth and announced, "By God I'm the one!" He pulled out his pistol and said, "That's the pistol that shot him." He took out a sword with dried blood on the blade: "There's blood of a damned Yankee."[32]

Spencer did his best to discredit the prosecution's witnesses. When Calvin Wilson, a Niagara River ferry operator, said he had heard McLeod boast about the *Caroline* raid, Spencer exposed him as a member of a Patriot lodge, asking if he had ever joined an enterprise to invade Canada. Judge Gridley warned that, because such an enterprise was against the law, the witness could refuse to answer. "I decline to answer, then," said Wilson. Had he ever entertained Benjamin Lett? After Gridley said he could be indicted for harboring Lett, a fugitive, Wilson again refused to answer. When Spencer took up the same line of questioning with another witness, Hall objected, charging the defense attorney with gathering evidence about the Patriots that he intended to use in his capacity as district attorney. Spencer bristled. He was not at the trial for any reason except to defend McLeod, he insisted, but he intended to show that the witnesses were connected with the Patriot movement, and that if they would tell the truth they would admit they wanted the conviction of McLeod, whether he was innocent or guilty. Hall lamely responded that he thought Spencer's remarks "somewhat extraordinary," but Judge Gridley ruled it was proper for the defense to draw out strong feelings in the witnesses.[33]

Spencer, professing astonishment at the feebleness of the prosecution's case, constructed his defense on two premises. The first was that the trial was inappropriate because the *Caroline* raid was a public act of the British state. Of course, New York's supreme court had ruled against this argument, but Spencer said he had the right to contest that decision. The *Caroline* raid was not an act of violence by one individual against another. It was a military act in time of war, during which ordinary civil principles of assault and battery did not apply. Britain may have been wrong to order the attack. Even so, it was "intolerable and revolting" to hold an individual responsible for the deed of a nation. The *Caroline* affair was an issue between governments, and because the federal executive had taken cognizance of the case, it lay beyond the jurisdiction of New York. The opinion of the state supreme court was "in no respect sound in this matter."

At this point, Attorney General Hall rose to object, but Judge Gridley waved him down. The ruling of the supreme court, he informed Spencer, was an "authoritative decision" he was bound to follow. The argument that McLeod could not be held personally responsible for an act of the British state could not be admitted in the trial.[34]

In the second part of his argument, Spencer asserted that, putting aside the question of whether an individual could be held responsible for an act of state, McLeod was an innocent man. He had not been a member of any of the boat crews that attacked the *Caroline* but had spent the night at the house of a friend several miles away. To prove that he had not participated in the raid, Spencer presented depositions he had obtained from at least one member of every boat in the raid swearing that McLeod had not been in his crew. The testimony, in the form of a lengthy and tedious series of defense interrogatories and prosecution cross-interrogatories, was read by Spencer over a two-day period and literally put the jury to sleep. One juror, apparently seeking to block out distracting sights as well as sounds, tied a handkerchief about his head, while others were content to lay their heads on the front of the jury box. "Altogether," the court reporter commented, "they looked more like twelve convicts . . . than a jury." After several hours, Judge Gridley, taking pity, adjourned until the next day.[35]

The depositions read, Spencer resumed oral testimony with witnesses who confirmed McLeod's story that he had not been in Chippewa on the night of the raid. According to his original statement, taken when he was arrested, he went to John Davis's inn at three that afternoon and left about seven-thirty for John Morrison's house at Stamford. William Press, a neighbor of McLeod's from Niagara, testified that on December 29, McLeod had traveled with him from Chippewa as far as Morrison's. Taking the stand after Press, Morrison, a retired British army officer, said that McLeod had arrived at his house at half past seven in the evening and stayed the night. He drank tea and a toddy with the family and retired at twelve-thirty. The next morning, a friend stopped at Morrison's gate and informed him that the *Caroline* had been burned. He went back to the house and told McLeod, who on hearing the news decided to return to Chippewa. Members of Morrison's family also testified that McLeod had spent the night. Later that morning of December 30, about eleven, Judge John McLean, of New York, had seen McLeod at Niagara Falls riding toward Chippewa.[36]

Because the Morrisons provided McLeod with an alibi during the time of the attack on the *Caroline*, the state attorneys wanted to crack their testimony. But in trying to do so Assistant Prosecutor Hawley so goaded Colonel Morrison that he angered Judge Gridley and probably irritated the jury. Whether his insults were calculated or simply inept is uncertain. Hawley asked Morrison if he had been drafted into the British army. With astonishment, the retired colonel replied, "Did you ever hear of an officer being drafted into his majesty's service?" When Hawley repeated the question, Morrison burst out, "I beg you will not talk to me about being drafted, for I cannot bear it, as a British officer!"[37]

When he tried to venture into the subject of McLeod's personal attachment to Morrison's daughter, Gridley intervened. Sometime after the *Caroline* raid, McLeod had established a romantic relationship with Ellen Morrison, who was married to an American from Buffalo. She left her husband to move in with McLeod, and once-cordial relations between McLeod and Morrison became strained. When Hawley brought up the embarrassing subject in court, Gridley upbraided him for asking Morrison questions calculated to insult him. His court, he told Hawley, "was not the place where a witness was to be showed up and insulted by uncalled for interrogatories." Hawley sulked that, if he could not ask questions he felt were essential, he would like to be excused from participating in the trial. Gridley replied, "Well, sir, then you must stop." Hall tried to smooth over the dispute by assuring the court that Hawley had intended no offense, but Gridley insisted he would not allow questions that had "no more to do with the case than the history of the Egyptians."[38]

Taking over for Hawley, the attorney general tried to impeach Morrison's testimony by summoning an unfriendly acquaintance of the colonel, William Defield, who claimed that in September 1839 Morrison had said he hoped the Americans would get hold of McLeod and "punish him for his participation in the burning of the *Caroline*." A few months later, however, in November 1840, Morrison had testified in Lewistown that McLeod had spent the night of the raid at his house. Defield said he asked Morrison at the time if he was certain of the fact and Morrison replied he was not, but that McLeod was a British subject and had to be protected. Spencer attacked Defield's credibility. A Queenston banker, Joseph Hamilton, testified that he had known Defield since he was a boy and, though he was an intelligent person, his reputation for honesty was not good; he had been a sergeant in the Canadian militia but had deserted to Navy Island. Hamilton had known Morrison for many years, too, and said his reputation was good.[39]

After six days, the lawyers finished presentation of evidence. Because it was Saturday, the jurors remained together through Sunday, and on Monday morning the court heard concluding arguments. Spencer's cocounsel, Alvin C. Bradley, began by blasting the prosecution's witnesses as, with few exceptions, "nothing but the collected idleness, vice, and profligacy of the border." Consider, he said, Henry Meyers, who alleged that ten days after the *Caroline* raid, in a crowded and noisy saloon, a clear voice had called out, "Where is the man that shot Amos Durfee?" Up stepped McLeod, who pulled out a gun and boasted, "I'm the man, and this is the pistol that did it!" And then, taking out a sword with dried blood continued: "This is Yankee blood!" Bradley scoffed: "Human blood so carefully hoarded!" The story was untrue and Meyers was a stupid, besotted wretch. As for Anson Quinby, who testified he heard McLeod say he had "killed two of the damned Yankees," Bradley remarked that, at his home in Warren County, Quinby was known as the man to call if anyone needed a witness to swear to anything. Whatever his reputation for truthfulness, his intelligence was at least as low as that of Meyers; the man, Bradley observed, was a "miserable idiot." At the beginning of the trial, Bradley had felt alarm about the consequences if McLeod were convicted, but he felt it no longer. He anticipated a "resolute acquittal."[40]

During the lawyers' final remarks, the number of spectators attending the trial steadily increased, drawn, said the court reporter, by the fame of the contestants and the anticipation of impressive oratory. They were well rewarded, he observed, with "splendid displays of forensic eloquence and elaborate argument."

When Bradley concluded his remarks, Spencer took the floor, and his treatment of the prosecution's witnesses was, if possible, less charitable than his associate's. Charging that the state's witnesses had committed the "blackest perjury that was ever brought to bear upon a trial," he alleged that the whole case against McLeod was "from beginning to end, an unholy and wicked combination of wicked men" directed toward causing war between the United States and Britain. These desperate men could find as many witnesses as they needed against McLeod— as fast as they could be discredited, new ones sprang up like hydras. Melt them all together in a crucible and one would see "how much virtue, dignity, and honesty of mind" remained. Their fabrications were incredible. McLeod never boasted about taking part in the *Caroline* expedition. When he heard those charges, he had asked Spencer if anyone could think him so foolish as to boast of such a thing when "every person living along the frontier" knew full well he had nothing to do with it. Could anyone believe, Spencer urged, that the Scotsman McLeod, from "a land where they are famed for their silence, would have been guilty of such an indiscretion?" While evidence on behalf of McLeod was conclusive, testimony against him was obviously false. Spencer had no hesitation, he said, in committing the case to the jury.[41]

When the defense concluded, Assistant Prosecutor Timothy Jenkins and Attorney General Hall presented their closing statements. Jenkins accused Spencer of addressing people in England rather than in America. Spencer had subjected state witnesses to sneers and insinuations, browbeaten them, and "put their characters in as great hazard as were the lives of those who were in the *Caroline*." McLeod's counsel had implied that the testimony of eminent men gathered by deposition was more worthy of belief than witnesses who appeared in person for the state. But why should a man's integrity be measured by the weight of his purse? Did the jury (which included nine farmers) not believe that the words of "men from the anvil and the plough" were as good as those of the speculating classes of Canada? Jenkins had little trust in depositions. In that kind of proceeding, witnesses could avoid admitting things that an opposing counsel could inquire about if they were on the stand. Besides, Jenkins said, why should the jury trust the word of those engaged in the *Caroline* raid? "Did they know when they were about to commit this murder, how many fathers they would render childless, and how many wives widows?" They did not. And yet "they were willing to go and fire indiscriminately on the boat. Now, I say, a man who will do this, is as hardened a villain, as ever swung on the gallows; they went and raised the murderous knife in the night-time, with a view of slaughtering those people indiscriminately." Depend on it, Jenkins said, those who participated in such an act had lost any moral sense and could be easily moved from the truth. Their statements that McLeod was not present could not be trusted.[42]

The attorney general also tried to discredit the testimony taken by commission. Given opportunity to closet with counsel and not subject to cross-examination, the "most perjured villain" could appear as truthful as the most "conscientious and upright man." If a witness lied during a trial, he could be punished for perjury, but there would be no penalty for false testimony from a foreign country. Defense depositions swearing that McLeod was not on the raid were entitled to no more credit than "mere voluntary statements, not taken under oath." As for McLeod's contention that he had spent the night of the *Caroline* raid at the Morrison home, it was well known that an alibi was the "common resort of all felons," and, because the state had shown that McLeod was related to the family—even though illegitimately—by his relationship with Ellen Morrison, the jury had to consider the control he had over them.[43] Perhaps, the attorney general concluded darkly, McLeod realized that as someone in public business he might find it harmful to be recognized as a participant in the raid. To disguise his involvement, he could have ridden to Morrison's with Press and returned to Chippewa in time to attack the *Caroline*.[44]

At last it was time to charge the jury, and Judge Gridley took two tedious hours. He advised the jurors that they had no concern with the large public issues that had been introduced, but only with the "ordinary charge of murder." Guilt belonged to everyone who aided or participated in the *Caroline* raid; it was not necessary to decide that McLeod personally had killed Durfee, only to determine whether he was on the expedition. At the same time, the judge cautioned the jurors to remember that in a criminal case, where a man's life was at stake, evidence for guilt must be overwhelming. If the defense had produced in their minds any reasonable doubt about McLeod's guilt, they should find in his favor.

When Gridley finally concluded, the jury retired. A half-hour later they returned with a verdict: not guilty.[45]

Suddenly, though it must have seemed nearly impossible to the participants, McLeod was a free man, after being held since November 1840. Attorney General Hall, who, according to Philip Hone had resorted to "every species of professional chicanery" to obtain a conviction, glumly reported to Seward, "I have saved you the trouble of pardoning McLeod."[46] The news was passed quickly to Washington, where Fletcher Webster officially informed the British minister. Fox, who had followed the course of the trial through the newspapers, had already informed Aberdeen, even before the verdict, that the prosecution's case had utterly failed.[47]

Credit for the result, of course, went primarily to McLeod's leading counsel, Joshua Spencer, and he promptly sent the British government a bill for $5,000. Aberdeen thought the fee excessive and considered refusing to authorize full payment, but Fox advised him that Spencer had handled the case with "skill, courage and entire honesty of purpose." Besides, he added, though the fee seemed high compared to British standards, the overcharge was not so great compared to the "enormous and incredible fees exacted upon ordinary occasions by American lawyers."[48]

With McLeod acquitted, a crucial task became returning him safely to Canada. General Scott informed the commander of the army's eastern division, Brigadier General John E. Wool, that part of a company of troops should escort McLeod from Utica to the Canadian border. The Oneida County sheriff, however, advised Wool that he could accomplish the task without a military escort. McLeod intended, Wool was informed, to proceed from Utica to New York City, where he hoped to obtain passage to England.[49] A few days later, his name appeared on the list for the steamer *Arcadia* to Liverpool, but the announcement was a ruse. Accompanied by a sheriff, he went to Canada by the usual route, from Utica to Lake Champlain and then by steamer to British territory. Upon reaching Canadian soil, he was received "with manifestations of joy and congratulations." In Montreal, looking "pale and sallow" from his confinement, he was greeted with loud cheers "amid the waving of hats and handkerchiefs."[50] A symbol of British loyalty had returned home.

9

THE CAULDRON COOLS

The outcome of McLeod's trial brought relief in the capitals of the United States and Britain, as well as on both sides of the Canadian-American frontier. Acquittal ended the danger of immediate war that his execution could have precipitated, and it broke the pattern of tension that had been building between the two countries ever since the Canadian rebellions. Although the possibility of war was not certain, mutual distrust and misunderstanding seemed to be pushing the nations toward a conflict that neither wanted. The *Caroline* affair had been an affront to honor that rankled even peace-loving Americans, and official British unconcern compounded the situation. The arrest of McLeod had the same effect in Britain. Parliamentary debate and public discussion of the trial showed how gravely this act wounded British honor. The American government's inability to control a state court added to British outrage.[1]

Still, the danger of McLeod's execution had always been less than people imagined. Governor Seward informed Attorney General Crittenden as early as March 1841 that "undeniable evidence" showed that the man was not guilty, and, even if he were convicted, Seward would use his executive power to prevent the sentence from being carried out. He had informed Philip Hone that he would never permit McLeod's execution, and others involved in the case, including General Scott and Assistant

Prosecutor Hawley, were confident Seward would pardon him if he were convicted.[2]

Misunderstanding between New York and the national government occurred because Seward's intentions were not clearly communicated to Washington. Perhaps because of confusion surrounding President Harrison's death and the succession of Tyler, Attorney General Crittenden failed to relay Governor Seward's assurances after meeting with him. In his report to the secretary of state, the attorney general mentioned Seward's desire to work with the national government, but he did not provide details because the governor had "himself communicated them in letters to you." The attorney general made no mention of a gubernatorial pardon. None of Seward's letters to Webster mentioned that possibility either. Instead, a distorted and sinister projection of Seward's aims was delivered to Washington by Simeon DeWitt Bloodgood, who suggested to Harrison and Webster that the governor's cooperation depended on how much "consideration" New York received from the administration.[3] At a time calling for frank and open dealing between New York and Washington, indirect and imperfect communication sowed seeds of distrust. Webster and Seward were understandably worried about the political hazards in the McLeod case, but they could have better achieved their ends through direct, explicit correspondence.

Although neither British nor American national leaders wanted war over the *Caroline* or McLeod, it might have been difficult to avoid one. Against the wishes of Tyler and Webster, as well as Peel and Aberdeen, the trial had become a point of honor. Public opinion and political posturing in the United States and Britain went far toward dictating the positions of both governments. Given the uncertainty of the situation, the abrasive level of military preparations in both countries, and the tendency of field commanders to act precipitately, conflict could have broken out despite peaceful intentions of the national governments. The *Caroline* raid itself was an example of excessive military ardor, as were Colonel Worth's actions at Brockville in 1839, departure of the *Brandywine* from the Mediterranean squadron in 1841, and the Grogan raid.

One reason for the poor relations between the countries was Minister Fox, who seemed to misunderstand not only the United States government but even his own Foreign Office. When, in February and September 1841, the British government had instructed him to withdraw from Washington if McLeod were executed, he took for granted that a break in relations meant war. He advised British officials and military personnel in North America and the West Indies to assume he was held against his will if he remained in the United States after McLeod's execution.[4]

Yet, evidence indicates that Peel hoped to avoid resort to arms, even if McLeod were condemned. Shortly after taking control of the Colonial Office, Lord Stanley warned Canadian Governor-General Sydenham that execution of McLeod would place Anglo-American affairs in a "critical and alarming position." Even so, breaking diplomatic relations did not necessarily mean war. Lord Stanley made clear that Sydenham was not authorized to take "any hostile steps" consequent to the withdrawal of Fox.[5]

Peel was surprised to learn that, if McLeod were executed, Tyler intended to refuse Fox's demand for his passport, even if it meant holding the minister by force. It would be better, Peel remarked, to let Fox go and send with him whatever explanations the United States had, along with proposals with reparations. But in the United States, when Tyler proposed explanations to England if McLeod were executed, Fox replied it would be too late.[6] Fox's incapacities as a diplomat were never so painfully obvious.

McLeod's acquittal helped avert war. It also opened the way for Britain and the United States to clear up other disagreements. Since the American Revolution, the two countries had argued about the boundary from Maine to the Great Lakes. Several efforts to resolve differences had failed. Other problem issues involved the African slave trade as well as the related visit-and-search controversy, the *Creole* incident of 1841—in which Britain had granted haven to escaped American slaves—and a complicated dispute regarding the Oregon territory.[7]

So long as McLeod's life was in danger, there could be no productive negotiation of issues between the countries, but, soon after news of his release reached London, Aberdeen took steps to end the disagreements. Calling the new American minister, Edward Everett, to the Foreign Office, he proposed a special diplomatic mission, which would have "full powers to make a definitive arrangement on every point in discussion between the two countries."

For the mission, Aberdeen had in mind Alexander Baring, Lord Ashburton, former head of Baring Brothers banking firm and an old friend of the United States.[8] He was an excellent choice. As a young man, he had traveled in the United States, and his wife, Anne Louisa Bingham, was the daughter of Senator William Bingham, of Pennsylvania. Under Ashburton's direction, the House of Baring had specialized in American accounts, and in Parliament and in government he had championed closer economic relations with the United States. He and Webster knew each other, for the secretary of state had been the Barings' counsel in the United States for years and the men had met during Webster's tour of England in 1839. When he learned of Ashburton's appointment, Webster wrote Everett that the mission was a welcome surprise. For himself, he said, no selection could be more agreeable.[9]

Prominent among the differences for Webster and Ashburton to discuss were questions remaining from the Canadian rebellions. No sooner had McLeod been acquitted than New York newspapers called on the government to renew demands regarding destruction of the *Caroline*. Philip Hone, commenting on the conclusion of the trial, observed that McLeod was free, but the question of whether or not he should have been tried remained open. "The fire," he said, "is only smothered[,] not extinguished." A guilty verdict might have been better, he thought, because then the issue would have fallen where it belonged all along, between the two governments.[10]

Minister Fox informed Aberdeen that McLeod's acquittal had not resolved the public question of whether he should have been tried at all. Federal legislation was necessary to protect others who had been involved in the *Caroline* raid, Fox observed, but, given the national government's disorganization and irresoluteness, such action seemed uncertain.[11] President Tyler acted as if McLeod's acquittal had reduced the question of individual liability for the *Caroline*'s destruction to a mere hypothetical issue. In a private talk with the president, the British minister expressed hope that the United States would take some action before someone else was arrested for the raid. Tyler protested that the "question was surrounded with extreme Constitutional difficulties." Fox believed that, instead of addressing the question fairly in his annual message, the president would throw it to Congress.[12]

In England, Aberdeen was concerned about the same problem. He ordered Fox to inform Webster, confidentially, that Britain expected measures to "correct the admitted anomaly in their Constitution" that allowed a state to assume jurisdiction over a federal matter.[13] In conversations with American minister Everett, Aberdeen asked what reparation the United States intended for "subjecting to criminal procedure a British subject," in a case the secretary of state admitted was unjustified. Aberdeen suggested the United States consider a constitutional amendment to prevent recurrence of such cases.[14]

In his first annual message, on December 7, 1841, Tyler urged Congress to pass legislation that would transfer cases involving "faithful observance and execution of our international relations" to the federal judiciary. The national government had responsibility for international relations and "ought to possess without question all the reasonable and proper means" of conducting them.[15] The chairman of the Senate Judiciary Committee, John M. Berrien, of Georgia, asked Webster whether he traced the authority of Congress to pass the law to any provision of the Constitution other than the last clause of Article I, Section 8, which gave Congress power to enact laws "necessary and proper" for the operation of government.[16] Webster sent Berrien suggestions for a draft of the bill, which he asked the senator to consider "private & wholly unofficial." Authority for the measure, he supposed, derived from the constitutional provision that the judicial power of the United States extended to all cases arising under the Constitution or laws and treaties made under its authority (Article III, Section 2), and from the implied proposition that questions involving the law of nations or affecting the relations of the United States with foreign countries came under the authority of the national government.[17]

The president and secretary of state had good cause to be concerned about another "McLeod case," for the Patriot Hunters, though disappointed by the outcome of the Canadian's trial, had not given up hope of provoking war. Two months after Tyler's message, Webster received word that another Canadian, John Sheridan Hogan, had been arrested in Lockport on charges of capturing and burning the *Caroline*. Hogan, a journalist, had been Sir Francis Bond Head's secretary during the Canadian rebellions, and Webster's informant had little doubt he had been a member of the *Caroline* expedition.[18] Recording the incident in his diary, New Yorker George Templeton Strong remarked: "Another unlucky hero of the *Caroline* affair fallen into the hands of our beastly borderers, and with a stronger chance this time than last that we've waked up the right passenger."[19] The day after his arrest, Hogan appeared before a judge, who discharged him. Proclaiming that "as a British subject, he had a right to traverse the universe," he returned home.[20]

Despite his brush with disaster, a few weeks later, Hogan was back in the United States, where again he was arrested, this time in Rochester. His lawyers solicited Webster's advice. They thought it inadvisable to seek habeas corpus because Hogan's enemies had another warrant ready for his arrest. By this time, some had begun to question his motives. Governor-General Sir Charles Bagot concluded that Hogan had conspired with the Patriots to bring about his own arrest. At his examination, several witnesses testified that he had boasted about his participation in the *Caroline* raid, but the public mood had changed since McLeod's arrest. The judge, declaring the evidence insufficient, ordered Hogan's discharge. Newspapers declared open season on Hogan. The Utica *Daily Gazette*, which during the examination had proclaimed the Canadian a miserable braggart, announced that he could be sent back to Canada now that he had convinced everyone of his stupidity. The Rochester *Democrat* called him a "contemptible, brainless coxcomb" who had nothing to do with the *Caroline* affair. He had tried to create the impression he was involved, the paper said, because the raid was popular in Canada. It was ridiculous that a few agitators could throw the frontier into commotion by "arresting every ass who may choose to come over and cut a swell in our city." The editor concluded, "This watching steamboats in order to seize obnoxious persons is disreputable in the extreme."[21]

Writing to Webster about Hogan's release, Joshua A. Spencer saw no rest on the frontier until some settlement was reached on the *Caroline* affair, including a stipulation that those who took part in the attack would not be prosecuted. President Tyler, responding to Hogan's arrests, sent a message to Congress urging legislation before the United States became embroiled in another controversy with Britain.[22]

Ashburton's arrival in the United States, occurring about the time of Hogan's release, lent urgency to the government's desire for a "McLeod law." The bill from Berrien's Judiciary Committee authorized federal judges to grant a writ of habeas corpus to any prisoner who claimed his offense was committed under authority of the law of nations or a foreign sovereign. The judge, if he decided the plea was valid, could discharge the prisoner; otherwise, the case would be remanded for trial. Even if the case were returned to the original court, the defendant could appeal to the circuit court or the Supreme Court.[23]

Senate Democrats lined up solidly against the proposal. It was, declared James Buchanan, "a dangerous and untried experiment," which would bring the states and national government into collision. From the beginning of the nation, he said, states had exercised jurisdiction over criminal offenses, and they would never peaceably submit to such an imposition on their sovereignty. Robert J. Walker, of Mississippi, argued that the proposal drew too much power to the national government and violated the Tenth Amendment of the Constitution, which reserved to the states those powers not delegated to the national government. The proposal's authors, he believed, had forgotten that "we are a confederate republic, *made by*, and *composed of*, sovereign States." John C. Calhoun warned his colleagues that Congress should not endanger the harmony and peace of the Union by extending federal authority.[24]

Despite the pleas of its opponents, the "McLeod bill" passed the Senate on July 8, 1842, by a straight party vote. The House delayed a few weeks, but on August 27, just as Webster and Ashburton were concluding their talks, passed the bill. Two days later, Tyler signed it.[25] Webster, a constitutional expansionist, probably would have preferred a measure that granted larger powers to the executive branch of the federal government: an act that gave the president authority to remove cases such as McLeod's from judicial proceedings altogether. The law was more limited than Webster desired, partly from congressional sensitivity to states' rights, but also because Southerners feared that foreign abolitionists might incite slaves to rebellion and claim the protection of their governments.

The Remedial Justice Act, as it was called, was a fitting conclusion to the McLeod affair. It repaired what many Americans regarded as a defect in the Constitution that allowed states to control the nation's foreign relations. Tyler and Webster, one a states'-rights Whig and the other a loose constructionist, agreed that foreign affairs were national matters. When New York asserted a right to try McLeod, the national government was compelled to declare its exclusive control over foreign relations. In passing the Remedial Justice Act, the United States assented to the principle of international law that nations must maintain a representative authority for other nations to deal with.[26]

In the larger perspective of constitutional history, the "McLeod law" occupies a place in a trend toward broadening federal power over habeas corpus. The original provision for habeas corpus, in Section 14 of the Judiciary Act of 1789, gave federal courts authority to inquire only into cases of persons imprisoned by federal order: federal courts could not issue a writ of habeas corpus for anyone held by a state. Because federal power over habeas corpus was statutory, each expansion of the principle required congressional action. The power expanded in 1833, when South Carolina nullified the tariff and threatened to jail anyone attempting to enforce the new law; Congress gave federal courts authority to issue writs of habeas corpus for federal officials whom states might imprison for carrying out their duties. The act further increased that power by permitting federal courts to order release of foreigners held by states for acts done on the orders of their government in accord with the law of nations.

The Remedial Justice Act cleared the way for even stronger federal authority over state courts after the Civil War. In 1867 federal courts were empowered to issue writs of habeas corpus for prisoners held "in violation of the Constitution or any treaty or law of the United States."[27] Since that time, federal courts have frequently removed suspects from state custody. In the best known case, *In re Neagle* (1890), the United States Supreme Court issued a writ of habeas corpus for a federal officer charged with homicide. David Neagle, a United States deputy marshal, was assigned to protect the life of Supreme Court Justice Stephen J. Field, who was in California on circuit court proceedings. While Field was eating breakfast, an armed man broke into the room. Neagle killed the assailant with his revolver and was charged with murder by the state. California maintained that, because no federal law specifically authorized bodily protection of judges, Neagle was responsible to the state for his actions. The United States Supreme Court took a broader view, upholding a writ of habeas corpus for the marshal.[28] Thus, over the years, federal authority to issue writs of habeas corpus has steadily increased.

Although an expanded statute of habeas corpus forestalled additional McLeod-type cases, the precipitating event, the *Caroline* raid, also had to be resolved to reestablish peace along the Canadian-American border. In their negotiations of 1842, Webster and Ashburton settled the affair through an exchange of notes. In his instructions to Ashburton, Lord Aberdeen had prepared the way. He said that, after reviewing dangers faced by loyal subjects in Canada, the British government still believed the attack necessary. Nonetheless, it lamented the necessity of the event and wished to assure the United States that, far from taking the incident lightly, it recognized that only urgent needs of self-defense brought about by the *Caroline*'s illegal acts justified it.[29] After a conference with Ashburton, Webster sent the British envoy a note: whether or not the activities of the *Caroline* were lawful, the invasion of American territory was "an offence to the sovereignty and the dignity of the United States," for which there had never been atonement or apology. The nation's self-respect, its sense of independence, equality, and honor, made it an issue of great importance.[30]

Ashburton's reply was balm for American feelings. "The inviolable character" of a nation's territory was the "most essential foundation of civilization." Britain was sensitive to its moral responsibility to support that principle by conduct and example. Sometimes, though, as Webster had intimated to Fox in his *Caroline* note of April 24, 1841, "overpowering necessity" might dictate suspension of that obligation. Self-defense was the first law of nations. Ashburton proposed that destruction of the *Caroline* met the criteria Webster had given to Fox: a "necessity of self-defence, instant, overwhelming, leaving no choice of means, and no moment for deliberation." In December 1837 Canadian territory had been invaded by "reckless and mischievous people," who employed the *Caroline* in furthering their evil designs. How long, Ashburton inquired, could the British government wait? After crossing the Niagara and unexpectedly discovering the *Caroline* on the American side of the river, the expedition, having "no moment for deliberation," went ahead with the attack.

In retrospect, Ashburton concluded, the most regrettable aspect of the affair was that "some explanation and apology for this occurrence was not immediately made: this with a frank explanation of the necessity of the case might and probably would have prevented much of the exasperation and of the subsequent complaints and recriminations to which it gave rise." He hoped the countries would bury unfortunate events of recent years and foster the harmony as well as friendship both peoples desired. Webster replied a few days later, acknowledging Ashburton's professions of respect for the United States and declaring the subject closed between the nations.[31] The *Caroline* affair was over.

The settlement had not been achieved without compromise. Webster later said it had taken him two days to convince the British minister to use the word "apology" in the note.[32] Ashburton informed his government that he had "interwoven" the apology with a "decided justification of what was done." He hoped Aberdeen would approve his July 28 note to Webster, for it had been a delicate task and he was certain that without a conclusion to the *Caroline* affair there would have been a "general indisposition to settle anything else."[33] In fact, President Tyler wanted the secretary of state to demand payment for the *Caroline*, but Webster never pressed the issue. Perhaps unknown to the president, Ashburton had already deleted from his note an explicit refusal to consider compensation for the *Caroline* because it was "notorious that it was part and parcel of the armament of the insurgent force."[34] On his part, Webster let pass without comment Ashburton's assertion that the *Caroline* raid was justifiable. Although the raid hardly met the requirements of self-defense set forth in Webster's note of April 24, 1841, the secretary simply remarked in his reply to Ashburton that, whether justifiable or not, it had happened a long time ago.[35] It was time, he seemed to say, for Britain and America to deal with the future instead of the past.

In succeeding years, Webster's *Caroline* doctrine has occupied an important place in international law and diplomacy. The concept of self-preservation and self-defense up to Webster's time came from customary international law, rules of conduct based on history and tradition. When questions arose, statesmen turned to such authorities as Grotius, Pufendorf, and Vattel, or to latter-day interpreters, among them the American Henry Wheaton. In no way was international law binding on any country. Nations studied it and applied or ignored its principles as they chose. Thus, when Jackson invaded Spanish Florida, Secretary of State Adams justified his deeds according to the international law of self-defense. But the general himself felt little necessity for exoneration. When he learned what Adams had done, Jackson is said to have vehemently proclaimed: "Damn Grotius! Damn Pufendorf! Damn Vattel! This is a mere matter between Jim Monroe and myself!"[36] Webster's contribution to international law was to articulate clearly the classical wisdom of the three scholars for modern circumstances. He built on the traditional law of nations, his own legal experience, and the work of his predecessor in the State Department, John Forsyth, to outline succinctly the conditions and limits of self-defense between nations.

In more recent times, too, nations have defended aggression by claiming the necessity of self-defense. After occupying Manchuria in 1931, Japan argued before the League of Nations that imminent necessity and its "special position" in Manchuria "justified measures of self-protection" according to the "standard principle laid down in the *Caroline* case."[37] After World War II, during the trials of the major German war criminals at Nuremberg, defense lawyers argued that Germany's invasion of Norway in 1940 was an act of self-defense, necessary to forestall Allied occupation of the territory. In rejecting the appeal, the International Military Tribunal specifically referred to Webster's *Caroline* note, holding that "preventive action in foreign territory is justified only in case of an instant and overwhelming necessity for self-defense, leaving no choice of means, and no moment for deliberation." At the trials of Japanese war criminals in Tokyo following World War II, the International Military Tribunal approved the claim that the Netherlands declared war on Japan in self-defense, for evidence revealed that a Japanese attack on the Netherlands East Indies was imminent.[38]

The role of law in the conduct of international affairs is itself a subject of debate. Since formation of the United Nations, specialists in international law have questioned the extent to which the organization's charter has affected customary international law. In particular, Article 2 of the United Nations Charter provides that member nations "shall refrain in their international relations from the threat or use of force against the territorial integrity or political independence of any state, or in any other manner inconsistent with the purposes of the United Nations." At the same time, Article 51 declares that nothing in the charter is intended to "impair the inherent right of individual or collective self-defense" in the event of armed attack.[39] Reconciling these two articles has proven to be difficult. In 1956, in an attempt to curtail Arab raids into its territory, Israel invaded the Sinai Peninsula. Critics charged that the move violated the United Nations proscription on the use of unilateral force. Defenders of the Israeli action argued that the right of self-defense specified in Article 51 was not limited to reaction to actual attacks, but included the right of response to overwhelming and imminent danger. They believed Webster's *Caroline* doctrine justified their interpretation.[40]

The *Caroline* formula has been revived on other occasions. When the Soviet Union placed nuclear missiles in Cuba during the Kennedy administration, the president ordered a quarantine—in essence a blockade—of the island. During the crisis, Assistant Attorney General Norbert A. Schlei advised Attorney General Robert F. Kennedy that the action could be justified by the *Caroline* doctrine. In 1976, when terrorists held Israeli citizens at Entebbe airport in Uganda, Israel attacked. Ambassador Chaim Herzog defended the action before the United Nations Security Council on the grounds of the *Caroline* doctrine.[41]

Clearly Webster's formulation of the doctrine of self-defense— the *Caroline* doctrine—as it came out of his experience in law and diplomacy, is closer to the view that the United Nations charter justifies self-defense only in the face of armed attack. In none of the cases cited, with the possible exception of Entebbe, was there need to initiate an attack in the name of self-defense. International lawyers who wish to use the *Caroline* case would be well advised to study the history of the affair, for the logic of Webster's argument has been pushed far beyond its intent. Studied in its original context, the *Caroline* doctrine is a model for international restraint rather than a license for action.

Some account remains to be made of the principals in the McLeod and *Caroline* affairs. Conclusion of his negotiations with Lord Ashburton gave Webster a chance to redeem his political career. Ever since the cabinet breakup of 1841, he had faced Whig pressure to renounce his office and the president. His former cabinet colleague John J. Crittenden found his inclination to remain with Tyler ignoble and degrading, and in Boston some charged that he kept his position because he was bankrupt and dependent. Webster justified his decision to continue with Tyler on the basis of the critical state of Anglo-American relations. He could not run the risk, he informed his friend Hiram Ketchum, of taking any "sudden or abrupt proceeding" regarding issues that so affected the peace of the country. Once his negotiations with Ashburton were concluded, there was little excuse to remain. As Tyler moved closer toward two goals Webster opposed—annexation of Texas and alliance with the Democrats—the secretary's discomfiture increased. One political friend advised him that he thought Tyler "would feel much relieved if you should resign your place." Webster delayed, hoping he could become minister to Britain, but at length he realized that would not happen, and on May 8, 1843, he submitted his resignation.[42]

The parting with Tyler seemed amicable. Webster expressed appreciation for the "friendly feelings and personal kindness" he had received from the president. Tyler thanked him for his "zeal and ability" in handling the nation's foreign affairs. Still, there is evidence that the Tyler-Webster alliance had been strained; within a few days of his resignation, Webster drafted an editorial for the Washington *National Intelligencer* criticizing the president for political opportunism.[43]

Webster's resignation did not mean the end of his career. He returned to Washington in 1845 as senator from Massachusetts. It was in this capacity that he delivered the famous Seventh of March speech favoring the Compromise of 1850. After President Zachary Taylor's death in July 1850, he was again chosen as secretary of state, under President Millard Fillmore. While in that position, his health failed, and he died October 24, 1852, at his home in Marshfield, Massachusetts. He was seventy years of age. Although he was one of the most illustrious leaders of the nineteenth century, he never realized his presidential ambitions.

When his term ended, Tyler retired to his plantation at Sherwood Forest, near Williamsburg, Virginia. He took no part in politics until the secession crisis. He opposed disunion, but when Virginia seceded he accepted a place in the Provisional Confederate Congress. He was elected to the Confederate House of Representatives, but died on January 18, 1862, before taking his seat.

William Henry Seward continued a long and influential political career. He retired from New York's governorship in 1842 but six years later was elected to the United States Senate, where he served as an uncompromising opponent of slavery. He harbored presidential ambitions, but, when Abraham Lincoln took office, he became his secretary of state and made his own mark in international affairs.

The British minister to the United States, Henry S. Fox, was removed from his position in 1843. Despite his often-expressed contempt for America, he continued to live in Washington until his death in 1846. Andrew Drew, the naval officer who led the *Caroline* raid, returned to England in 1842. Later, he commanded HMS *Wasp* in the West Indies and served as a naval storekeeper in South Africa. He was promoted to rear admiral before his death in 1878.[44]

As for McLeod, after returning to Canada, he married Ellen Morrison and became a storekeeper in Drummondville, near Niagara Falls. The couple had several children, and, though McLeod almost certainly would not have approved, some of his descendants moved to New York. In 1844 he petitioned the Canadian government to compensate him for injuries suffered during his imprisonment. A special legislative committee, taking particular care to remark that he had never boasted of his participation in the *Caroline* raid, recommended that the Crown grant him a pension. But the British government did not approve the request. McLeod also filed a claim for damages against the United States with the 1853 London Arbitration Commission, and went to England to plead his cause in person. The American and British commissioners disagreed, and the case was referred to an umpire, who disallowed the claim. Finally, in 1855, the British government awarded McLeod an annual pension of £200 for his hardships while imprisoned. On September 27, 1871, he died—the tumultuous events of the intervening three decades since his trial having nearly obliterated his brief but considerable fame.[45]

Abbreviated Forms
used in Notes

Arthur, *Papers*: Sir George Arthur. *The Arthur Papers, Being the Canadian Papers, mainly confidential, Private, and Demi-Official of Sir George Arthur.* Edited by Charles R. Sanderson. 3 vols. Toronto, 1943–1959.

ASPFR: Walter Lowrie and Matthew St. Clair Clarke, eds. *American State Papers: Foreign Relations.* 6 vols. Washington, D.C., 1832–1859.

B.L. Add. Ms.: British Library, Additional Manuscripts.

CO: Colonial Office, Great Britain.

DS: Department of State, United States.

FO: Foreign Office, Great Britain.

LC: Library of Congress.

NA: National Archives, United States.

PAC: Public Archives of Canada.

PRO: Public Record Office, Great Britain.

RG: Record Group.

WD: War Department, United States.

NOTES

CHAPTER 1: "BLOOD HAS BEEN SHED"

1. Christopher Ward, *The War of the Revolution* (2 vols., New York, 1952), 1: 317; Alfred Leroy Burt, *A Short History of Canada for Americans* (Minneapolis, 1942), 67–71; George Rawlyk, "The 1770s," in *Colonists and Canadians, 1760–1867*, ed. J. M. S. Careless (Toronto, 1971), 33–34.

2. Ward, *War of Revolution*, 1: 137–38.

3. Ibid., 1: 138–39, 197; Burt, *Short History of Canada*, 78, 79; Rawlyk, "The 1770s," 38.

4. John Adams to Samuel Adams, July 26, 1778, Benjamin Franklin to David Hartley, October 26, 1778, both in Francis Wharton, ed., *Revolutionary Diplomatic Correspondence of the United States* (6 vols., Washington, D.C., 1889), 2: 667–68, 810–12.

5. Leslie Upton, "The 1780s," in *Colonists and Canadians*, 49–50; Marcus Lee Hansen, *The Mingling of the Canadian and American Peoples* (New Haven, 1940), 52.

6. Hansen, *Mingling of Canadian and American Peoples*, 61, 64.

7. Quoted in ibid., 91, 84.

8. Carl Wittke, *A History of Canada*, rev. ed. (New York, 1928), 85; Marshall Smelser, *The Democratic Republic, 1801–1815* (New York, 1968), 227, 232; Alan Wilson, "The 1810s," in *Colonists and Canadians*, 142–43; Burt, *Short History of Canada*, 101.

9. Burt, *Short History of Canada*, 104; J. H. Stewart Reid, Kenneth McNaught, and Harry S. Crowe, eds., *A Source-book of Canadian History*, rev. ed. (Toronto, 1964), 67; Wittke, *History of Canada*, 85; Smelser, *Democratic Republic*, 239–44. In the aftermath of Hull's surrender, an army

court-martial sentenced the general to death for cowardice, but President James Madison pardoned him.

10. Smelser, *Democratic Republic*, 239; Wilson, "The 1810s," 143.

11. Charles W. Humphries, "The Capture of York," *Ontario History* 51 (1959): 1–21; Wittke, *History of Canada*, 87–88; Burt, *Short History of Canada*, 104–05: Smelser, *Democratic Republic*, 258, 269–70.

12. Wilson, "The 1810s," 144.

13. Burt, *Short History of Canada*, 106; Hansen, *Mingling of Canadian and American Peoples*, 95–97.

14. Wilson, "The 1810s," 145–46; Michael Cross, "The 1820s," in *Colonists and Canadians*, 161–63.

15. Morse quoted in Richard W. Van Alstyne, *The Rising American Empire* (New York, 1974), 78; Jefferson to Monroe, November 24, 1801, in Thomas Jefferson, *Writings of Thomas Jefferson*, ed. Paul L. Ford (10 vols., New York, 1892–99), 8: 103–06.

16. Sir George Arthur to Sir John Colborne, October 14, 1838, in Arthur, *Papers*, 1: 303–05; Henry S. Fox to Lord Aberdeen, March 8, 1843, quoted in Van Alstyne, *Rising American Empire*, 104.

17. Carl Wittke, *A History of Canada*, rev. ed. (New York, 1928), 65–67.

18. Ibid., 99–100; S. D. Clark, *Movements of Political Protest in Canada, 1640–1840* (Toronto, 1959), 320–21; Stanley B. Ryerson, *Unequal Union: Confederation and the Roots of Conflict in the Canadas, 1815–1873* (New York, 1968), 39–40, 106.

19. Ryerson, *Unequal Union*, 48–56.

20. Wittke, *Canada*, 101–03.

21. Ibid., 98; Joseph Schull, *Rebellion: The Rising in French Canada, 1837* (Toronto, 1971), 43–44.

22. Schull, *Rebellion*, 61–62, 80–84, 115–22.

23. On the Upper Canadian rebellion from its outbreak to the assault on Montgomery's Tavern, see John C. Dent, *The Story of the Upper Canadian Rebellion* (2 vols., Toronto, 1885), 1: 359–83, 2: 10–155.

24. Albert B. Corey, *The Crisis of 1830–1842 in Canadian-American Relations* (New Haven, 1941), 30.

25. Dent, *Upper Canadian Rebellion*, 2: 198–99.

26. Ibid., 2: 197–98.

27. On Van Buren's career, see James C. Curtis, *The Fox at Bay: Martin Van Buren and the Presidency, 1837–1841* (Lexington, Ky., 1970); Robert V. Remini, *Martin Van Buren and the Making of the Democratic Party* (New York, 1970); Donald B. Cole, *Martin Van Buren and the American Political System* (Princeton, N.J., 1984); John Niven, *Martin Van Buren: The Ro-*

mantic Age of American Politics (New York, 1983); and Major L. Wilson, *The Presidency of Martin Van Buren* (Lawrence, Kansas, 1984).

28. James D. Richardson, comp., *A Compilation of the Messages and Papers of the Presidents, 1789–1897* (10 vols., Washington, D.C., 1896–99), 3: 314, 319–20.

29. John Forsyth to Daniel Kellogg et al., December 7, 1837, in *House Executive Documents*, 25th Cong., 2d sess., Serial 323, No. 74, p. 29.

30. J. Trowbridge to Martin Van Buren, December 14, 1837, Secretary of the Treasury to Collectors, December 19, 1837, John Forsyth to Nathaniel S. Benton, December 21, 1837, all in *House Executive Documents*, Serial 323, No. 74, pp. 30–31, 41–42.

31. Nathaniel S. Benton to John Forsyth, December 26, 1837, in *House Executive Documents*, Serial 323, No. 74, pp. 43–44; Nathaniel Garrow to Martin Van Buren, December 28, 1837, in Richardson, *Messages and Papers*, 3: 399–400. Garrow is erroneously identified as "Ganon" in the document.

32. Dent, *Upper Canadian Rebellion*, 2: 202.

33. A brief sketch of McLeod is in John C. Dent, *The Last Forty Years: Canada since the Union of 1841* (2 vols., Toronto, 1881), 1: 170–71. See also the entry in the *Dictionary of Canadian Biography* (Toronto, 1972), 10: 481–82. On McLeod's activities in the United States, see Alastair Watt, "The Case of Alexander McLeod," *Canadian Historical Review* 12 (June 1931), 163–64.

34. Dent, *Upper Canadian Rebellion*, 2: 203–04.

35. This account of the attack on the *Caroline* is drawn from many accounts of the participants and witnesses, who frequently vary in their descriptions of the event. These include: affidavits enclosed in Henry W. Rogers to Martin Van Buren, December 30, 1837, in NA, DS, RG 59, Misc. Letters; Andrew Stevenson to Daniel Webster, September 18, 1841, containing depositions of Andrew Drew and other Canadians, NA, DS, RG 59, Despatches from U.S. Ministers in Britain; and testimony given at the trial of Alexander McLeod for murder and arson in connection with the *Caroline* affair, reported in 2 *Gould's Stenographic Reporter* 45–61 (New York, 1841). The official British view of the raid is in Head to Glenelg, February 9, 1838, PAC, RG 7, G 12, vol. 28. The poem is quoted from Robert H. Ferrell, *American Diplomacy*, 3d ed. (New York, 1975), 207.

36. Andrew Drew to Allan MacNab, December 30, 1837, in *Journal of the House of Assembly of Upper Canada*, 3d session, 13th Parliament, 1st Queen Victoria, 90; Special Message of Governor William L. Marcy to the Legislature, January 2, 1838, in Albany *Argus*, January 3, 1838;

Buffalo *Commercial-Advertiser*, December 30, 1837, quoted in Washington *National Intelligencer*, January 9, 1838; *Niles' National Register*, January 20, 1838; George Templeton Strong, *The Diary of George Templeton Strong*, ed. Allan Nevins and Milton Halsey Thomas, Vol. 1, *Young Man in New York* (4 vols., New York, 1952), 81.

37. Rochester *Democrat*, December 30, 1837, quoted in Washington *National Intelligencer*, January 9, 1838; Albany *Argus*, January 4, 5, 1838; Smith Stilwell to Martin Van Buren, January 8, 1838, NA, DS, RG 59, Misc. Letters.

38. Buffalo correspondent to the Albany *Evening Journal*, January 1, 1838, quoted in *Albany Argus*, January 5, 1838.

39. Anonymous note, circa December 30, 1837, published in Arthur, *Papers*, 1: 44–45.

40. Winfield Scott, *Memoirs of Lieut.-General Scott, LL. D.* (2 vols., New York, 1864), 1: 305–07.

CHAPTER 2: NEUTRALITY FALLS SHORT

1. Secretary of War Joel Poinsett to Secretary of State John Forsyth, January 6, 1838 (and enclosures: Poinsett to Scott, January 5, 1838; Poinsett to William L. Marcy and Silas H. Jenison, January 5, 1838), NA, DS, RG 59, Misc. Letters; James C. Curtis, *The Fox at Bay: Martin Van Buren and the Presidency, 1837–1841* (Lexington, Ky., 1970), 171.

2. Winfield Scott, *Memoirs of Lieut.-General Scott, LL. D.* (2 vols., New York, 1864), 1: 308–17; Charles W. Elliott, *Winfield Scott: The Soldier and the Man* (New York, 1937), 338–57; New York *Herald*, January 11, 1838.

3. James D. Richardson, comp., *A Compilation of the Messages and Papers of the Presidents, 1789–1897* (10 vols., Washington, D.C., 1896–99), 3: 399, 481; 3 U.S. Stats., 370–77, 447–50.

4. Forsyth to Fox, both notes dated January 5, 1838, NA, DS, RG 59, Notes to Britain.

5. Cleveland Collector to J. W. Allen, January 8, 1838, NA, DS, RG 59, Misc. Letters.

6. John C. Dent, *The Story of the Upper Canadian Rebellion, Largely Derived from Original Sources and Documents* (2 vols., Toronto, 1885), 2: 228–31; ——— Goodwin to Forsyth, January 17, 1838, NA, DS, RG 59, Misc. Letters.

7. Scott to Poinsett, February 3, 1838, quoted in Elliott, *Winfield Scott*, 339; "Rensselaer Van Rensselaer's Own Notes on his Military Life," in

Catharina V. R. Bonney, comp., *A Legacy of Historical Gleanings*, 2d ed. (2 vols., Albany, N.Y., 1975), 2: 84, 90.

8. *Niles' National Register*, January 27, 1838; Bonney, *Gleanings*, 2: 89, 123–26.

9. Scott, *Memoirs*, 313–17.

10. Elliott, *Scott*, 146–48, 157–65, 342–43; Scott, *Memoirs*, 342–43.

11. Beckles Willson, *Friendly Relations: A Narrative of Britain's Ministers and Ambassadors to America, 1791–1930* (Boston, 1934), 144–45.

12. Philip Hone, *Diary of Philip Hone*, ed. Allan Nevins (2 vols., New York, 1927), 1: 457, 2: 526; Willson, *Friendly Relations*, 151.

13. Alvin L. Duckett, *John Forsyth, Political Tactician* (Athens, Ga., 1962), 5–8.

14. Ibid., 49–50, 70.

15. Forsyth to Fox, January 5, January 19, February 13, 1838, all in NA, DS, RG 59, Notes to Britain; Fox to Forsyth, February 6, 1838, NA, DS, RG 59, Notes from Britain.

16. Opinion of the Law Officers of the Crown, February 21, 1838, enclosed in Palmerston to Fox, March 6, 1838, PRO, FO, Series 115, Vol. 68 (hereafter 115/68 etc.).

17. Emerich de Vattel, *The Law of Nations, or the Principles of Natural Law*, tr. Charles G. Fenwick (3 vols., Washington, D.C., 1916), Vol. 3, Book 1, Chapter 2, Sections 16–18.

18. Geoffrey Brun, *Europe and the French Imperium, 1799–1814* (New York, 1938), 128; Asa Briggs, *The Making of Modern England, 1783–1867: The Age of Improvement* (New York, 1965), 151; Will and Ariel Durant, *The Age of Napoleon: A History of European Civilization from 1789 to 1815* (New York, 1975), 665.

19. Richardson, *Messages and Papers*, 2: 13–14, 23–25.

20. John C. Calhoun to Andrew Jackson, December 26, 1817, in Andrew Jackson, *Correspondence of Andrew Jackson*, ed. John Spencer Bassett (7 vols., Washington, D.C., 1926–35), 2: 341–42; Luis de Onís to John Quincy Adams, July 8, 1818, in *ASPFR*, 4: 496; John Quincy Adams, *Memoirs of John Quincy Adams*, ed. Charles Francis Adams (12 vols., Philadelphia, 1874–77), 4: 102–15; Samuel Flagg Bemis, *John Quincy Adams and the Foundations of American Foreign Policy* (New York, 1949), 315–16; George Dangerfield, *The Era of Good Feelings* (New York, 1952), 131–36.

21. Adams to George W. Erving, November 28, 1818, in *ASPFR*, 4: 539–45; Bemis, *Foundations of American Foreign Policy*, 326.

22. *Niles' National Register*, January 13, 1838; *Congressional Globe*, 25th Cong., 2d sess., 79.

23. Richardson, *Messages and Papers*, 3: 401–04; *Niles' National Register*, January 13, 1838; *Cong. Globe*, 25th Cong., 2d sess., 82–83.

24. *Cong. Globe*, 25th Cong., 2d sess., 88, 103, 119, 184.

25. Ibid., 192–93, 199, appendix 144–45.

26. Ibid., 185, 196, appendix 143–44.

27. Ibid., 199.

28. Ibid., 205–06, 214–15, 223–24, 230–31; 5 U.S. Stats., 212–14.

29. Fox to Head, March 11, 1838, in Arthur, *Papers*, 1: 59–61; Dent, *Upper Canadian Rebellion*, 2: 241–42.

30. Arthur, *Papers*, 1: ix; Arthur to Colborne, March 13, 1838, in ibid., 61–62.

31. George G. Johnson to Francis Thomas, March 31, 1838, A. E. Wing to Forsyth, September 15, 1838, John Oakland et al. to Forsyth, September 15, 1838, John Norvell to Forsyth, April 24, 1838, Ann Theller to Martin Van Buren [September 16, 1838], all in NA, DS, RG 59, Misc. Letters.

32. Statement of Benjamin Chittenden, June 22, 1838, enclosed in Silas Wright to Forsyth, July 2, 1838, NA, DS, RG 59, Misc. Letters; Arthur to C. A. Hagerman [Attorney General], April 7, 1838, in Arthur, *Papers*, 1: 74; Albert B. Corey, *The Crisis of 1830–1842 in Canadian-American Relations* (New Haven, 1941), 35, 39–40.

33. See the biographical sketch of Vail by E. Wilder Spaulding in *Dictionary of American Biography* (20 vols., New York, 1928–1936), Vol. 10, Part 1, p. 136.

34. Forsyth to Fox, April 3, 1838, NA, DS, RG 59, Notes to Britain; Fox to Forsyth, April 3, 1838, NA, DS, RG 59, Notes from Britain; Forsyth to Vail, April 3, 1838, NA, DS, RG 59, Special Missions; Arthur to Colborne, April 25, 1838, in Arthur, *Papers*, 1: 87–90.

35. Vail to Forsyth, April 11, 1838, NA, DS, RG 59, Misc. Letters; Arthur to Glenelg, April 24, 1838, PAC, RG 7, G 12, Vol. 29; Vail to Forsyth, May 5, 1838, NA, DS, RG 59, Communications from Special Agents.

36. Fox to Arthur, June 26, 1838, in Arthur, *Papers*, 1: 210–12; Arthur to Glenelg, July 15, 1838, PAC, RG 7, G 12, Vol. 29.

CHAPTER 3: VAN BUREN CAVES IN

1. Stevenson to Forsyth, March 6, 1838, NA, DS, RG 59, Despatches, Britain; Opinion of the Law Officers of the Crown, February 21, 1838, enclosed in Palmerston to Fox, March 6, 1838, PRO, FO 115/68.

2. Forsyth to Stevenson, March 12, 1838, NA, DS, RG 59, Instructions, Britain.

3. Martin Van Buren to Palmerston, May 16, 1838, Martin Van Buren Papers-LC (hereafter MVB-LC).

4. Fox to Palmerston, April 20, August 10, 1839, both in PRO, FO 115/69.

5. Stevenson to Palmerston, May 22, 1838, enclosed in Stevenson to Forsyth, May 24, 1838, NA, DS, RG 59, Despatches, Britain.

6. Hugo Grotius, *De Jure Belli ac Pacis Libri Tres*, trans. Francis W. Kelsey (2 vols., Oxford, 1925), Book 2, Chapter 1, Section 5, pp. 173–75; Samuel Pufendorf, *De Jure Naturae et Gentium Libri Octo*, trans. C. H. and W. A. Oldfather (Oxford, 1934), Book 2, Chapter 5, Sections 6–8, pp. 272–77.

7. George H. McWhorter to Woodbury, September 14, 1838, enclosed in Woodbury to Forsyth, September 27, 1838, NA, DS, RG 59, Misc. Letters; B. ? to Van Buren, November 4, 1838, MVB-LC.

8. Oscar A. Kinchen, *The Rise and Fall of the Patriot Hunters* (New York, 1956), 56–59; Fox to Durham, October 5, 1838, Fox Papers, PRO 97/17.

9. Arthur to Fox, May 22, 1838, in Arthur, *Papers*, 1: 123. On the *Peel* affair, see Christopher Ripley to Forsyth, May 30, 1838, Proclamation of Sir George Arthur, May 31, 1838, John Fine to Silas Wright, Jr., June 2, 1838, Bishop Perkins and Smith Stilwell to Silas Wright, Jr., June 3, 1838, and enclosures, all in NA, DS, RG 59, Misc. Letters. See also *House Executive Documents*, 25th Congress, 2d sess., Serial 331, No. 440, and the accounts in the Albany *Argus*, June 16, 17, 1838; Petition of William Johnston, April 18, 1838, NA, DS, RG 59, Misc. Letters; London *Times*, July 9, 1838, September 11, 1838.

10. Proclamation of Governor William L. Marcy, June 4, 1838, Marcy to Poinsett, June 3, 5, 1838, all in *House Executive Documents*, Serial 331, No. 440, pp. 23–27; London *Times*, July 3, 23, August 8, 1838.

11. Sir George Arthur Proclamation, May 31, 1838, Perkins and Stilwell to Wright, June 3, 1838, and enclosures, all in *House Executive Documents*, Serial 331, No. 440, pp. 5–6, 11–14.

12. Joel R. Poinsett to Van Buren, June 19, 1838, in ibid., 22–23; *Congressional Globe*, 25th Cong., 2d sess., 445; Van Buren's message in Richardson, *Messages and Papers*, 3: 478–79.

13. Benton to Van Buren, May 31, 1838, McWhorter to Woodbury, September 19, 1838, both in NA, DS, RG 59, Misc. Letters; Vail to Fox,

September 28, 1838, NA, DS, RG 59, Notes to Britain; Fox to Arthur, October 4, 21, 1838, both in Arthur, *Papers*, 1: 294–95, 312–13; Fox to Vail, November 3, 1838, NA, DS, RG 59, Notes from Britain.

14. See the accounts in *Niles' National Register*, November 24, 1838.

15. Fox to Forsyth, November 3, 1838, NA, DS, RG 59, Notes from Britain; Forsyth to Fox, November 15, 1838, NA, DS, RG 59, Notes to Britain; Richardson, *Messages and Papers*, 3: 482–83; George Rudé, *Protest and Punishment: The Story of the Social and Political Protestors Transported to Australia, 1788–1868* (Oxford, 1978), 86. Linus W. Miller, one of the American prisoners, was released from the penal colony in 1845 and returned to the United States, where he published *Notes of an Exile to Van Diemen's Land* (New York, 1846).

16. Lucius V. Bierce to Van Buren, July 13, 1838, NA, DS, RG 59, Misc. Letters; Kinchen, *Patriot Hunters*, 79–84.

17. J. W. Turner to George McWhorter, September 15, 1838, enclosed in McWhorter to Levi Woodbury, September 19, 1838, Acting Secretary of War Samuel Cooper to Macomb, September 28, 1838, enclosed in Cooper to Vail, September 28, 1838, both in NA, DS, RG 59, Misc. Letters; Lt. John T. W. Jones to Arthur, November 5, 1838, in Arthur, *Papers*, 347–50.

18. Winfield Scott, *Memoirs of Lieut.-General Scott, LL. D.* (2 vols., New York, 1864), 2: 332; Charles W. Elliott, *Winfield Scott: The Soldier and the Man* (New York, 1937), 356–57; Confidential Circular, April 15, 1838, NA, WD, RG 108, Headquarters of the Army, Letters Sent; Fox to Arthur, October 21, 1838, Fox Papers, PRO 97/17; Fox to Arthur, October 5, 1838, Arthur to Sir John Colborne, November 1, 1838, Fox to Arthur, December 6, 1838, all in Arthur, *Papers*, 1: 297, 341–42, 420–23.

19. Benton to Forsyth, June 21, October 1, 1838, both in NA, DS, RG 59, Misc. Letters.

20. Circular Instructions to Collectors of Districts Bordering on the Frontiers of Canada, April 6, 1838, Benton to Van Buren, June 5, 1838, Garrow to Forsyth, December 3, 1838, Ann Theller to Van Buren, September 16, 1838, Ten Eyck to Forsyth, November 23, 1838, Wilkins to Van Buren, January 7, 1839, all in NA, DS, RG 59, Misc. Letters.

21. Garrow to Forsyth, November 29, December 3, 1838, undated but received in Washington December 28, 1838, all in NA, DS, RG 59, Misc. Letters.

22. Jones to Arthur, November 5, 1838, Fox to Arthur, November 5, 1838, both in Arthur, *Papers*, 1: 347–50; Ivor D. Spencer, *The Victor and the Spoils: A Life of William L. Marcy* (Providence, R.I., 1959), 95–97, 107;

Glyndon G. Van Deusen, *William Henry Seward* (New York, 1967), 50–52.

23. Flagg to Van Buren, November 23, 1838, Croswell to Van Buren, November 25, 1838; Joel Turrill to Van Buren, December 23, 1838, all in MVB-LC; Van Buren to Flagg, quoted in Curtis, *Fox at Bay*, 181; Richardson, *Messages and Papers*, 3: 485–87.

24. *Cong. Globe.*, 25th Cong., 3d sess., 150, 216–18, 230–33, 238–44.

25. Newspaper clipping, June 21, 1838, MVB-LC; Fox to Palmerston, August 10, 1839, PRO, FO 115/69.

26. Mackenzie to Van Buren, October 23, 1839, MVB-LC.

27. Richardson, *Messages and Papers*, 3: 351; Norvell to Forsyth, December 28, 1839 (with enclosure), Morgan L. Gage to Norvell, December 13, 1839, both in NA, DS, RG 59, Misc. Letters; George M. Keim to William Gilmore and Robert Christy, December 28, 1839, MVB-LC.

28. Mackenzie to Van Buren, January 10, 1840, MVB-LC.

29. Mackenzie to William H. Seward, January 14, 1840, William H. Seward Papers, Rush Rhees Library, University of Rochester; Seward to Mackenzie, January 27, 1840, Mackenzie to Van Buren, February 10, 1839, both in MVB-LC.

30. William Dunbar to B. Latham, February 10, 1840, MVB-LC; *Cong. Globe*, 26th Cong., 1st sess., 292, 327, 368, 370, 377, 385.

CHAPTER 4: BRITAIN DRAWS THE LINE

1. Quoted in David P. Crook, *American Democracy in English Politics, 1815–1850* (Oxford, 1965), 77, 83.

2. Wilbur D. Jones, *The American Problem in British Diplomacy, 1841–1861* (Athens, Ga., 1974), 2; Donald Southgate, *'The Most English Minister . . . ': The Policies and Politics of Palmerston* (New York, 1966), 172–73; Herbert C. F. Bell, *Lord Palmerston* (2 vols., Hamden, Conn., 1966), 1: 238–48.

3. Head to Glenelg, January 30, March 6, 1838, PAC, RG 7, G 12, Vol. 28; Fox to Colborne, January 19, 1838, Fox Papers, PRO 97/17.

4. Fox to Head, March 11, 1838, Fox to Arthur, June 26, 1838, Arthur to Lord Fitzroy, October 30, 1838, Arthur to Colborne, November 1, 1838, all in Arthur, *Papers*, 1: 59–61, 210–12, 334–36, 341–42; Arthur to Fox, November 15, 1838, Fox Papers, PRO 97/18.

5. Fox to Palmerston, November 24, December 4, 1838, both in PRO,

FO 115/69; Fox to Palmerston, December 6, 1838, in Arthur, *Papers*, 1: 420–23.

6. Fox to Vice Admiral Sir Charles Paget, March 15, 1838, Fox to Consul W. Gray, May 9, 1838, Fox to Paget, May 18, 1838, all in Fox Papers, PRO 97/17; Palmerston to Fox, April 4, 1838, PRO, FO 115/68.

7. Kenneth Bourne, *Britain and the Balance of Power in North America, 1815–1908* (Berkeley and Los Angeles, 1967), 78–79; Colonel William Napier, "Project of Warfare against America," March 10, 1839, Wellington Papers-2/57/82–84 and Supplement 2/57/85–86—University of Southampton; John Russell to Sir Hussey, September 14, 1839, Lord John Russell Papers, PRO 30/22/3D.

8. Sandom to Lord Colchester, September 15, 1839, January 25, 1841, February 13, 1846, all in Colchester Papers, PRO 30/9/2/4 and 30/9/6/ 13; Bourne, *Britain and the Balance of Power*, 79.

9. Fox to Arthur, November 10, 1838, in Arthur, *Papers*, 1: 261–63; Fox to Forsyth, November 25, 1838, NA, DS, RG 59, Notes from Great Britain; Albert B. Corey, *The Crisis of 1830–1842 in Canadian-American Relations* (New Haven, 1941), 66–67, 111.

10. Fox to Arthur, November 10, 1838, in Arthur, *Papers*, 1: 361–63; Fox to Vail, November 3, 1838, NA, DS, RG 59, Notes from Britain; Forsyth to Fox, November 15, 1838, NA, DS, RG 59, Notes to Britain.

11. Fox to Palmerston, November 19, 1838, PRO, FO 115/69.

12. Melbourne to Palmerston, December 15, 1838, Palmerston Papers-General Correspondence/Melbourne/260—University of Southampton; Palmerston to Fox, December 15, 1838, PRO, FO 115/68.

13. Copy of Grand Jury Indictment against Howland Hastings, January 10, 1839, enclosed in Stephens T. Mason to Forsyth, January 11, 1839, Minutes of the Trial of Hastings, undated, enclosed in D. Goodwin to Forsyth, April 13, 1839, both in NA, DS, RG 59, Misc. Letters.

14. Forsyth to Fox, January 28, 1839, NA, DS, RG 59, Notes to Britain; Minutes of the Trial of Hastings, Arthur to Mason, February 14, [1839], McDonell to Mason, February 21, 1839, all enclosed in Goodwin to Forsyth, April 13, 1839, NA, DS, RG 59, Misc. Letters; Stevenson to Palmerston, June 24, 1839, enclosed in Stevenson to Forsyth, June 26, 1839, Palmerston to Stevenson, February 14, 1840, enclosed in Stevenson to Forsyth, February 18, 1840, both in NA, DS, RG 59, Despatches, Britain.

15. The Jay Treaty is in Hunter Miller, ed., *Treaties and Other International Acts of the United States of America* (8 vols., Washington, D.C., 1931–48), 2: 245–74 (see especially p. 263). Robbins committed murder

on board the British warship *Hermione* and fled to the United States, which returned him to British custody. The case is discussed in John Bassett Moore, *A Digest of International Law*, (8 vols., Washington, D.C., 1906), 4: 270, 281.

16. John Bassett Moore, *A Treatise on Extradition and Interstate Rendition* (2 vols., Boston, 1891), 1: 55–56, 59, 313–15.

17. Colborne to Jenison, January 1, 1839, Depositions of John Gibson and Sarah Waters, January 2, 1839, Lt. Col. N. F. Williams to Charles Gore, December 30, 1838, Deposition of Thomas Donaldson, January 1, 1839, all enclosed in Fox to Forsyth, February 15, 1839, NA, DS, RG 59, Notes from Britain; Capt. John Grattan to Lt. Griffin, February 3, 1839, Deposition of Mrs. Charolotte Vosburgh, February 3, 1839, both enclosed in Fox to Forsyth, February 15, 1839, NA, DS, RG 59, Notes from Britain.

18. Jenison to Colborne, January 10, February 26, 1839, both enclosed in Jenison to Forsyth, February 7, 1839, NA, DS, RG 59, Misc. Letters; Fox to Forsyth, February 15, 1839, NA, DS, RG 59, Notes from Britain.

19. Colborne to Jenison, February 12, 1839, enclosed in Fox to Forsyth, March 18, 1839, NA, DS, RG 59, Notes from Britain; Charles Adams to Martin Van Buren, February 16, 1839, NA, DS, RG 59, Misc. Letters.

20. Fox to Forsyth, March 18, 1839, NA, DS, RG 59, Notes from Britain; Forsyth to Fox, March 20, 1839, NA, DS, RG 59, Notes to Britain. The *Holmes v. Jennison* case is in 14 Peters 540 (1840). Like John Sanford in *Dred Scott v. Sandford*, the court reporter gave Jenison an additional letter for his name. See the discussion of the case in Moore, *Extradition*, 1: 57–59, and in Carl B. Swisher, *History of the Supreme Court of the United States*, Vol. 5, *The Taney Period, 1836–64* (New York, 1974), 175–77. See also *ex parte Holmes*, 12 Vermont 631 (1840).

21. Robert B. Ross, "The Patriot War," in *Collections and Researches Made by the Michigan Pioneer and Historical Society* 21 (1912–13), 532, 541, 607–08; Spencer to Forsyth, June 10, 1839, NA, DS, RG 59, Misc. Letters.

22. Vail to Seward, June 20, 1839, Spencer to Forsyth, July 11, 1839, both in NA, DS, RG 59, Domestic Letters; London *Times*, July 17, 1840.

23. Deposition of Ira Richards, March 12, 1839, Deposition of Baily Weldon and Wesley Weeks, March 18, 1839, Deposition of Andrew Oliver, Jr., March 23, 1839, all enclosed in Seward to Martin Van Buren, March 30, 1839, NA, DS, RG 59, Misc. Letters; Proclamation of Governor Seward, March 30, 1839, William H. Seward Papers, Rush Rhees Li-

brary, University of Rochester. Seward issued another proclamation on July 11, 1839, offering a $200 reward.

24. Affidavit of Thomas James Stewart, April 15, 1839, enclosed in Smith Stilwell to Forsyth, April 15, 1839, Affidavit of Joseph Whitney, April 19, 1839, enclosed in Stilwell to Forsyth, April 19, 1839, both in NA, DS, RG 59, Misc. Letters.

25. Forsyth to Stevenson, June 5, 1839, NA, DS, RG 59, Instructions, Britain; Stevenson to Palmerston, July 2, 1839, enclosed in Stevenson to Forsyth, July 6, 1839, NA, DS, RG 59, Despatches, Britain. On the belief that James was a Patriot, see Brockville Citizens to Arthur, circa May 29, 1839, in Arthur, *Papers*, 2: 158–59.

26. Deposition of William Harrison (master of the *Weeks*), May 18, 1839, Worth to Collector of Customs, Brockville, May 18, 1839, Worth to Turner, May 19, 1839, all enclosed in Col. William J. Worth to Gen. Abraham Eustis, May 20, 1839, NA, DS, RG 59, Misc. Letters; Eustis to Adjutant General, U.S. Army, May 22, 1839, NA, DS, RG 59, Misc. Letters.

27. Opinion of Charles A. Hagerman, Attorney General, and William Draper, Solicitor General, enclosed in Palmerston to Fox, September 10, 1839, PRO, FO 115/70; Arthur to Fox, circa May 29, 1839, Arthur to Colborne, June 17, 1839, Arthur to Brockville Citizens, circa May 29, 1839, all in Arthur, *Papers*, 2: 158, 159–60, 169–71.

28. Opinion of Hagerman and Draper, June 29, 1839, enclosed in Palmerston to Fox, September 10, 1839, PRO, FO 115/70.

29. Forsyth to Stevenson, June 5, 1839, NA, DS, RG 59, Instructions, Britain; Stevenson to Palmerston, July 2, 1839, enclosed in Stevenson to Forsyth, July 6, 1839, NA, DS, RG 59, Despatches, Britain.

30. Palmerston to Stevenson, September 19, 1839, enclosed in Stevenson to Forsyth, September 28, 1839, NA, DS, RG 59, Despatches, Britain. Palmerston made a mistake. The law he referred to (3 and 4 William IV, Chapter 59, Section 7) provided for the forfeiture of vessels weighing less than seventy tons. The *Weeks*, as all the documents available at the time showed, exceeded one hundred tons.

31. Ibid.

32. Stevenson to Forsyth, September 28, 1839, NA, DS, RG 59, Despatches, Britain.

33. Palmerston to Fox, September 10, 1839, PRO, FO 115/70; Fox to Forsyth, October 21, 1839, NA, DS, RG 59, Notes from Britain; Forsyth to Fox, October 31, 1839, NA, DS, RG 59, Notes to Britain; Fox to Palmerston, November 13, 1839, PRO, FO 115/69.

CHAPTER 5: THE ARREST OF ALEXANDER MCLEOD

1. John C. Dent, *The Story of the Upper Canadian Rebellion* (2 vols., Toronto, 1885), 2: 128–29; Alastair Watt, "The Case of Alexander McLeod," *Canadian Historical Review* 12 (June 1931), 163–64; Arthur to James B. B. Estcourt, December 4, 1838, in Arthur, *Papers*, 1: 413.

2. Buchanan to C. A. Hagerman, June 10, 1837, Arthur, *Papers*, 1: 17.

✓3. Howard Jones, *To the Webster-Ashburton Treaty: A Study in Anglo-American Relations, 1783–1843* (Chapel Hill, N.C., 1977), 49. See the letter from McLeod to the editor of the Niagara *Chronicle,* undated, in PRO, CO 42/483. It was frequently reputed that Alexander McLeod had a brother named Angus, who was on the *Caroline* raid. In a letter published in the London *Times,* March 17, 1841, Angus denied that either he or his brother participated in the raid. See Watt, "McLeod," 164.

4. Arthur to Fox, January 12, 1841, in Arthur, *Papers*, 3: 239–41; Draper to Harrison, January 9, 1841, PAC, RG 5, B43 (reel C15691); Watt, "McLeod," 153.

5. Arthur to Glenelg, May 11, September 18, 1838, both in PAC, RG 7, G 12, Vol. 29 (reel H1104); Arthur to Sydenham, November 30, 1840, Jackson to Arthur, January 11, 1841, both in Arthur, *Papers*, 3: 191–93, 238.

6. Arthur to Sydenham, January 11, 1841, Arthur to Fox, January 12, 1841, Arthur to R. D. Jackson, January 18, 1841, Jackson to Arthur, January 23, 1841, Arthur to Sydenham, February 1, 1841, all in Arthur, *Papers*, 3: 236–38, 239–41, 249–50, 261–62, 291–92.

7. Fox to Palmerston, August 19, 1839, November 28, 1840, both in PRO, FO 115/69.

8. Fox to Forsyth, December 13, 1840, NA, DS, RG 59, Notes from Britain; Stevenson to Palmerston, May 22, 1838, NA, DS, RG 59, Notes to Britain.

9. C. K. Webster, "Lord Palmerston at Work, 1830–41," *Politica* (August 1934): 129–44; Asa Briggs, *The Making of Modern England, 1783–1867: The Age of Improvement* (New York, 1965), 359; Jasper Ridley, *Lord Palmerston* (New York, 1971), 107–21; Kenneth Bourne, *Palmerston: The Early Years, 1784–1841* (New York, 1982), 552, 586–87, 597; Wilbur D. Jones, *The American Problem in British Diplomacy, 1841–1861* (Athens, Ga., 1974), 2–3.

10. Forsyth to Fox, December 26, 1840, NA, DS, RG 59, Notes to Britain.

11. Fox to Palmerston, December 27, 1840, PRO, FO 115/69.

12. Fox to Forsyth, December 29, 1840, NA, DS, RG 59, Notes from Britain; Forsyth to Fox, December 31, 1840, NA, DS, RG 59, Notes to Britain.

13. Fox to Palmerston, January 10, 1841, PRO, FO 115/69.

14. Emerich de Vattel, *The Law of Nations, or the Principles of Natural Law*, trans. Charles G. Fenwick (Washington, D.C., 1916), Book 2, Chapter 8, Sections 101–02, 104; Abraham Gridley to William H. Seward, December 23, 1840, Seward Papers, Rush Rhees Library, University of Rochester (hereafter Seward Papers-UR).

15. John B. Moore, *A Digest of International Law* (8 vols., Washington, D.C., 1906), 2: 23–24; "Opinions of Attorneys General," in *House Executive Documents*, 31st Cong., 2d sess., No. 55, pp. 21–22. The case, *Waters v. Collot*, is in 2 Dallas 247.

16. *House Executive Documents*, 31st Cong., 2d sess., No. 55, pp. 24–26.

17. Jefferson to Genêt, September 9, 1793, quoted in Francis Wharton, ed., *A Digest of the International Law of the United States* (3 vols., Washington, D.C., 1886), 2: 675.

18. *Congressional Globe*, 26th Cong., 2d sess., 44; Richardson, *Messages and Papers*, 3: 622–24. The correspondence is published in *House Executive Documents*, 26th Cong., 2d sess., Serial 383, No. 33.

19. *Cong. Globe*, 26th Cong., 2d sess., 73–75, 79–81.

20. Arthur to Fox, January 12, 1841, Arthur to Sydenham, January 18, 1841, both in Arthur *Papers*, 3: 239–41, 250–51; Arthur to Lord John Russell, January 25, 1841, PAC, RG 7, G 12, Vol. 33 (reel H1104).

21. Gardner and Bradley to W. H. Draper, February 13, 1841, in Arthur, *Papers*, 3: 329–33.

22. Sydenham to Arthur, January 15, 1841, in ibid., 3: 244–45.

23. McLeod to Draper, January 11, 1841, in ibid., 3: 239.

24. Secker Brough to Draper, January 28, 1841, in ibid., 3: 283–85; Elias Ransom to George H. Broughton, January 29, 1841, Seward Papers-UR.

25. Brough to Draper, January 28, 1841, Arthur to Sydenham, February 1, 1841, Arthur to Sydenham, February 2, 1841, Arthur to Russell, February 4, 1841, all in Arthur, *Papers*, 3: 283–85, 291–92, 293–94, 297–98; Forsyth to Fox, February 10, 1841, NA, DS, RG 59, Notes to Britain.

26. London *Times*, February 11, 16, 20, March 4, 5, 1841; Buffalo *Commercial Advertiser*, January 29, 1841, extract published in Arthur, *Papers*, 3: 286–87; Marvin to Seward, February 5, 1841, Seward to Marvin, February 12, 1841, both in Seward Papers-UR.

27. Seward to Forsyth, February 27, 1841, NA, DS, RG 59, Misc.

Letters; Joseph Hamilton to Samuel B. Harrison, February 8, 1841, Arthur to Sydenham, February 13, 1841, both in Arthur, *Papers*, 3: 307, 318–19. See also Fox to Palmerston, February [1]7, 1841, PRO, FO 115/69. Fox's dispatch is marked the 7th, but this is obviously a mistake because he refers in it to his dispatch of the 10th and to the Pickens Report (discussed below), which appeared on the 13th.

28. The Pickens Report and the discussion on it are in *Cong. Globe*, 26th Cong., 2d sess., 170–75. The report is also published in *House Reports*, 26th Cong., 2d sess., Serial 388, No. 162; John B. Edmunds, *Francis W. Pickens and the Politics of Destruction* (Chapel Hill, N.C., 1986), 61–63.

29. Ridley, *Palmerston*, 244–45, 253–58; P. H. Colomb, *Naval Warfare: Its Ruling Principles and Practice Historically Treated* (London, 1899), 410–11; C. J. Bartlett, *Great Britain and Sea Power, 1815–1853* (Oxford, 1963), 144–46; *Cong. Globe*, 26th Cong., 2d sess., 171.

30. Fox to Palmerston, February [1]7, 1841, PRO, FO 115/69.

31. Stevenson to Forsyth, February 9, 1841, NA, DS, RG 59, Despatches, Britain; London *Morning Herald*, March 17, 1841, quoted in Corey, *Crisis of 1830–1842*, 139; London *Times*, March 9, 18, April 10, 1841.

32. *Hansard's Parliamentary Debates*, 3d series, Vol. 56, Columns 364–74, 456–59.

33. Palmerston to Fox, January 19, February 9, 1841, both in PRO, FO 115/75.

34. Stevenson to Van Buren, February 9, 1841, MVB-LC.

35. Palmerston to Fox, February 9, 1841, PRO, FO 115/75; Palmerston to William Temple, February 9, 1841, in Evelyn Ashley, *The Life and Correspondence of Henry John Temple, Viscount Palmerston* (2 vols., London, 1879), 1: 406–07; Admiralty to Vice Admiral Sir Thomas Harvey, March 3, 1841, PRO, Admiralty Outletters and Instructions, 2/1696; Fox to Sir Thomas Harvey, March 13, 1841, Fox Papers, PRO 97/17.

36. W. D. Jones, *American Problem in British Diplomacy*, 4–6; *Hansard's Parliamentary Debates*, 3d series, Vol. 56, Columns 1386–1387.

37. Fox to Palmerston, January 10, February 21, 1841, both in PRO, FO 115/69; Sydenham to Arthur, February 18, 1841, in Arthur, *Papers*, 3: 326–27.

38. Philip Hone, Diary of Philip Hone, January 12, 1841, microfilm manuscript, New-York Historical Society; Sydenham to Arthur, February 18, 1841, in Arthur, *Papers*, 3: 326–27; Fox to Palmerston, February 24, March 7, 1841, both in PRO, FO 115/69.

CHAPTER 6: TIPPECANOE AND TYLER, TOO

1. John C. Calhoun to Virgil Maxcy, February 19, 1841, in John C. Calhoun, *The Papers of John C. Calhoun*, Vol. 15, 1839–1841, ed. Clyde N. Wilson (Columbia, S.C., 1983), 507–09; Richard M. Blatchford to William H. Seward, February 14, 1841, Seward Papers-UR. On the election of William Henry Harrison, see Robert G. Gunderson, *The Log-Cabin Campaign* (Lexington, Ky., 1957). For a comprehensive view of Webster's long and varied career, see Maurice G. Baxter, *One and Inseparable: Daniel Webster and the Union* (Cambridge, Mass., 1984).

2. Peter Harvey, *Reminiscences and Anecdotes of Daniel Webster* (Boston, 1877), 162–63. The text of Harrison's inaugural address is in the *National Intelligencer*, March 5, 1841.

3. Fox to Palmerston, March 9, 1841, No. 23, PRO, FO 115/69.

4. Forsyth to Fox, December 26, 1840, NA, DS, RG 59, Notes to Britain.

5. Fox to Palmerston, March 7, 1841, No. 21, PRO, FO 115/69. Even Governor Arthur, usually a Cassandrian voice, felt encouraged because McLeod's lawyers informed the Canadians that he had received intimations of the new government's interest in securing McLeod's release. See Arthur to Sydenham, March 11, 13, 1841, in Arthur, *Papers*, 3: 379–80, 382–84. See also Arthur to Lord John Russell, March 17, 1841, in ibid., 3: 388–89.

6. Memorandum on the Northeastern Boundary Negotiations, March 9, 1839, Memorandum of Proposal for Special Mission to England, March 10, 1839, both in Daniel Webster, *The Papers of Daniel Webster: Correspondence*, Vol. 4, 1835–1839, ed. Charles M. Wiltse and Harold D. Moser (Hanover, N.H., 1980), 346–50. The most thorough discussion of the boundary controversy is Howard Jones, *To the Webster-Ashburton Treaty: A Study in Anglo-American Relations, 1783–1843* (Chapel Hill, N.C., 1977).

7. Baring Brothers to Webster, October 12, 1839, Webster to Baring Brothers, October 16, 1839, both in Wiltse and Moser, *Webster Correspondence*, 4: 401–02, 404–07; Baxter, *One and Inseparable*, 258–74. On Webster's Anglophilia, see Charles M. Wiltse, "Daniel Webster and the British Experience," *Massachusetts Historical Society Proceedings* 85 (1973), 58–77.

8. Webster to Duke of Rutland, November 16, 1839, in Wiltse and Moser, *Webster Correspondence*, 4: 409–10.

9. Stevenson to Palmerston, May 22, 1838, enclosed in Stevenson to Forsyth, May 24, 1838, No. 49, NA, DS, RG 59, Despatches, Britain.

10. Fox to Palmerston, March 12, 1841, No. 25, PRO, FO 115/69.

11. Webster to John C. Spencer, March 11, 1841, NA, DS, RG 59, Domestic Letters.

12. Fox to Webster, March 12, 1841, NA, DS, RG 59, Notes from Britain.

13. Bell to Scott, March 12, 1841, in Charles W. Elliott, *Winfield Scott: The Soldier and the Man* (New York, 1937), 398; Bell to Seward, March 12, 1841, NA, WD, RG 107, Letters Sent, Military Book No. 23.

14. Albany *Argus*, March 18, 1841; Elliott, *Winfield Scott*, 398–99; William H. Seward, *William H. Seward: An Autobiography from 1801 to 1834, with a Memoir of his Life, and Selections from his Letters, 1831–1846*, ed. Frederick W. Seward (New York, 1891), 527.

15. Seward to Forsyth, February 27, 1841, NA, DS, RG 59, Misc. Letters; Webster to Crittenden, March 15, 1841, Crittenden Papers-Duke University; Fox to Arthur, March 20, 1841, Fox Papers, PRO 97/17.

16. Crittenden to Robert P. Letcher, March 14, 1841, in Mrs. Chapman Coleman, ed., *The Life of John J. Crittenden, with Selections from the Correspondence and Speeches* (2 vols., Philadelphia, 1871), 1:149–50.

17. Paper relating to McLeod found among Crittenden's Letters, undated, Crittenden to Webster, undated, both in ibid., 1: 150–54; John C. Spencer to John J. Crittenden, memorandum, undated, Webster Papers-LC.

18. Seward to Crittenden, March 31, 1841, in William H. Seward, *The Works of William H. Seward*, ed. George E. Baker (3 vols., New York, 1853), 2: 586–88.

19. Webster to Seward, March 17, 1841, Seward Papers-UR.

20. Seward to Webster, March 22, 1841 (public), NA, DS, RG 59, Misc. Letters; Seward to Webster, March 22, 1841 (private), Webster Papers-LC.

21. Bloodgood to Seward, February 22, 1841, Seward Papers-UR. A biographical sketch of Bloodgood is in James G. Wilson and John Fiske, eds., *Appleton's Cyclopaedia of American History* (6 vols., New York, 1887), 1: 296.

22. Bloodgood to Seward, March 2, 1841, Seward Papers-UR.

23. Bloodgood to Seward, March 6, 1841, ibid.

24. Ibid.

25. Seward to Tyler, July 10, 1841 (draft), Seward to Morgan, July 26, 1841, both in ibid. Possibly Seward sent the letter to both Tyler and Morgan, and the copies have not been preserved, but, given the deplorable relations that existed between the governor and the president, it seems more likely that Seward, after writing the draft, decided to rely on Morgan.

26. London *Sun*, March 10, 1841; London *Times*, March 17, 1841.

27. Harcourt to Webster, March 12, 1841, Webster Papers-LC.

28. Stevenson to Hull, March 8, March 12, 1841, enclosed in Stevenson's despatch No. 125 of June 18, 1841, in William R. Manning, ed., *Diplomatic Correspondence of the United States: Canadian Relations, 1784–1860* (4 vols., Washington, D.C., 1940–45), 3:638.

29. Stevenson to Webster, March 9, 1841, No. 118, NA, DS, RG 59, Despatches to Britain.

30. Stevenson to Webster, March 18, 1841, No. 119, ibid.

31. Stevenson to Webster, April 7, 1841, No. 120, ibid.

32. John H. Powell to Hull, March 11, 1841, Minutes of Council of Commanders, March 24, 1841, Orders of March 25, 1841, all in *Senate Documents*, 27th Cong., 1st sess., Serial 390, No. 33; Linda M. Maloney, *The Captain from Connecticut: The Life and Naval Times of Isaac Hull* (Boston, 1986), 470–76.

33. Bolton to Secretary of the Navy George E. Badger, May 9, 1841, in *Senate Documents*, 27th Cong., 1st sess., Serial 390, No. 33; newspaper accounts cited from Francis F. Wayland, *Andrew Stevenson: Democrat and Diplomat, 1785–1857* (Philadelphia, 1949), 190; *Congressional Globe*, 27th Cong., 1st sess., 79.

34. Lewis Cass to Webster, March 5, 1841, Webster Papers-Dartmouth College.

35. Cass to Webster, March 15, 1841, ibid. The letter is also published in George T. Curtis, *Life of Daniel Webster* (2 vols., New York, 1870), 2:63–64, but Curtis misconstrues the meaning of Cass's remark by incorrectly transcribing "excite" as "quiet."

36. Nesselrode to Alexander de Bodisco, March 18/30, 1841, NA, DS, RG 59, Notes from Russia. Regarding the offer through the Russian minister in London, see Palmerston to Fox, April 18, 1841, No. 15, PRO, FO 115/75. Rumors about Russian interference in Canadian affairs were persistent. In 1839 Henry S. Fox had employed a confidential agent, Stewart Derbishire, to gather intelligence on Canadian rebels. Derbishire reported that the Russian government was promoting disaffection in British colonies. When Fox informed John Quincy Adams of Derbi-

shire's report, Adams said he was not aware of such activity, but believed this was the course a power as "active and intriguing as Russia" would take. Stewart Derbishire Report, July 20, 1839, Fox Papers, PRO 97/17.

37. Gardner and Bradley to W. H. Draper, February 13, 1841, in Arthur, *Papers*, 3: 329–34.

38. Arthur to Sydenham, February 19, 1841, ibid., 3: 327–29.

39. Arthur to Sydenham, March 4, 1841, ibid., 3: 357–58; Joseph Hamilton to Arthur, March 9, 1841, ibid., 3: 374–75; *Niles' National Register*, April 10, 1841.

40. Porter to Seward, March 25, 1841, Seward to Porter, March 31, 1841, both in Seward Papers-UR.

41. Seward to Hall, March 16, 1841, ibid.

42. Nelson to Seward, March 15, 1841, enclosed in Seward to Webster, March 18, 1841, NA, DS, RG 59, Misc. Letters.

43. Willis Hall to Seward, April 1, 1841, enclosed in Seward to Webster, April 12, 1841, ibid.; *Niles' National Register*, April 3, 1841.

44. Fox to Palmerston, March 20, 1841, No. 32, PRO, FO 115/69. Fox's dispatch is dated the twentieth, but McLeod's case did not come before the court until the twenty-first.

45. Albany *Argus*, April 6, 1841; *Niles' National Register*, April 10, 1841.

46. Stephen W. Stathis, "John Tyler's Presidential Succession: A Reappraisal," *Prologue* 8 (Winter 1976), 226; *Niles' National Register*, April 10, 1841.

47. Oliver P. Chitwood, *John Tyler: Champion of the Old South* (New York, 1939), 184.

48. John Quincy Adams, *Memoirs of John Quincy Adams*, ed. Charles Francis Adams (12 vols., Philadelphia, 1874–77), 10: 456–57.

49. Poinsett to Van Buren, April 4, 1841, MVB-LC.

50. Fox to Webster, March 12, 1841, NA, DS, RG 59, Notes from Britain; Fox to Palmerston, April 7, 1841, No. 35, April 14, 1841, No. 38, PRO, FO 115/69.

51. Lyon G. Tyler, ed., *The Letters and Times of the Tylers* (3 vols., Richmond, Va., 1884–96), 2: 206–07.

52. Webster to Fox, April 24, 1841, NA, DS, RG 59, Notes to Britain. On the importance of Webster's note in international law, see J. L. Brierly, *The Law of Nations: An Introduction to the International Law of Peace* (6th ed., Oxford, 1963), 405–06.

53. Hugo Grotius, *De Jure Belli ac Pacis Libri Tres*, trans. Francis W. Kelsey (2 vols., Oxford, 1925), Book 2, Chapter 1, Section 5, pp. 173–75; Samuel Pufendorf, *De Jure Naturae et Gentium Libri Octo*, trans. C. H.

and W. A. Oldfather (Oxford, 1934), Book 2, Chapter 5, Sections 6–8, pp. 272–77; Emerich de Vattel, *The Law of Nations, or the Principles of Natural Law,* trans. Charles G. Fenwick (3 vols., Washington, D.C., 1916), Vol. 3, Book 1, Chapter 2, Section 18, p. 14, and Book 3, Chapter 3, Section 44, p. 249. On Vattel's influence in the United States, see the introduction by Fenwick, xxxv–xxxviii.

54. Maurice G. Baxter, *Daniel Webster and the Supreme Court* (Amherst, Mass., 1966), 4–5, 39–43.

55. The case is in 11 Wheaton 1–58 (1826).

56. Gardner and Bradley to Webster, March 21, 1841, NA, DS, RG 59, Misc. Letters; Scott to Seward, March 27, 1841, Seward Papers-UR.

57. Webster to Tyler, [circa April 1841], Webster Papers-Dartmouth College. The letter is published in C. H. Van Tyne, ed., *The Letters of Daniel Webster* (New York, 1902), 232–33, where it is dated, I think erroneously, circa July 1841. By July, Joshua A. Spencer, in whom Webster had great confidence, had joined the defense and was seeking a writ of habeas corpus from the New York Supreme Court.

58. Chester Alden, *Courts and Lawyers of New York: A History, 1609–1925* (3 vols., New York and Chicago, 1925), 3: 1153.

59. F. W. Seward, ed., *Seward,* 239–40, 393.

60. Coleman, *Crittenden,* 150.

61. Scott to Seward, March 27, 1841, Seward Papers-UR.

62. Webster to Fox, April 12, 1841, NA, DS, RG 59, Notes to Britain.

63. Webster to J. A. Spencer, April 16, 1841, Gratz Collection-Historical Society of Pennsylvania.

64. Webster to J. A. Spencer, April 19, 1841, NA, DS, RG 59, Domestic Letters.

65. Albany *Argus,* March 20, 1841; *Niles' National Register,* May 1, 1841.

66. Seward to Tyler, May 4, 1841, NA, DS, RG 59, Misc. Letters.

67. Tyler to Seward, May 7, 1841, NA, DS, RG 59, Domestic Letters; Seward to Tyler, May 10, 1841, NA, DS, RG 59, Misc. Letters.

68. Tyler to Webster, May 15, 1841, Webster Papers-LC; Tyler to Seward, May 15, 1841, in L. G. Tyler, *Tylers,* 2: 208–09.

69. Seward to Tyler, May 20, 1841, NA, DS, RG 59, Misc. Letters.

70. Tyler to Seward, May 25, 1841, ibid.

71. Seward to Tyler, June 1, 1841, ibid.

72. Seward to Ewing, May 17, 1841, Seward Papers-UR.

73. Seward to Morgan, July 21, 1841, ibid.

74. Glyndon G. Van Deusen, *William Henry Seward* (New York, 1967), 5.

75. Blatchford to Seward, May 16, 1841, Seward Papers-UR.

76. Webster to Ketchum, [July 1841], Webster Papers-Dartmouth College.

77. Blatchford to Seward, August 8, 1841, Seward Papers-UR.

78. Seward to Morgan, July 21, August 9, 1841, both in ibid. See also Seward to Weed, undated, in F. W. Seward, ed., *Seward*, 555.

CHAPTER 7: ARGUMENT, ARGUMENT

1. *Niles' National Register*, May 8, 1841; Philip Hone, Diary of Philip Hone, May 6, 1841, microfilm manuscript, New-York Historical Society.

2. Daniel Webster to Fletcher Webster, May 10, 1841, Webster-Healy Papers—New-York Historical Society; Daniel Webster to Fletcher Webster, May 16, 1841, in Daniel Webster, *The Private Correspondence of Daniel Webster*, ed. Fletcher Webster (2 vols., Boston, 1857), 2: 104–05.

3. The case, including the arguments of the prosecution and defense attorneys, is in 25 Wendell's (New York) Reports 483–603 (1841).

4. Ibid., 483.

5. Ibid., 519–33, 536, 540, 543.

6. Emerich de Vattel, *The Law of Nations, or the Principles of Natural Law*, trans. Charles G. Fenwick (3 vols., Washington, D.C., 1916), Vol. 3, Book 3, Chapter 8, Section 137, p. 279.

7. Ibid., Chapter 4, Section 61, p. 256; Chapter 8, Section 147, p. 283; Chapter 15, Section 226, p. 318.

8. Ibid., Chapter 4, Sections 67–68, pp. 257–58.

9. 25 Wendell 543–48.

10. Vattel, Vol. 3, Book 1, Chapter 1, Sections 26, 53, pp. 17, 25; Vol. 3, Book 3, Chapter 2, Section 6, p. 237; Vol. 3, Book 2, Chapter 6, Section 74, p. 136.

11. 25 Wendell 548–56.

12. Constitution of the United States, Article 2, Section 2; Article 1, Section 10; Article 1, Section 8.

13. 9 Wheaton 1 (1824); 25 Wendell 561–65. In *Gibbons* v. *Ogden*, the Court did not limit state powers if they did not interfere with those of Congress.

14. Richard M. Blatchford to William H. Seward, May 19, 1841, Seward Papers-UR.

15. Fox to Palmerston, May 28, 1841, No. 49, June 12, 1841, No. 51, both in PRO, FO 115/69.

16. Special Session Message, June 1, 1841, in James D. Richardson, comp., *A Compilation of the Messages and Papers of the Presidents, 1789–1897* (10 vols., Washington, D.C., 1896–99), 4: 41.

17. *Congressional Globe*, 27th Cong., 1st sess., 14; appendix 14–18.

18. Peter Harvey, *Reminiscences and Anecdotes of Daniel Webster* (Boston, 1877), 222–24; Arthur M. Schlesinger, Jr., *The Age of Jackson* (Boston, 1953), 59–61.

19. *Cong. Globe*, 27th Cong., 1st sess., appendix 42–46.

20. Ibid., appendix 110–13.

21. Ibid., appendix 417–19.

22. Aaron V. Brown to James K. Polk, June 12, 1841, in James K. Polk, *Correspondence of James K. Polk*, Vol. 5, *1839–1841*, ed. Wayne Cutler et al. (Nashville, Tenn., 1979), 692–96; Fox to Palmerston, June 27, 1841, No. 60, PRO, FO 115/69.

23. Daniel Webster, *The Papers of Daniel Webster: Correspondence*, Vol. 2, *1825–1829*, ed. Charles M. Wiltse and Harold D. Moser (Hanover, N.H., 1976), 78–79; Webster to Clay, March 25, 1827, ibid., 175–77. It was Ingersoll who initiated the famous misconduct charges against Webster in 1846. See Kenneth R. Stevens, "The Webster-Ingersoll Feud: Politics and Personality in the New Nation," *Historical New Hampshire* 37 (Summer/Fall 1982), 174–92, and Howard Jones, "The Attempt to Impeach Daniel Webster," *Capitol Studies* 3 (Fall 1975), 31–44.

24. *Cong. Globe*, 27th Cong., 1st sess., appendix 75–79.

25. Ibid., 173–74.

26. Ibid., appendix 153–55.

27. Ibid., appendix 419–22.

28. Ibid., 121–22.

29. Ibid., appendix 422–24.

30. Ibid., 200.

31. Ibid., 4ll and appendix 432–34.

32. John Quincy Adams, *Memoirs of John Quincy Adams*, ed. Charles Francis Adams (12 vols., Philadelphia, 1874–77), 11: 20.

33. Spencer to Webster, July 6, 1841, Webster Papers-New Hampshire Historical Society (hereafter NHHS); Hall to Seward, July 11, 1841, Seward Papers-UR.

34. 25 Wendell 567–73. For the entirety of Cowen's opinion, see 567–603.

35. Ibid., 588.

36. Fox to Palmerston, July 28, 1841, PRO, FO 115/76; Fox to Sydenham, September 5, 1841, Fox Papers, PRO 97/17.

37. William H. Seward to Frances Seward, July 21, 1841, in William H. Seward, *William H. Seward: An Autobiography from 1801 to 1834, with a Memoir of his Life, and Selections from his Letters, 1831–1846,* ed. Frederick W. Seward (New York, 1891), 555; Blatchford to Seward, July 21, 1841, Seward Papers-UR.

38. Webster to Story, July 16, 1841, Webster Papers-Massachusetts Historical Society; Story to Webster, July 21, 1841, Webster Papers-Dartmouth College.

39. See Daniel B. Tallmadge, "Review of the Opinion of Judge Cowen . . . in the Case of Alexander McLeod," 26 Wendell 663–706 (1842); Webster to Tallmadge, January 31, 1842, in ibid., 703.

40. Joshua A. Spencer to Webster, July 12, 1841, Webster Papers-NHHS; Gardner and Bradley to Draper, July 19, 1841, enclosed in Sydenham to Fox, August 3, 1841, Fox Papers, PRO 97/18.

41. Webster to Joshua A. Spencer, August 6, 1841, NA, DS, RG 59, Domestic Letters.

42. Tyler to Webster, circa September 7–8, 1841, in Lyon G. Tyler, ed., *The Letters and Times of the Tylers* (3 vols., Richmond, Va., 1884–1896), 2: 212–13; Hall to Seward, July 24, 1841, Seward Papers-UR.

43. Jacob M. Howard to Webster, April 6, 1841, Webster Papers-Dartmouth College; Webster to Tyler, circa April–July 1841, Webster Papers-NHHS; unsigned conversations with John St. John, July 6, 1841, NA, DS, RG 59, Misc. Letters; General Hugh Brady to General Winfield Scott, July 15, 1841, NA, DS, RG 59, Misc. Letters; Captain John Munroe to General Scott, July 16, 1841, NA, DS, RG 59, Misc. Letters; Fox to Palmerston, July 27, 1841, No. 67, PRO, FO 115/69.

44. Webster to Tyler, circa April–July 1841, Webster Papers-NHHS.

45. Seward to Colonel James Bankhead, August 4, 1841, Seward Papers-UR; "A Friend" to Seward, August 8, 1841, Seward Papers-UR; unidentified informant to Fox, August 8, 1841, NA, DS, RG 59, Notes from Britain.

46. Seward to A. Chandler, August 10, 1841, Seward Papers-UR; S. Blatchford to Collectors at Oswego, Utica, and Montezuma, New York, August 10, 1841, Seward Papers-UR; A. Chandler to Seward, August 31, September 11, 1841, both in Seward Papers-UR.

47. Samuel Blatchford to Timothy Jenkins (draft in Seward's hand), August 10, 1841, Webster to Seward, August 24, 1841, Seward to First Judge, District Attorney, and Sheriff of Oneida County, August 31, 1841, all in Seward Papers-UR; Seward to Webster, September 3, 1841,

NA, DS, RG 59, Misc. Letters; S. Blatchford to Seward, September 20, 1841, Seward Papers-UR.

48. On Lett, see Robert B. Ross, "The Patriot War," in *Collections and Researches Made by the Michigan Pioneer and Historical Society* 21 (1912–13), 432, 541, 607–08, reprinted from a series of articles by Ross published in the Detroit *Evening News* in 1890; Proclamation offering reward for Lett, July 23, 1841, Seward to Norman Rowe, September 1, 1841, both in Seward Papers-UR; Seward to Webster, September 3, 1841, NA, DS, RG 59, Misc. Letters; Henry W. Rogers to Seward, September 6, 1841, Seward Papers-UR.

49. Seward to Webster, September 21, 1841, NA, DS, RG 59, Misc. Letters; Seward to Webster, September 22, 1841, Webster to Seward, September 23, 1841, both in Seward Papers-UR.

50. Proclamation of September 25, 1841, in Richardson, *Messages and Papers*, 4: 72–73.

51. Confidential Circular, October 2, 1841, NA, Treasury Department, RG 56, Letters sent to Collectors of Small Ports.

52. C. Anthony [U.S. Attorney, Ohio] to Webster, October 2, 1841, J. Howard [U.S. Marshal, Detroit] to Webster, October 6, 1841, Demas Adams [U.S. Marshal, Ohio] to Webster, October 7, 1841, J. K. Livingston [U.S. Collector, Rochester] to Webster, October 11, 1841, all in NA, DS, RG 59, Misc. Letters; Fox to Aberdeen, September 25, 1841, No. 94, FO 115/76.

53. See Fox's despatches to Palmerston, July 28, 1841, No. 68, August 5, 1841, No. 70, August 18, 1841, No. 73, all in PRO, FO 115/76.

54. See Charles S. Campbell, *From Revolution to Rapprochement: The United States and Great Britain, 1783–1900* (New York, 1974), 59; Howard Jones, *To the Webster-Ashburton Treaty: A Study in Anglo-American Relations, 1783–1843* (Chapel Hill, N.C., 1977), 60–61; Glyndon G. Van Deusen, *The Jacksonian Era, 1828–1848* (New York, 1959), 173.

55. For a thorough and thoughtful study of Aberdeen's foreign policy, see Wilbur D. Jones, *The American Problem in British Diplomacy, 1841–1861* (Athens, Ga., 1974), especially 1–8, and *Lord Aberdeen and the Americas* (Athens, Ga., 1958), especially 83–87. For general studies of Aberdeen, see Lucille Iremonger, *Lord Aberdeen: A Biography of the Fourth Earl of Aberdeen, K.G., K.T., Prime Minister, 1852–1855* (London, 1978), especially 166–84, and Muriel E. Chamberlain, *Lord Aberdeen: A Political Biography* (London, 1983).

56. Stevenson to Palmerston, May 22, 1838, enclosed in Stevenson to Forsyth, May 24, 1838, Palmerston to Stevenson, September 18, 1841, both in NA, DS, RG 59, Despatches, Britain.

57. Stevenson to Webster, August 31, 1841, Stevenson to Palmerston, August 31, 1841, enclosed in Stevenson to Webster, September 18, 1841, both in NA, DS, RG 59, Despatches, Britain.

58. Stevenson to Forsyth, July 2, 1839, NA, DS, RG 59, Despatches, Britain; Forsyth to Stevenson, September 11, 1839, NA, DS, RG 59, Instructions, Britain.

59. Palmerston to Fox, August 18, 1841, No. 22, PRO, FO 115/75.

60. Fox to Webster, September 5, 1841, NA, DS, RG 59, Notes from Britain.

61. Fox to Palmerston, September 12, 1841, No. 84, PRO, FO 115/76.

62. Webster to Fox, September 10, 1841, NA, DS, RG 59, Notes to Britain.

63. Hansard's Parliamentary Debates, 3d series, Vol. 59, Columns 265–70; W. D. Jones, American Problem in British Diplomacy, 7.

64. Stevenson to Webster, September 18, 1841, NA, DS, RG 59, Despatches, Britain.

65. C. Hughes to Webster, September 18, 1841, Webster Papers-NHHS.

66. Palmerston to Fox, February 9, 1841, No. 5, Aberdeen to Fox, September 18, 1841, No. 1, both in PRO, FO 115/75.

67. Fox to Aberdeen, October 1, 17, 1841, both in PRO, FO 115/76; Fox to Vice Admiral Sir Charles Adams, October 5, 1841, Fox Papers, PRO 97/17.

68. Peel to Queen Victoria, October 28, 1841, in Victoria Regina, The Letters of Queen Victoria: A Selection from Her Majesty's Correspondence between the Years 1837 and 1861, ed. Arthur C. Benson and Viscount Esher (3 vols., London, 1907), 1: 355–56.

69. Cabinet Memorandum No. 5, September 6, 1841, and Colonial Office to Sydenham, September 10, 1841, cited in Kenneth Bourne, Britain and the Balance of Power in North America, 1815–1908 (Berkeley and Los Angeles, 1967), 94; Lieutenant H. D. Fanshawe reports of October 15, November 30, and December 14, 1841, cited in ibid., 95; Peel to Stanley, September 20, 1841, Peel Papers, B.L. Add. Ms. 40467/60–61; Peel Memorandum to Aberdeen, Haddington, and Stanley, October 17, 1841, in C. S. Parker, ed., Sir Robert Peel, from his Private Papers (3 vols., London, 1891–99), 3: 387–88; Haddington to Peel, September 13, 1841, Peel to Wellington, October 18, 1841, both in Peel Papers, B.L. Add. Ms. 40459/60–62.

70. Albert Fitz, July 21, 1842, NA, DS, RG 59, Communications from Special Agents; Anthony M. Brescia, " 'Defences Strong Enough to Defy the World': The Visit of a U.S. State Department Special Agent to Ber-

muda in 1841," *Bulletin of the Institute of Maritime History and Archaeology* 10 (December 1987): 11–12, 14, 16, 25–26.

71. Bourne, *Britain and the Balance of Power*, 79; Fox to Forsyth, November 25, 1838, NA, DS, RG 59, Notes from Britain.

72. John Norvell to Martin Van Buren, May 24, 1840, NA, DS, RG 59, Misc. Letters.

73. Robinson to Bell, September 13, 1841, NA, DS, RG 59, Misc. Letters.

74. Hawley to Seward, September 17, 21, 1841, enclosed in Seward to Webster, September 24, 1841, both in NA, DS, RG 59, Misc. Letters.

75. Scott to Bell, September 15, 1841, Seward Papers-UR.

76. Webster to Seward, September 23, 1841, ibid.; Webster to Fox, September 25, 1841, NA, DS, RG 59, Notes to Britain.

77. *Cong. Globe*, 27th Cong., 1st sess., 160, 278–82, 429.

78. Ibid., appendix, 46.

79. Gilpin to Martin Van Buren, June 18, 1841, MVB-LC.

Chapter 8: Trial

1. Clayton's conversation is reported in Christopher Morgan to Seward, August 1, 1841, Seward Papers-UR; Andrew B. Dickinson to Seward, August 2, 1841, Christopher Morgan to Seward, August 10, 1841, both in Seward Papers-UR. On the bank veto and the cabinet crisis, see Maurice G. Baxter, *One and Inseparable: Daniel Webster and the Union* (Cambridge, Mass., 1984), 299–317.

2. Thurlow Weed to George W. Patterson, August 26, 1841, Weed Papers, Rush Rhees Library, University of Rochester (hereafter Weed Papers-UR); Richard M. Blatchford to Seward, August 29, 1841, Seward Papers-UR.

3. John Quincy Adams, *The Memoirs of John Quincy Adams*, ed. Charles Francis Adams (12 vols., Philadelphia, 1874–77), 11: 13–14.

4. Philip Hone, *The Diary of Philip Hone*, ed. Allan Nevins (2 vols., New York, 1927), 2: 560–66.

5. Webster to Hiram Ketchem, September 10, 1841, in Fletcher Webster, ed., *The Private Correspondence of Daniel Webster* (2 vols., Boston, 1857), 2: 110.

6. Fox to Palmerston, September 13, 1841, No. 85, PRO, FO 115/76.

7. See Grogan to Tyler, October 12, 1841, Sworn Deposition of Grogan, October 13, 1841, enclosed in Charles Davis [U.S. Marshal, Ver-

mont] and William Barron [U.S. Attorney, Vermont] to Webster, October 15, 1841, both in NA, DS, RG 59, Misc. Letters.

8. Colborne to Jenison, January 1, 1839, Depositions of John Gibson and Sarah Waters, January 2, 1839, Lt. Col. N. F. Williams to Charles Gore, December 30, 1839, Deposition of Thomas Donaldson, January 1, 1839, all enclosed in Fox to Forsyth, February 15, 1839, NA, DS, RG 59, Notes from Britain.

9. Jenison to Colborne, January 10, February 6, 1839, both enclosed in Jenison to Forsyth, February 7, 1839, NA, DS, RG 59, Misc. Letters; Fox to Forsyth, February 15, 1839, NA, DS, RG 59, Notes from Britain.

10. This account of Grogan's seizure, detention, and release is written from the following documents: William W. White, A. C. Butler, and D. Moll to John Tyler, September 25, 1841 (and enclosures), NA, DS, RG 59, Misc. Letters. Of the enclosures, see especially Affidavit of Alexander Manning, September 22, 1841; Depositions enclosed in Jenison to Webster, October 12, 1841, James W. Grogan to John Tyler, October 12, 1841, Deposition of James W. Grogan, October 13, 1841, enclosed in Charles Davis and William Barron to Webster, October 15, 1841, all in NA, DS, RG 59, Misc. Letters. See also the report of Davis and Barron to Webster, October 16, 1841, NA, DS, RG 59, Misc. Letters.

11. Orlando Stevens et al. to John Tyler, September 23, 1841, William W. White et al., to Tyler, September 25, 1841, William W. White to Webster, September 25, 1841, all in NA, DS, RG 59, Misc. Letters.

12. Jenison to Webster, September 29, 1841, ibid.

13. Jenison to Jackson, September 29, 1841, in *Journal of the House of Representatives of the State of Vermont*, October Session, 1841 (Montpelier, 1841), appendix 91–92.

14. Fox to Aberdeen, September 29, 1841, No. 100, PRO, FO 115/76; Webster to Seward, October 1, 1841, Seward Papers-UR.

15. Fletcher Webster to Fox, September 28, 1841, NA, DS, RG 59, Notes to Britain; Fletcher Webster to Daniel Webster, October 9, 1841, Webster Papers-NHHS; Fox to Aberdeen, September 28, 1841, No. 99, September 29, 1841, No. 101, PRO, FO 115/76.

16. Jackson to Jenison, October 6, 1841, in *Vermont House Journal*, October 1841, appendix 92–93; Jackson to Jenison, October 6, 1841, in ibid., appendix 93.

17. Duke of Wellington to Peel, October 19, 1841, Peel Papers, B.L. Add. Ms. 40459/63–64. Peel to Duke of Wellington, October 20, 1841, Peel Papers, B.L. Add. Ms. 40459/65–66; Stanley to Bagot, October 20, 1841, No. 8, enclosed in Aberdeen to Fox, October 20, 1841, No. 2, PRO, FO 115/76.

18. Aberdeen to Fox, November 3, 1841, No. 5, PRO, FO 115/75.

19. Fox to Fletcher Webster, October 21, 1841, NA, DS, RG 59, Notes from Britain; Fox to Aberdeen, November 26, 1841, No. 131, PRO, FO 115/76.

20. Seward to Weed, September 1, 1841, Seward Papers-UR; Hawley to Weed, September 2, 3, 1841, both in Weed Papers-UR.

21. Joshua A. Spencer to Webster, September 24, 29, 1841, both in Webster Papers-NHHS.

22. Joshua A. Spencer to Webster, September 24, October 1, 1841, both in Webster Papers-NHHS; S. Blatchford to Seward, September 20, 1841, Seward Papers-UR.

23. Scott to John Bell, September 21, 1841, NA, DS, RG 59, Misc. Letters.

24. Willis Hall to J. C. Spencer, September 28, 1841, George W. Bull to Willis Hall, September 20, 1841, both in Seward Papers-UR.

25. Hawley to Seward, August 27, 1841, Seward to Hawley, August 30, 1841, Blatchford to Seward, September 20, 1841, Nelson to Seward, September 20, 1841, all in Seward Papers-UR; Hawley to Weed, October 1, 1841, Weed Papers-UR; Hawley to Seward, October 2, 1841, Seward to Hall, October 4, 1841, both in Seward Papers-UR.

26. Henry Underwood [Seward's secretary] to General John E. Wool, September 26, 1841, Robert Anderson [Wool's adjutant general] to Underwood, September 27, 1841, Fortune C. White [First Judge, Oneida County] to Seward, September 28, 1841, all in Seward Papers-UR; Adj. Gen. R. Anderson to Lt. Horace Brooks, September 29, 1841, NA, Department of War Records, RG 393, Records of the U.S. Army Continental Commands, 1821–1920, Eastern Division Letters Sent.

27. 2 *Gould's Stenographic Reporter* (1841), 11–18. The following account of McLeod's trial is from the second volume of *Gould's Stenographic Reporter* (3 vols., Washington, D.C., 1841), which is a 416-page transcript. Marcus T. C. Gould commissioned stenographers, who attended trials that attracted wide public interest, and sent his reports to subscribers. Only three volumes were published. The *Reporter* is not generally available, but a less full, and still substantial, account of McLeod's trial is in John D. Lawson, ed., *American State Trials*, Vol. VII (St. Louis, 1917), 61–323. The trial was widely reported in newspapers of the day. See the accounts in *Niles' National Register*, October 16, 23, 1841.

28. 2 *Gould's Reporter*, 22–24, 41–42.

29. Ibid., 59–61.

30. Ibid., 45–47.

31. Ibid., 51–57. This is contrary to the popular legend of the flaming *Caroline* sweeping over the falls intact.

32. Ibid., 61–64, 71–72, 80.

33. Ibid., 73–78.

34. Ibid., 85–86, 99–105.

35. Ibid., 108–89 (depositions).

36. Ibid., 190–92, 201–02.

37. Ibid., 192.

38. Ibid.

39. Ibid., 229–31.

40. Ibid., 231, 242–43, 244, 246.

41. Ibid., 255, 267, 274, 275, 284.

42. Ibid., 290, 299, 300.

43. Ibid., 321–22, 331.

44. Ibid., 339.

45. Ibid., 342, 357–58.

46. Philip Hone, Diary of Philip Hone, October 11, 1841, microfilm manuscript, New-York Historical Society; Hall to Seward, October 12, 1841, Seward Papers-UR.

47. Fletcher Webster to Fox, October 18, 1841, NA, DS, RG 59, Notes to Britain; Fox to Aberdeen, October 11, 1841, No. 104, PRO, FO 115/76.

48. Fox to Aberdeen, June 28, 1842, No. 16, PRO, FO 115/79.

49. Scott to Wool, October 8, 1841, NA, WD, RG 393, Eastern Division Letters Sent.

50. Hone, manuscript Diary, October 18, 21, 1841; Montreal *Herald*, cited in *National Intelligencer*, October 23, 1841; Milledge L. Bonham, Jr., "Alexander McLeod: Bone of Contention," *New York History* 18 (April 1937), 215; London *Times*, November 15, 17, 1841.

CHAPTER 9: THE CAULDRON COOLS

1. The London *Times*, on August 5, 1841, for example, expressed its sense of humiliation that a British subject was "rotting in a foreign gaol, under a charge of having done an act which the British Government acknowledges and applauds." On October 12, 1841, the *Times* stated that "whatever the fate of M'LEOD, the day of reckoning with Great Britain remains," when the United States would be "taught a lesson."

2. Seward to Crittenden, May 31, 1841, in William H. Seward, *The*

Works of William H. Seward, ed. George E. Baker (3 vol., New York, 1853), 2: 586–88; Seward to Richard Blatchford, March 23, 1846, in C. H. Van Tyne, ed., *The Letters of Daniel Webster* (New York, 1902), 311–16; Hawley to Weed, September 2, 1841, Weed Papers-UR; Scott to John Bell, September 21, 1841, NA, DS, RG 59, Misc. Letters; Philip Hone, *Diary of Philip Hone*, October 13, 1841, microfilm manuscript, New-York Historical Society.

3. Crittenden to Webster, undated, in Mrs. Chapman Coleman, ed., *The Life of John J. Crittenden* (2 vols., Philadelphia, 1871), 1: 151–54; Bloodgood to Seward, March 6, 1841, Seward Papers-UR.

4. Palmerston to Fox, February 9, 1841, Aberdeen to Fox, September 18, 1841, both in PRO, FO 115/75, Fox to Sir Harvey and others, March 13, 1841, Fox Papers, PRO, 97/16; Fox to Vice Admiral Charles Adams, October 5, 1841, Fox Papers, PRO, 97/17.

5. Stanley to Sydenham, September 10, 1841, Fox Papers, PRO, 97/18.

6. Peel to Queen Victoria, October 28, 1841, in *Victoria Regina, The Letters of Queen Victoria: A Selection from Her Majesty's Correspondence between the Years 1837 and 1861*, ed. Arthur C. Benson and Viscount Esher (3 vols., London, 1907), 1: 355–56; Fox to Aberdeen, October 1, 1841, No. 102, October 17, 1841, No. 112, both in PRO, FO 115/76.

7. For a complete review of Anglo-American diplomatic problems, see Howard Jones, *To the Webster-Ashburton Treaty: A Study in Anglo-American Relations, 1783–1843* (Chapel Hill, N.C., 1977).

8. Aberdeen to Peel, December 29, 1841, B.L. Add. Ms. 40453/77–78; Everett to Webster, December 31, 1841, NA, DS, RG 59, Despatches, Britain.

9. H. Jones, *To the Webster-Ashburton Treaty*, 96–98; Claude M. Fuess, *Daniel Webster* (2 vols., Boston, 1930), 2: 105–06; Sydney Nathans, *Daniel Webster and Jacksonian Democracy* (Baltimore, 1973), 190; Webster to Everett, January 29, 1842, Everett Papers-Massachusetts Historical Society.

10. John C. Spencer to Webster, October 16, 1841, Webster Papers-LC; Hone, manuscript Diary, October 13, 1841.

11. Fox to Aberdeen, October 28, 1841, No. 118, PRO, FO 115/76.

12. Fox to Aberdeen, November 20, 1841, No. 127, November 28, 1841, No. 134, both in PRO, FO 115/76.

13. Aberdeen to Fox, November 18, 1841, No. 8, ibid.

14. Everett to Webster, December 15, 1841, Everett Papers-Massachusetts Historical Society; Everett to Webster, December 28, 1841, NA, DS, RG 59, Despatches, Britain.

15. James D. Richardson, comp., *A Compilation of the Messages and*

Papers of the Presidents, 1789–1897 (10 vols., Washington, D.C., 1896–99), 4: 74–75.

16. Berrien to Webster, January 19, 1842, NA, DS, RG 59, Misc. Letters.

17. Webster to Berrien, January 14, 1842, Webster Papers-New Hampshire Historical Society.

18. Lot Clark to Webster, March 1, 1842, NA, DS, RG 59, Misc. Letters.

19. George Templeton Strong, *The Diary of George Templeton Strong*, ed. Allan Nevins and Milton Halsey Thomas, Vol. 1, *Young Man in New York* (4 vols., New York, 1952), 175–76.

20. Lot Clark to Webster, March 2, 1841, NA, DS, RG 59, Misc. Letters; Albany *Argus*, April 4, 1842.

21. Graham H. Chapin and James W. Gilbert to John Tyler, April 1, 1842, James W. Gilbert to Webster, April 2, 1842, both in NA, DS, RG 59, Misc. Letters; Bagot to Stanley, April 19, 1842, cited in Oscar A. Kinchen, *The Rise and Fall of the Patriot Hunters* (New York, 1956), 119; Albany *Argus*, April 4, 1842; Utica *Daily Gazette*, April 6, 8, 1842; Rochester *Democrat*, undated, in *National Intelligencer*, April 7, 1842; Rochester *Democrat*, April 6, 1842, in *National Intelligencer*, April 12, 1842. His reputation considerably bruised, Hogan returned to Canada, where he became a well-known journalist. He applied to his government for compensation for his American adventure, but it was refused. In December 1859 he was murdered by unknown assassins. John C. Dent, *The Last Forty Years: Canada since the Union of 1841* (2 vols., Toronto, 1881), 1: 188–89.

22. Joshua A. Spencer to Webster, April 8, 1842, NA, DS, RG 59, Misc. Letters; Special Message of March 8, 1842, in Richardson, *Messages and Papers*, 4: 103.

23. *Congressional Globe*, 27th Cong., 2d sess., pt. 1, pp. 443–44.

24. Ibid., pt. 1, p. 557; pt. 2, appendix 382–88; appendix, 611–19.

25. Ibid., pt. 1, p. 558; pt. 1, pp. 891–92; 5 U.S. Stats., 539–40.

26. Quincy Wright, *The Control of American Foreign Relations* (New York, 1922), 15.

27. 14 U.S. Stats., 384–86.

28. *In re Neagle*, 135 U.S. 1.

29. Aberdeen to Ashburton, February 8, 1842, in William R. Manning, ed., *Diplomatic Correspondence of the United States: Canadian Relations, 1784–1860* (4 vols., Washington, D.C., 1940–45), 3: 688–93.

30. Webster to Ashburton, July 27, 1842, NA, DS, RG 59, Notes to Britain.

31. Ashburton to Webster, July 28, 1842, NA, DS, RG 59, Notes from Britain; Webster to Ashburton, August 6, 1842, NA, DS, RG 59, Notes to Britain.

32. George T. Curtis, *Life of Daniel Webster* (2 vols., New York, 1870), 2: 121. To what extent Ashburton apologized to the United States for the *Caroline* raid has been a subject of debate. Webster clearly regarded Ashburton's use of the word "apology" to be literally that, and Ashburton felt he had hedged any apology by justifying the attack. Howard Jones, in *To the Webster-Ashburton Treaty*, describes Ashburton's remarks as "something close to an apology" without actually being one (pp. 153–54). I regard the tone and substance of Ashburton's words as an apology, despite his subsequent qualifications on the topic. Peel also regarded Ashburton's note as an apology; see Peel to Aberdeen, January 27, 1844, cited in Wilbur D. Jones, *Lord Aberdeen and the Americas* (Athens, Ga., 1958), 15, 90n.

33. Ashburton to Aberdeen, July 28, 1842, in Manning, *Canadian Relations*, 3: 771.

34. Tyler to Webster, August 3, 1842, Webster Papers-LC; Ashburton to Aberdeen, August 13, 1842, in Manning, *Canadian Relations*, 3: 770.

35. Webster to Ashburton, August 6, 1842, NA, DS, RG 59, Notes to Britain.

36. Henry A. Wise, *Seven Decades of the Union* (Philadelphia, 1872), 151–52.

37. Philip Marshall Brown, "Japanese Interpretation of the Kellogg Pact," *American Journal of International Law* 27 (January 1933), 100–102.

38. Lawrence D. Egbert, ed., "International Military Tribunal (Nuremberg), Judgment and Sentences," *American Journal of International Law* 41 (January 1947), 203–07; Myres S. McDougal and Florentino P. Feliciano, *Law and Minimum World Public Order: The Legal Regulation of International Coercion* (New Haven, 1961), 231–32; D. W. Bowett, *Self-Defense in International Law* (New York, 1958), 143–44.

39. The United Nations charter is published in Rosalyn Higgins, *The Development of International Law through the Political Organs of the United Nations* (London, 1963), 347–70.

40. Louis Henkin, *How Nations Behave: Law and Foreign Policy* (New York, 1979), 141, 258–62; Bowett, *Self-Defense in International Law*, 182–99.

41. United Nations, *Verbatim Record of the 1939th Meeting of the United Nations Security Council, July 9, 1976* (New York, 1976); "Memorandum for the Attorney General. Re: Legality under International Law of Remedial Action against use of Cuba as a Missile Base by the Soviet

Union," in Abram Chayes, *The Cuban Missile Crisis and the Role of Law* (New York, 1974), 108–16, especially 108–11.

42. Crittenden to Robert P. Letcher, September 13, 1841, George Bancroft to William L. Marcy, November 4, 1841, both quoted in Sydney Nathans, *Daniel Webster and Jacksonian Democracy* (Baltimore, 1973), 184; Webster to Hiram Ketchum, September 11, 1841, H. Shaw to Webster, February 23, 1843, both in Daniel Webster, *The Papers of Daniel Webster: Correspondence*, Vol. 5, *1840–1843*, ed. Harold D. Moser (Hanover, N.H., 1982), 149–50, 276–77.

43. Webster to Tyler, May 8, 1843, Tyler to Webster, May 8, 1843, both in Daniel Webster, *The Papers of Daniel Webster: Diplomatic Papers*, Vol. 1, *1841–1843*, ed. Kenneth E. Shewmaker, Kenneth R. Stevens, and Anita McGurn (Hanover, N.H., 1983), 931–32. The editorial, which appeared in the May 13, 1843, Washington *National Intelligencer*, is published in Moser, *Webster Correspondence*, 5: 304–06.

44. Peel to Aberdeen, November 17, 1841, Peel Papers, B.L. Add. Ms. 40453/58–59; Aberdeen to Fox, November 2, 1843, Aberdeen Papers, B.L. Add. Ms. 43123/225–226; John Ireland, "Andrew Drew: The Man who Burned the *Caroline*," *Ontario History* 59 (September 1967): 154–55.

45. Milledge L. Bonham, Jr., "Alexander McLeod: Bone of Contention," *New York History* 18 (April 1937): 217; Alastair Watt, "The Case of Alexander McLeod," *Canadian Historical Review* 12 (June 1931): 160–61; J. E. Rea, "Alexander McLeod," *Dictionary of Canadian Biography*, Vol. 10 (Toronto, 1972): 482–83; John B. Moore, *History and Digest of International Arbitrations to which the United States has been a part* (6 vols., Washington, D.C., 1898), 1: 398, 412, 423; 3: 2419–28.

Bibliography

I. Manuscript Sources

A. United States Official Papers, National Archives (NA)

1. State Department (RG 59)
   Instructions to United States Ministers.
   Despatches from United States Ministers.
   Notes to Foreign Legations.
   Notes from Foreign Legations.
   Domestic Letters.
   Miscellaneous Letters.
   Instructions, Special Missions.
   Communications from Special Agents.
2. Navy Department (RG 45)
   Letters Received by the Secretary of the Navy from Captains.
3. War Department
   Letters Sent, Military Book No. 23 (RG 107).
   Records of the U.S. Army Continental Commands, 1821–1920,
      Eastern Division, Letters Sent (RG 393).
4. Treasury Department (RG 56)
   Letters Sent to Collectors of Small Ports (RG 56).

B. Great Britain Official Papers, Public Record Office (PRO)

1. Foreign Office
   Series 115 (United States), vols. 67–76. Library of Congress microfilm and photostats.
2. Admiralty
   Admiralty Outletters and Instructions.

C. Public Archives of Canada (PAC)

1. Colonial Office Records. Original Correspondence-Secretary of State. Foreign Arrest and Trial of Mr. McLeod (CO42/483). PAC, MG11, Microfilm Reel B371.
2. Colonial Office Records. Supplementary Original Correspondence (CO537/139). PAC, MG11, Microfilm Reel B827.
3. Governor-General's Office. Letterbooks of Despatches to the Colonial Office, Upper Canada to Secretary of State, 1837–39. PAC, RG7, G12, vols. 28–29, Microfilm Reels 1103-H1104.
4. Governor-General's Office. Lt.-Governor's Correspondence, Upper Canada. PAC, RG7, G14, Microfilm Reel H1178.
5. Upper Canada Records Relating to the Rebellion of 1837–1838. Prosecution of Alexander McLeod. PAC, RG5, B43, Microfilm Reel C15691.

D. Private Papers (British and American)

Earl of Aberdeen (George Hamilton-Gordon) Papers. British Library, Additional Manuscripts.
Colchester Papers. Public Record Office, Series 30/9.
John J. Crittenden Papers. Duke University (microfilm).
Edward Everett Papers. Massachusetts Historical Society (microfilm).
Henry Stephen Fox Papers. Public Record Office, Series 97.
Philip Hone, Diary of Philip Hone. New-York Historical Society (microfilm).
Lord Melbourne Papers. University of Southampton, England.

Viscount Palmerston Papers. British Library, Additional Manuscripts.

Viscount Palmerston (Henry John Temple) Papers. University of Southampton, England.

Sir Robert Peel Papers. British Library, Additional Manuscripts.

William Henry Seward Papers. Rush Rhees Library, University of Rochester (now available on microfilm).

Martin Van Buren Papers. Library of Congress (microfilm).

Daniel Webster Papers, microfilm edition (Ann Arbor, Mich., University Microfilms, Inc., 1971).

Thurlow Weed Papers. Rush Rhees Library, University of Rochester.

Duke of Wellington Papers. University of Southampton, England.

II. PUBLISHED PAPERS—PRIMARY

A. Official Papers

1. United States
   25th Congress, 2d Session. House Executive Documents 74 and 440.
   26th Congress, 2d Session. House Executive Document 383 and House Report No. 162.
   27th Congress, 1st Session. Senate Document 33.
   31st Congress, 2d Session. House Executive Document 55.
   Congressional Globe.

Lowrie, Walter, and Matthew St. Clair Clarke, eds. *American State Papers: Foreign Relations.* 6 vols. Washington, D.C.: Gales & Seaton, 1832–59.

Manning, William R., ed. *Diplomatic Correspondence of the United States: Canadian Relations, 1784–1860.* 4 vols. Washington, D.C.: Carnegie Endowment for International Peace, 1940–45.

Miller, Hunter, ed. *Treaties and Other International Acts of the United States of America.* 8 vols. Washington, D.C.: Government Printing Office, 1931–48.

Richardson, James D., comp. *A Compilation of the Messages and Papers of the Presidents, 1789–1897.* 10 vols. Washington, D.C.: Government Printing Office, 1896–1899.

United States Statutes at Large.

2. Great Britain and Canada

Hansard's Parliamentary Debates. 3d series, 356 vols. London: Wyman, 1830–91.

Journal of the House of Assembly of Upper Canada.

B. Memoirs, Correspondence, and Collections

Adams, John Quincy. *The Memoirs of John Quincy Adams, comprising Portions of his Diary from 1795 to 1848*. Edited by Charles Francis Adams. 12 vols. Philadelphia: J. B. Lippincott & Co., 1874–77.

Arthur, Sir George. *The Arthur Papers, being the Canadian Papers, mainly Confidential, Private, and Demi-Official of Sir George Arthur*. Edited by Charles R. Sanderson. 3 vols. Toronto: Toronto Public Library, 1943–59.

Ashley, Evelyn. *The Life and Correspondence of Henry John Temple, Viscount Palmerston*. 2 vols. London: Richard Bentley & Son, 1879.

Bonney, Catharina V. R., comp. *A Legacy of Historical Gleanings*. 2 vols. 2d ed. Albany, N.Y.: J. Munsell, 1875.

Calhoun, John C. *The Papers of John C. Calhoun*. Vol. 15, *1839–1841*. Edited by Clyde N. Wilson. Columbia, S.C.: University of South Carolina Press, 1983.

Coleman, Mrs. Chapman, ed. *The Life of John J. Crittenden, with Selections from the Correspondence and Speeches*. 2 vols. Philadelphia: J. B. Lippincott & Co., 1871.

Hone, Philip. *Diary of Philip Hone, 1828–1851*. Edited by Allan Nevins. 2 vols. New York: Dodd, Mead & Company, 1927.

Jackson, Andrew. *Correspondence of Andrew Jackson*. Edited by John Spencer Bassett. 7 vols. Washington, D.C.: Carnegie Institution, 1926–35.

Miller, Linus W. *Notes of an Exile to Van Diemen's Land*. Fredonia, N.Y.: W. McKinstry & Co., 1846.

Peel, Sir Robert. *Sir Robert Peel, from his Private Papers*. Edited by C. S. Parker. 3 vols. London: J. Murray, 1891–99.

Polk, James K. *Correspondence of James K. Polk*. Vol. 5, *1839–1841*. Edited by Wayne Cutler et al. Nashville, Tenn.: University of Tennessee Press, 1979.

Scott, Winfield. *Memoirs of Lieut.-General Scott, LL.D.* 2 vols. New York: Sheldon & Company, 1864.

Seward, William H. *William H. Seward: An Autobiography from 1801 to 1834, with a Memoir of his Life, and Selections from his Letters, 1831–*

1846. Edited by Frederick W. Seward. New York: Derby & Miller, 1891.

———. *The Works of William H. Seward*. Edited by George E. Baker. 3 vols. New York: Redfield, 1853.

Strong, George Templeton. *The Diary of George Templeton Strong*. Edited by Allan Nevins and Milton Halsey Thomas. Vol. 1, *Young Man in New York*. New York: Macmillan, 1952.

Tyler, Lyon G., ed. *The Letters and Times of the Tylers*. 3 vols. Richmond, Va.: Whittet & Shepperson, 1884–96.

Victoria Regina. *The Letters of Queen Victoria: A Selection from Her Majesty's Correspondence between the Years 1837 and 1861*. Edited by Arthur C. Benson and Viscount Esher. 3 vols. London: J. Murray, 1907.

Webster, Daniel. *The Letters of Daniel Webster*. Edited by C. H. Van Tyne. New York: McClure, Phillips & Co., 1902.

———. *The Private Correspondence of Daniel Webster*. Edited by Fletcher Webster. 2 vols. Boston: Little, Brown & Co., 1857.

———. *The Papers of Daniel Webster: Correspondence*. Edited by Charles M. Wiltse et al. 7 vols. Hanover, N.H.: University Press of New England, 1974–86.

———. *The Papers of Daniel Webster: Diplomatic Papers*. Vol. 1, *1841–1843*. Edited by Kenneth E. Shewmaker, Kenneth R. Stevens, and Anita McGurn. Hanover, N.H.: University Press of New England, 1983.

Wise, Henry A. *Seven Decades of the Union*. Philadelphia: J. B. Lippincott & Co., 1872.

C. Legal Collections and Treatises on International Law

Bowett, D. W. *Self-Defense in International Law*. New York: Praeger, 1958.

Brierly, J. L. *The Law of Nations: An Introduction to the International Law of Peace*. 6th ed. Oxford: Oxford University Press, 1963.

Brown, Philip Marshall. "Japanese Interpretation of the Kellogg Pact." *American Journal of International Law* 27 (1933): 100–02.

Chayes, Abram. *The Cuban Missile Crisis and the Role of Law*. New York: Oxford University Press, 1974.

Egbert, Lawrence D., ed. "International Military Tribunal (Nuremberg), Judgment and Sentences." *American Journal of International Law* 41 (1947): 203–07.

Gould, Marcus T. C. *Gould's Stenographic Reporter*. 3 vols. New York: Marcus T. C. Gould, 1841.

Grotius, Hugo. *De Jure Belli ac Pacis Libri Tres*. Translated by Francis W. Kelsey. 2 vols. Oxford: Clarendon Press, 1925.

Henkin, Louis. *How Nations Behave: Law and Foreign Policy*. New York: Columbia University Press, 1979.

Higgins, Rosalyn. *The Development of International Law through the Political Organs of the United Nations*. London: Oxford University Press, 1963.

Journal of the House of Representatives of the State of Vermont, 1841. Montpelier, Vt.: State of Vermont, 1841.

Lawson, John D. *American State Trials*. Vol. 7, *McLeod Trial*. St. Louis, Mo.: Thomas Law Book Co., 1917.

McDougal Myres S., and Florentino P. Feliciano. *Law and Minimum World Public Order: The Legal Regulation of International Coercion*. New Haven, Conn.: Yale University Press, 1961.

Moore, John Bassett. *A Digest of International Law*. 8 vols. Washington, D.C.: Government Printing Office, 1906.

———. *History and Digest of International Arbitrations to which the United States has been a Party*. 6 vols. Washington, D.C.: Government Printing Office, 1898.

———. *A Treatise on Extradition and Interstate Rendition*. 2 vols. Boston: Boston Book Co., 1891.

Pufendorf, Samuel. *De Jure Naturae et Gentium Libri Octo*. Translated by C. H. and W. A Oldfather. Oxford: Clarendon Press, 1934.

United Nations. *Verbatim Record of the 1939th Meeting of the United Nations Security Council, July 9, 1976*. New York: United Nations, 1976.

Vattel, Emerich de. *The Law of Nations, or the Principles of Natural Law*. Translated by Charles G. Fenwick. 3 vols. Washington, D.C.: Carnegie Institution, 1916.

Wharton, Francis, ed. *A Digest of International Law of the United States*. 3 vols. Washington, D.C.: Government Printing Office, 1886.

Wright, Quincy. *The Control of American Foreign Relations*. New York: Macmillan, 1922.

D. Newspapers

Albany (N.Y.) *Argus*.
Albany (N.Y.) *Evening Journal*.

Buffalo (N.Y.) *Commercial-Advertiser.*
London *Sun.*
London *Times.*
New York *Herald.*
Niles' National Register.
Rochester (N.Y.) *Democrat.*
Washington (D.C.) *National Intelligencer.*

III. PUBLISHED SOURCES—SECONDARY

A. Books

Allen, Harry C. *Conflict and Concord: The Anglo-American Relationship since 1783.* New York: St. Martin's Press, 1959.
————. *Great Britain and the United States: A History of Anglo-American Relations, 1783–1952.* New York: St. Martin's Press, 1955.
Bartlett, C. J. *Great Britain and Sea Power, 1815–1853.* Oxford: Clarendon Press, 1963.
Baxter, Maurice G. *Daniel Webster and the Supreme Court.* Amherst, Mass.: University of Massachusetts Press, 1966.
————. *One and Inseparable: Daniel Webster and the Union.* Cambridge, Mass.: Harvard University Press, 1984.
Bell, Herbert C. F. *Lord Palmerston.* 2 vols. Hamden, Conn.: Archon Books, 1966.
Bemis, Samuel Flagg. *John Quincy Adams and the Foundations of American Foreign Policy.* New York: Alfred A. Knopf, 1949.
Bourne, Kenneth. *Britain and the Balance of Power in North America, 1815–1908.* Berkeley and Los Angeles: University of California Press, 1967.
————. *Palmerston: The Early Years, 1784–1841.* New York: Free Press, 1982.
Burt, Alfred Leroy. *A Short History of Canada for Americans.* Minneapolis: University of Minnesota Press, 1942.
Callahan, James M. *American Foreign Policy in Canadian Relations.* New York: R. S. Barnes, 1937.
Campbell, Charles S. *From Revolution to Rapprochement: The United States and Great Britain, 1783–1900.* New York: John Wiley & Sons, 1974.

Careless, J. M. S., ed. *Colonists and Canadiens, 1760–1867.* Toronto: Macmillan of Canada, 1971.

Chamberlain, Muriel E. *Lord Aberdeen: A Political Biography.* London and New York: Longman, 1983.

Chitwood, Oliver P. *John Tyler: Champion of the Old South.* New York: Appleton-Century Co., 1939.

Clark, S. D. *Movements of Political Protest in Canada, 1640–1840.* Toronto: University of Toronto Press, 1959.

Cole, Donald B. *Martin Van Buren and the American Political System.* Princeton, N.J.: Princeton University Press, 1984.

Colomb, P. H. *Naval Warfare: Its Ruling Principles and Practice Historically Treated.* London: W. H. Allen, 1899.

Corey, Albert B. *The Crisis of 1830–1842 in Canadian-American Relations.* New Haven, Conn.: Yale University Press, 1941.

Crook, David Paul. *American Democracy in English Politics, 1815–1850.* Oxford: Oxford University Press, 1965.

Current, Richard N. *Daniel Webster and the Rise of National Conservatism.* Boston: Little, Brown & Co., 1955.

Curtis, George T. *Life of Daniel Webster.* 2 vols. New York: D. Appleton and Company, 1870.

Curtis, James C. *The Fox at Bay: Martin Van Buren and the Presidency, 1837–1841.* Lexington, Ky.: University Press of Kentucky, 1970.

Dangerfield, George. *The Era of Good Feelings.* New York: Harcourt, Brace & World, 1952.

Dent, John C. *The Last Forty Years: Canada since the Union of 1841.* 2 vols. Toronto: George Virtue, 1881.

———. *The Story of the Upper Canadian Rebellion, Largely Derived from Original Sources and Documents.* 2 vols. Toronto: C. B. Robinson, 1885.

Duckett, Alvin L. *John Forsyth, Political Tactician.* Athens, Ga.: University of Georgia Press, 1962.

Dunham, Aileen. *Political Unrest in Upper Canada, 1815–1836.* London: Longmans, Green, and Co., 1927.

Edmunds, John B. *Francis W. Pickens and the Politics of Destruction.* Chapel Hill, N.C.: University of North Carolina Press, 1986.

Elliott, Charles W. *Winfield Scott: The Soldier and the Man.* New York: Macmillan, 1937.

Frothingham, Paul R. *Edward Everett, Orator and Statesman.* Boston: Houghton Mifflin Co., 1925.

Fuess, Claude M. *Daniel Webster.* 2 vols. Boston: Little, Brown & Co., 1930.

Gash, Norman. *The Life of Sir Robert Peel after 1830*. London: Rowman and Littlefield, 1972.

Guillet, Edwin C. *The Lives and Times of the Patriots: An Account of the Rebellion in Upper Canada, 1837–38, and of the Patriot Agitation in the United States, 1837–1842*. Toronto: T. Nelson & Sons, 1938.

Hansen, Marcus Lee. *The Mingling of the Canadian and American Peoples*. New Haven, Conn.: Yale University Press, 1940.

Harvey, Peter. *Reminiscences and Anecdotes of Daniel Webster*. Boston: Little, Brown & Co., 1877.

Hidy, Ralph W. *The House of Baring in American Trade and Finance*. Cambridge, Mass.: Harvard University Press, 1949.

Iremonger, Lucille. *Lord Aberdeen: A Biography of the Fourth Earl of Aberdeen, K.G., K.T., Prime Minister, 1852–1855*. London: Collins, 1978.

Jones, Howard. *To the Webster-Ashburton Treaty: A Study in Anglo-American Relations, 1783–1843*. Chapel Hill, N.C.: University of North Carolina Press, 1977.

Jones, Wilbur D. *The American Problem in British Diplomacy, 1841–1861*. Athens, Ga.: University of Georgia Press, 1974.

———. *Lord Aberdeen and the Americas*. Athens, Ga.: University of Georgia Press, 1958.

Kilbourn, William. *The Firebrand: William Lyon Mackenzie and the Rebellion in Upper Canada*. Toronto: Clarke, Irwin, 1956.

Kinchen, Oscar A. *The Rise and Fall of the Patriot Hunters*. New York: Bookman, 1956.

Kirwan, Albert D. *John J. Crittenden*. Lexington, Ky.: University Press of Kentucky, 1962.

McInnis, Edgar W. *The Unguarded Frontier: A History of American-Canadian Relations*. Garden City, N.Y.: Doubleday, Doran, 1942.

Maloney, Linda M. *The Captain from Connecticut: The Life and Naval Times of Isaac Hull*. Boston: Northeastern University Press, 1986.

Merk, Frederick. *Fruits of Propaganda in the Tyler Administration*. Cambridge, Mass.: Harvard University Press, 1971.

Morgan, Robert J. *A Whig Embattled: The Presidency under John Tyler*. Lincoln, Nebr.: University of Nebraska Press, 1954.

Nathans, Sydney. *Daniel Webster and Jacksonian Democracy*. Baltimore: Johns Hopkins University Press, 1973.

Niven, John. *Martin Van Buren: The Romantic Age of American Politics*. New York: Oxford University Press, 1983.

Reeves, Jesse S. *American Diplomacy under Tyler and Polk*. Baltimore: Johns Hopkins University Press, 1907.

Reid, J. H. Stewart, Kenneth McNaught, and Harry S. Crowe, eds. *A Source-book of Canadian History: Selected Documents and Personal Papers.* Rev. ed. Toronto: Longmans Canada Ltd., 1964.

Remini, Robert V. *Martin Van Buren and the Making of the Democratic Party.* New York: W. W. Norton & Co., 1970.

Ridley, Jasper. *Lord Palmerston.* New York: E. P. Dutton & Co., 1971.

Rudé, George. *Protest and Punishment: The Story of the Social and Political Protestors Transported to Australia, 1788–1868.* Oxford: Oxford University Press, 1978.

Ryerson, Stanley B. *Unequal Union: Confederation and the Roots of Conflict in the Canadas, 1815–1873.* New York: International Publishers, 1968.

Schlesinger, Arthur M., Jr. *The Age of Jackson.* Boston: Little, Brown & Co., 1953.

Schull, Joseph. *Rebellion: The Rising in French Canada, 1837.* Toronto: Macmillan of Canada, 1971.

Seager, Robert, II. *And Tyler, Too: A Biography of John and Julia Gardiner Tyler.* New York: McGraw-Hill, 1963.

Smelser, Marshall. *The Democratic Republic, 1801–1815.* New York: Harper & Row, 1968.

Soulsby, Hugh G. *The Right of Search and the Slave Trade in Anglo-American Relations, 1814–1862.* Baltimore: Johns Hopkins University Studies, 1933.

Southgate, Donald. *'The Most English Minister . . . ': The Policies and Politics of Palmerston.* New York: St. Martin's Press, 1966.

Spencer, Ivor D. *The Victor and the Spoils: A Life of William L. Marcy.* Providence, R.I.: Brown University Press, 1959.

Swisher, Carl B. *History of the Supreme Court of the United States.* Vol. 5, *The Taney Period, 1836–64.* New York: Macmillan, 1974.

Tiffany, Orrin E. *The Relations of the United States to the Canadian Rebellion of 1837–38.* Buffalo, N.Y.: Buffalo, Historical Society Publication, No. 8, 1905.

Van Alstyne, Richard W. *The Rising American Empire.* New York: W. W. Norton & Co., 1974.

Van Deusen, Glyndon G. *The Jacksonian Era, 1828–1848.* New York: Harper & Row, 1959.

————. *William Henry Seward.* New York: Oxford University Press, 1967.

Ward, Christopher. *The War of the Revolution.* 2 vols. New York: Macmillan, 1952.

Wayland, Francis P. *Andrew Stevenson: Democrat and Diplomat, 1785–1857.* Philadelphia: University of Pennsylvania Press, 1949.
Wilson, Major L. *The Presidency of Martin Van Buren.* Lawrence, Kans.: University Press of Kansas, 1984.
Willson, Beckles. *Friendly Relations: A Narrative of Britain's Ministers and Ambassadors to America, 1791–1930.* Boston: Little, Brown & Co., 1934.
Wittke, Carl. *A History of Canada.* Rev. ed. New York: Alfred A. Knopf, 1928.
Woodford, Frank B. *Lewis Cass: The Last Jeffersonian.* New Brunswick, N.J.: Rutgers University Press, 1950.

B. Articles and Essays

Bonham, Milledge L., Jr. "Alexander McLeod: Bone of Contention." *New York History* 18 (1937): 189–217.
Brescia, Anthony M. "'Defences Strong Enough to Defy the World': The Visit of a U.S. State Department Special Agent to Bermuda in 1841." *Bulletin of the Institute of Maritime History and Archaeology* 10 (December 1987): 11–12, 14, 16, 25–26.
Corey, Albert B. "Public Opinion and the McLeod Case." *Canadian Historical Association Report* (1936): 53–64.
Creighton, D. G. "The Economic Background of the Rebellions of Eighteen Thirty-Seven." *Canadian Journal of Economics and Political Science* 3 (1937): 322–34.
Hand, Augustus N. "Local Incidents of the Papineau Rebellion." *New York History* 15 (1934): 376–87.
Humphries, Charles W. "The Capture of York." *Ontario History* 51 (1959): 1–21.
Ireland, John. "Andrew Drew: The Man who Burned the *Caroline.*" *Ontario History* 59 (1967): 137–56.
Jones, Howard. "The *Caroline* Affair." *Historian* 38 (1976): 485–502.
———. "The Attempt to Impeach Daniel Webster." *Capitol Studies* 3 (1975): 31–44.
Longley, R. S. "Emigration and the Crisis of 1837 in Upper Canada." *Canadian Historical Review* 17 (1936): 29–40.
Mackay, R. A. "The Political Ideals of William Lyon Mackenzie." *Canadian Journal of Economics and Political Science* 3 (1937): 1–22.

Musham, H. A. "Early Great Lakes Steamboats: The Battle of the Windmill and Afterward, 1838–1842." *American Neptune* 8 (1948): 37–60.

New, Chester W. "The Rebellion of 1837 in its Larger Setting." *Canadian Historical Association Report* (1937): 5–17.

Ross, Robert B. "The Patriot War." In *Collections and Researches Made by the Michigan Pioneer and Historical Society* 21 (1912–13): 432, 541, 607–08.

Shortridge, Wilson P. "The Canadian-American Frontier during the Rebellion of 1837–1838." *Canadian Historical Review* 7 (1926): 13–26.

Stacey, C. P. "The Myth of the Unguarded Frontier, 1815–1871." *American Historical Review* 56 (1950): 1–18.

Stathis, Stephen W. "John Tyler's Presidential Succession: A Reappraisal." *Prologue* 8 (1976): 223–36.

Stevens, Kenneth R. "James Grogan and the Crisis in Canadian-American Relations, 1837–1842." *Vermont History* 50 (1982): 219–26.

———. "The Webster-Ingersoll Feud: Politics and Personality in the New Nation." *Historical New Hampshire* 37 (1982): 174–92.

Tyler, Lyon G. "President Tyler and the Ashburton Treaty." *William and Mary College Quarterly Historical Magazine* 25 (1916): 1–8.

Van Alstyne, Richard W. "The British Right of Search and the African Slave Trade." *Journal of Modern History* 2 (1930): 37–47.

Watt, Alastair. "The Case of Alexander McLeod." *Canadian Historical Review* 12 (1931): 145–67.

Webster, C. K. "Lord Palmerston at Work, 1830–41." *Politica* (August 1934): 129–44.

Wiltse, Charles M. "Daniel Webster and the British Experience." *Proceedings of the Massachusetts Historical Society* 85 (1973): 58–77.

Zorn, Roman J. "Criminal Extradition Menaces the Canadian Haven for Fugitive Slaves, 1841–1861." *Canadian Historical Review* 38 (1957): 284–94.

INDEX

217